The
WASHINGTONS
of
WESSYNGTON
PLANTATION

The

WASHINGTONS

of

WESSYNGTON
PLANTATION

———◆———

Stories of My Family's Journey to Freedom

John F. Baker Jr.

ATRIA BOOKS

NEW YORK   LONDON   TORONTO   SYDNEY

ATRIA BOOKS

A Division of Simon & Schuster, Inc.
1230 Avenue of the Americas
New York, NY 10020

First Atria Books hardcover edition February 2009

ATRIA BOOKS and colophon are trademarks of Simon & Schuster, Inc.

For information about special discounts for bulk purchases,
please contact Simon & Schuster Special Sales at
1-800-456-6798 or business@simonandschuster.com.

Designed by Paul Dippolito

Manufactured in the United States of America

1   3   5   7   9   10   8   6   4   2

Library of Congress Cataloging-in-Publication Data
Baker Jr., John F., date.
The Washingtons of Wessyngton Plantation: stories of my family's journey to
freedom / by John F. Baker Jr. — 1st Atria Books hardcover ed.
p. cm.
Includes bibliographical references.
1. Wessyngton Plantation (Tenn.)—History. 2. Washington family. 3. Baker Jr.,
John F., date—Family. 4. African American families. 5. African Americans—
Genealogy. 6. African Americans—Tennessee—Robertson County—Biography.
7. Slaves—Tennessee—Robertson County—Biography. 8. Plantation life—
Tennessee—Robertson County—History. 9. Tobacco farms—Tennessee—
Robertson County—History. 10. Robertson County (Tenn.)—Antiquities. I. Title.

F444.W425B35 2009
929'.20973—dc22   2008018742

ISBN-13: 978-1-4165-6740-0
ISBN-10: 1-4165-6740-2

In honor of Emanuel, Henny, Allen, and Granville Washington, whose photograph led me on a thirty-year journey to discover their stories and those of the hundreds of others enslaved on Wessyngton Plantation

I don't care what anybody says, the Lord meant for you to do all this. Look at all the Washingtons and others that have come along long before you and gone and never thought about this. This story had to be told before the end of time about what our people went through and He sent you to do it.

—MAGGIE POLK WASHINGTON,
99 YEARS OLD

You really love to talk about your ancestors and all the other people from Washington that you have traced down. As long as you are living, they will never be dead.

—MATTIE TERRY, 93 YEARS OLD

I think you are doing a fine job looking up all this history. Our people need to know what all those people went through back then for us to get to where we are now, especially the young folks.

—HENRY POLK, 85 YEARS OLD

Contents

Prologue

———•◦•———

I am one of the tens of thousands of descendants of the hundreds of African Americans who were once enslaved on Wessyngton Plantation, the largest tobacco plantation in America. My ancestors were among the first to come to the plantation and the oldest who can be traced to present-day descendants. As many as ten generations of my family have lived in the area since the arrival of my first ancestors.

The human need to know where you come from and whom you come from runs deep in the African American psyche. The phenomenon that was Alex Haley's *Roots* is evidence of that, but so is the common practice of African American parents to raise their children emphasizing the importance of knowing your kin: those present as well as those who have passed away. We don't care if someone is our third cousin or our fiftieth cousin; we're still family. I know that my family certainly instilled these values in me. And from that grew my passion for learning about the history of all the families on Wessyngton Plantation. This passion led me on a thirty-year journey of discovery.

I can only hope that each reader will come to see that the story of the African Americans on Wessyngton Plantation is a special story of individuals—a proud history of family, hard work, and achievement. It is a perfect way for future generations to honor our ancestors.

Seated left: Emanuel Washington (1824–1907), the cook; seated right: Henny Washington (1839–1913), the head laundress; standing left: Allen Washington (1825–1890s), the head dairyman; standing right: Granville Washington (1831–1898), George A. Washington's valet. Taken at Wessyngton Plantation, ca. 1891.

CHAPTER 1

The Photo in My Textbook

As a young child in the 1960s, my maternal grandfather took me for a ride in the country nearly every Sunday afternoon after church. We would drive about ten miles northwest of Springfield, Tennessee, and would pass by an impressive mansion, which sat some distance off the road. My grandfather would say, "That's Washington, where your people came from on your grandmother's side."

I discovered the story of my ancestors by accident while flipping through the pages of my seventh-grade social studies book, *Your Tennessee*. At the beginning of the chapter "Black Tennesseans," I spotted a photograph of four African Americans. In the 1970s little was taught in public schools about black history other than the Civil War period, so the picture really intrigued me. I kept being drawn to this photograph and examined it carefully. The people were dressed well and looked dignified. I knew from their clothing that the photo was nearly one hundred years old. Each time I went to class, I would turn to the photo because the couple seated reminded me of some of my family members—the woman and my maternal grandmother especially.

My grandmother Sallie Washington Nicholson moved to Indianapolis in 1941 and from there to Chicago. Each year she would come home to visit. On her visit, in 1976, when I was thirteen years old, she spent the weekend with her brother and sister-in-law Bob and Maggie Washington in Cedar Hill. She called my mother and told her to have me bring a camera when we came to pick her up because she had something she wanted me to photograph. When my mother and I arrived, my grandmother showed us an article from the *Robertson County Times*, published in Springfield. I immediately realized that this was the same photograph I had seen in my school textbook. The caption under the photograph listed the names of the former slaves, the owner, and the name of the plantation: Wessyngton. The caption read: "Another of the pictures from Wessyngton. Seated left: Emanuel Washington, Uncle Man the cook, seated right: Hettie Washington, Aunt Henny the head laundress (Uncle Man's wife), standing left: Allen Washington, the head dairyman, standing right: Granville Washington (George A. Washington's valet or body servant). Taken at Wessyngton [1891]."

I remember to this day what happened next:

"Who are these people, Big Mama?" I asked.

"That's my grandfather and grandmother," she said, pointing to the seated couple. "My grandfather was the cook at Washington." I knew that she was really talking about Wessyngton because most black people in the area refer to the plantation as Washington. "And that is where we got the Washington name."

Although I had seen the photograph in the textbook many times, it assumed a different meaning once I knew that those people were my ancestors. I was in shock. I could hardly wait to get back to school and tell my classmates that my ancestors were in our history book. I looked at each person in the photograph carefully. I looked at Emanuel, Henny, Allen, and then Granville. Pointing to Granville, I asked, "Who is this white man? Was he the slave owner?" My grandmother and uncle replied at the same time, "He's not white, he is related to us too! Granville was our cousin. Papa used to talk about him all the time. He said George

Washington who owned the Washington farm was his father by a slave girl. Granville's mother was kin to Papa on his mother's side of the family."

Sallie Washington Nicholson, My Grandmother, 1909–1995

I was the youngest child in the family. My mother died having twins when I was three. My parents were Amos and Callie White Washington. My father was born at Washington in 1870, his parents were Emanuel and Henny Washington, who were born slaves on the Washington plantation. My grandfather died before I was born, and our grandmother died when I was too little to remember her, but Papa used to talk about them and our other relatives all the time. His daddy was the cook at Washing-

*Sallie Washington Nicholson
(1909–1995).*

ton [Wessyngton] and when Papa was just a small boy he used to follow his daddy around the Big House and played in the kitchen at Washington while his daddy worked. Papa could make corn-bread that was as good as cake. I guess he learned that from his daddy. Papa said he was taught to read and write by some of the Washington children he played with as a child.

Did they ever say how the slaves were treated at Washington?

Papa said they always treated his daddy like he was part of the family because he was the cook and used to tell all the children ghost stories. Papa said his daddy was the best cook there was. I don't know if they treated them all like they did him or not. They say the Washingtons never caused the breakup of families by selling slaves from the plantation. Our grandmother Henny was part Indian and so was our mother's father, Bob White. After our grandfather got too old to cook and went blind, John Phillips cooked at Washington. He married our cousin Annie Washington who was Cousin Gabe Washington's daughter. I think Cousin Gabe was the last of the slaves that stayed there after they were freed. I used to talk to him all the time when we went down there. The Washingtons were really fond of him too. When we were children just about all older people were called "uncle" or "auntie" whether they were related or not. This made it that much harder to tell how everybody was kin. We even had to address our older sisters and brothers with a title. You could not just call them by their first names. That is why I say Sister Cora.

I always wondered why you called Aunt Cora "Sister Cora" and she didn't say "sister" when she was talking to you.

That's because she was the oldest. I called my brother Baxter and sister Henrietta by their names because they were closer to my age.

A lot of our cousins lived down at Washington when we were growing up. Allen Washington that's on the picture with our grandparents was Guss Washington's grandfather. Guss married our cousin Carrie, and both of them worked down at Washington for years and years. You can probably talk to Carrie, because she can remember lots of things and so will Sister Cora.

When we were children Papa used to make sure we went to church. We went to the Antioch Baptist Church in Turnersville. Papa always sent us, but he never went there, he always said he belonged to a white Catholic church [possibly St. Michael's]. He later joined South Baptist Church in Springfield and was baptized when he was in his eighties. When I was a child Papa always told us to pray at night as if it was our last time to make sure we went to Heaven, and never go to bed angry with anyone without making things right. He said that's how his parents taught him to pray.

I went to school in Sandy Springs at Scott's School and some at Antioch School. Our cousin Clarine Darden was my first teacher. My mother died when I was small, so they started me to school early. I can't even remember what Mama looked like. When I first married your grandfather, I woke up in the middle of the night and looked toward the foot of my bed and there Mama stood. I was afraid and hid my head under the covers. I looked out a second time and she was still there. I could not wake your grandfather, so I was afraid to look out again. After I described her to my brother and sister they said it was our mother.

After Mama died, my father married Jenny Scott, she was the daughter of Mr. Joe Scott and Mrs. Fannie Scott, who lived down by Scott's Cemetery. Mr. Joe Scott was a Washington slave too.

My mama's mother lived near us. Her name was Fannie Connell White Long. She was a midwife who delivered black and white babies. We called her Granny Fanny. She died in 1920 during the flu epidemic. A whole lot of people died with the flu back then and tuberculosis. My sister Henrietta died from tuberculosis one month before your mother was born in 1928. Henrietta always looked after me after Mama died, and so did Bob. Some of our family was buried in White's Cemetery, which was owned by our family. My great-grandfather Henry White bought that property right after he was freed.

On the fourth Sunday in May they hold Antioch Baptist Church's homecoming. There would be people from everywhere. I used to go often to get to see our relatives and friends who had moved up North.

They used to have a hayride in town in Springfield that used to go down to Washington when I was young. When I was carrying your mother, we went down there and a boy fell off the wagon, Curtis "Six Deuce" Meneese, and had to have his leg amputated. I never went on the ride after that. Several of our cousins still lived at Washington then.

Our family came here with the first Washington that started the plantation. I don't know what year it was, but I think our family was there the whole time or close to the start of it. Most of our family stayed there after they were set free.

Bob Washington, My Great-uncle, 1897–1977

I remember my granddaddy and grandmamma. Everybody called my granddaddy 'Uncle Man,' but his name was Emanuel. Our grandmother was named Henny. Our sister Henrietta was named after her. Our mother died having twins in 1913, and Grandpa Man's sister, Aunt Sue, stayed with us to help Papa out with the children. I remember her burning the toast when she cooked and wanted us to eat it anyway. She was born a slave down at Washington and was older than our grandfather. She was probably close to one hundred when she died. Grandpa

Bob Washington (1897–1977) and Maggie
Polk Washington (1904–2003), on their
fiftieth anniversary.

Man had another sister, Clara Washington; she died in 1925 and was nearly one hundred when she died; she was Jenny Hayes's mother. Most of our people have lived to get pretty old. Papa had a brother named Grundy Washington who lived in Clarksville, Tennessee. He had ten or twelve children too. We have relatives everywhere. Many of them moved up North. Our oldest brother, Willie, moved up North, then our brother Baxter and your grandmother later moved up there. Some of them tried to get me to move, but I never did.

Our father said our family came from Virginia with the Washingtons. They were some kin to the president, and that's where we got our family name. Some of the family still lives down in the old Washington house. If you call down there and tell them who you are, they may be able to help you find something. They still have some of the old slave houses and everything else down there. [My great-uncle told me the plantation was not far from his house. My great-aunt Maggie confirmed what my grandmother and great-uncle said about the family. Her maternal ancestors also came from the Wessyngton Plantation.]

I questioned them all I could about the people in the photograph that night. My mother finally interrupted and told them I would keep asking questions as long as they would answer them and that I should be a lawyer. This ended my first of many interviews. I had heard bits and pieces about our family growing up as I always hung around older relatives. I suppose the old adage that a picture is worth a thousand words is really true. Now I was determined to get every shred of information I could to find out more about our distant past.

CHAPTER 2

That's Washington, Where Your People Came From

———— ·•·• ————

After the discovery of my ancestors in the photograph, I was so excited I could hardly sleep. The next morning I looked in the phone book and called out to Wessyngton. Anne Talbott, a descendant of the plantation's original owner, answered the phone. I introduced myself and told her that I had seen the article in our local newspaper and that I was the great-great-grandson of Emanuel and Henny Washington who were born at Wessyngton. Anne told me that Emanuel's family had remained on the plantation after they were freed, and they had many records of the slaves' births, photographs, and, she said, a portrait of my great-great-grandfather was still hanging in the mansion. She told me that she operated a bookstore in Springfield and she would gladly meet me there and show me some of the records and photographs.

When I arrived at the bookstore, Anne greeted me and showed me an old photo album with several pictures of my great-great-grandparents and a beautiful portrait of my great-great-grandfather painted by a famous artist, [Maria] Howard Weeden. I was amazed. Then she showed me copies of a list of about eight legal-sized pages of names. These were the names of slaves who had been born on the Wessyngton Plantation from 1795 through 1860.

Wessyngton Plantation birth register, 1795 through 1860.

On the second page of the document I found "Manuel born April 23rd 1824"—my great-great-grandfather! I continued searching and found "Henny was borne May 26, 1839"—my great-great-grandmother! It was exciting to see my family history unfold before my eyes. Anne asked if I saw any other names I was familiar with. There were more than two hundred names on the document. Since the names of the slaves were recorded by several Washington family members during a sixty-five-year span, their spellings varied. Anne then looked further and found "General born December 25, 1854 Hena's child," then "born November 23rd 1856, Grunday, Henna's child," then "1859 born January 22nd Henna's child Cornelia." She said, "These should be your great-great-grandparents' children—have you ever heard of them?" I had never heard of General or Cornelia, but I remember many times hearing that my great-grandfather Amos Washington had a brother named Grundy, so that must have been him. Anne made copies of the lists and the photographs for me. I could hardly wait to get home and share this information with my family. Anne invited me out to Wessyngton, so I went the following Sunday.

Wessyngton was located only ten miles from my home in Springfield, so my mother took me out there. As we arrived at the impressive stone entrance gate, I had a flashback from my early childhood when my grandfather Joe Cobbs said, "That's Washington. That's where your people came from on your grandmother's side of the

Emanuel Washington, portraits by [Maria] Howard Weeden.

family." Then I fully understood the magnitude of my grandfather's words. We followed the winding driveway and came to the stately old mansion. It was hard to believe that my ancestors had actually built it one hundred sixty years earlier.

Anne explained that her grandmother had married a Northerner, and she and her family had only recently moved to Wessyngton. Felix "Ditt" Terry, a descendant of Wessyngton slaves, also lived in the mansion with his family. For decades, he had helped run the farm, grew tobacco, and had cared for George A. Washington 2d until his death in 1964.

Visiting Wessyngton was like stepping back in time. The mansion had old portraits hanging everywhere, including one of my great-great-grandfather and a few other slaves. Most of the furniture was from the 1800s, and I imagined it looked like it did when my ancestors were enslaved there.

Anne gave me a tour of the plantation, which encompassed more than one thousand acres, with its smoke house, tobacco-

John and Anne Talbott with daughters Polly, Thayer, and Kemp at Wessyngton, 1973.

Wessyngton mansion, 1976.

curing barns, and large kitchen. On a hill behind the Wessyngton mansion several log slave cabins were still standing. I was
intrigued and wondered which one my family might have lived
in. Anne then led me to the slave cemetery, some distance from
the main house. We had to go down a steep hill and climb a few
vine-covered fences. My mother was right behind until I climbed
the second fence. The cemetery was located on a small hill in a
large grove of trees. Simple stones and a few wild roses marked the
graves. I thought about the hundreds of slaves who had lived on
the plantation and were buried in that cemetery. I felt their presence. At the end of my visit Anne urged me to come back any time
I wanted to; over the years I did so and we forged a warm friend-
ship. While Anne had been showing me around, she told me that
her family had deposited all the plantation records in the Tennessee State Library and Archives in Nashville, and I could probably
find lots of information there. My mother looked at me as if to say,
"I know you want me to take you to Nashville next."

Of course, she was right.

My father joined my mother and me on my first of many trips

to the state archives. The trip took about thirty minutes. I remember my excitement as I walked into the majestic building next to the State Capitol building. I asked to see the Washington Family Papers. When I opened the first storage carton, I was amazed to see fragile old papers. The Washington Family Papers was (and still is) the largest collection of family records in the state, including those of presidents Jackson, Polk, and Johnson. It is the only complete collection pertaining to a Tennessee plantation. Apparently, the Washingtons saved every piece of paper they ever laid their hands on. Many of the documents had not been seen since they were created more than one hundred years earlier. I found the original slave birth register with the names of my ancestors that Anne had shown me a copy of. The documents were light yellow in color, and the ink had turned brown from aging. As I touched the fragile papers, I knew that I would learn about not only my family history but all the hundreds of others enslaved on Wessyngton.

I have always been an avid reader and really liked history, but now it had a much different meaning. I purchased all the black history books I could find: books on slavery, plantations, Tennessee history, Southern history, African history, the slave trade, the Civil War, and anything else that might shed light on my ancestors' lives. I studied the history of my own county, which had lots of information about Wessyngton and the Washington family. I researched the genealogy of the Washington family because that was necessary to trace the origins of the early slave families.

Anne Talbott suggested that I talk to Mattie Terry, Carrie Williams Washington, and Lady Terry because they had been around Wessyngton most of their lives and knew many of the slaves personally. My plan was to question some of my older relatives and others whose ancestors came from the plantation. Most of the information we have on slavery in the United States has been written by slave owners, taken from court documents, diaries, or plantation account books. Very little reflects how the slaves felt about their condition. Few slaves left any written record of their lives and the harsh conditions they endured. The history of slavery from an African American perspective has been passed down to successive generations in the form of oral history or narratives, which date back to African customs. In addition to my family members, I have had the privilege of personally interviewing more than twenty-five children and grandchildren of former Wessyngton slaves, ranging in age from eighty-five to one hundred six years old. Their stories have been passed down directly from their parents, grandparents, and great-grandparents. This gives voice to a history that would otherwise be forgotten. These stories were related to me in a candid manner, sparing no details, whether good, bad, or indifferent. I found that most of their stories could be supported by original documents. In turn, these conversations expanded my research since each person had information that added to what I was finding in the official records. Once I began hearing these stories, I knew that I must preserve all this information.

When I started my research I was too young to drive, so either my mother or father took me, usually my mother. I recall her telling her friends that she would be glad when I was old enough to get my license because I was dragging her all over the county. I really appreciate her taking me; I know I was a nuisance at times. As soon as I found one bit of information, I wanted to go somewhere else and do more research or another interview.

Fortunately for my parents, many of our relatives and others who had ties to Wessyngton lived within walking distance of my house or we attended the same church. My great-aunt Maggie Washington often told me, "I guess the Good Lord is just keeping all of us around here to help you tell our people's story."

One of the first people I visited was Mattie Terry, who lived less than a five-minute walk down my street. Miss Matt proved to be a veritable gold mine of information. She and I both attended the Greater South Baptist Church in Springfield then and we became

Mattie Terry (1889–1982).

great friends. I visited Miss Matt weekly. She was a tall, slim woman with a loving spirit. When she was over ninety years old she still walked straight as an arrow with her head held high and proud, and got around better than many people half her age. Witty and humorous, she was constantly cracking jokes. Her memory was very sharp until her death. In the course of several years, she told me many stories of her ancestors' lives, her early life, and her travels when she left the South.

When I arrived at Miss Matt's the first time, I brought along the photograph of my ancestors featured in our local newspaper. I showed it to her and told her that I was trying to find information about my family and the Washington's plantation, Wessyngton. She then said, "Hold on just a minute," and she got the same picture and showed it to me. I asked, "Did you know my great-

great-grandparents?" She told me that they were still working at Wessyngton when she was a young girl and started working there. She shared the history of her own family at Wessyngton and all the others she remembered from her childhood. Many lines of Mattie's ancestors came from Wessyngton going back five generations. This included the Washingtons, Cheathams, Terrys, and Lewises.

Mattie Terry, 1889–1982

I'm Mattie Terry, my father was Austin B. Terry, and my mother was Margaret Lewis Terry. They were both born down at Washington during slavery times. I worked at Washington from the time I was a young woman until I moved to the North with the Blagden branch of the Washington family.

Some of the old slaves would tell us stories about slavery times when we were children. They told me that some of their ancestors had been captured and taken aboard ships and were brought to America. They said that the first Washington, George A. Washington's daddy, brought their ancestors to Tennessee with him from Virginia, some of them walking every step of the way. I think some of them said there were fourteen when they first came out here. Those slaves really had it hard back then.

Sarah Washington Cheatham, 1810–1914

TOLD BY MATTIE TERRY

My great-grandma Sarah, even when she was over one hundred years old, would gather up all us grandchillun and great-grandchillun and tell us about slavery times. Sometimes when she would tell us what all they went through, me and the other children would all be crying. Thank the Lord He delivered them.

Grandma Sarah was born a slave at Washington. She married another slave, Tom. He was owned by Archer Cheatham and came to Washington when his owner died. I remember her telling us about building the Big House at Washington when she was just a girl. She said her and the other slaves would have to pack [carry] clay from down there in the bottom where the creek is up to where the Big House is now, and the other slave men made bricks to build that house, and it is still standing after all these years, so you know they knew what they were doing. She told us about landscaping that big ol' front yard and flower garden at Washington.

Grandma Sarah told us that prayer meetings had to be held in secret on the plantation and that slaves put overturned kettles and pots at their doors to muffle the sound of praying and singing. Grandma Sarah had seen slaves whipped with a wooden paddle with holes bored in it and salt and straw was rubbed in the wounds if they were caught praying for their freedom. The slaves would be held by other slaves, and others would be summoned to observe. Yet she said this still didn't stop 'em from holding the meetings.

Grandma Sarah lived to be one hundred four years old. At that age, she could thread a needle without the use of glasses and was still able to chop her own firewood.

Mattie Terry (*continued*)

My great-grandmother Sarah was Grandma Melissa's [1829–1911] mother. Melissa was my mother's mother. They both helped raise us children when my mother died, but Grandma Sarah did the most of our raising.

Melissa married one of the Lewis slaves who were brought to Wessyngton in 1843. After his death, Melissa married Edmund White Washington, who after emancipation became the first pastor of the Antioch Baptist Church in Turnersville. Melissa's daughter Margaret Lewis was my mother.

My father, Austin B. Terry [1844–1916], was born a Washington slave too. His daddy was Dick Terry [1818–1879]. He was brought to the plantation in 1838 from the plantation of Nathaniel Terry in Todd County, Kentucky. My daddy's mother's name was Aggy. They tell me that George A. Washington bought her and fourteen other slaves from a bank in Nashville. I heard lots of stories about Dick Terry. He was really mean. [Dick refused to be called by the Washington surname and was always referred to as Terry in all the Washington papers prior to his emancipation. Dick was of a very stubborn and determined disposition even during the days of slavery.] They couldn't do anything with him no matter how much they whipped him. [Shortly before the end of the Civil War, Dick sent word to the plantation that he was soon to return from Nashville and was to be boss of the place and he would be running the "damned plantation." He claimed that his friends, meaning agents from the Freedmen's Bureau, had met and would be dividing the estate among the former slaves.]

Right after slavery times some of our family moved to Cheatham County, where I was born. My mother died from childbirth when I was two years old. When I was a child, a white man accused my father of stealing wheat and had him arrested, but he was innocent. My father prayed so hard while in jail that the jailor became scared and released him.

My family returned to the Washington farm in the early 1900s. I did not get to attend school much because I had to help work in the fields. I would get to go a few days and would have to stop and help out on the farm, so I told my daddy it was no need for me to go a few days and have to stop, so I would just stop going altogether. He thought going a few days was better than nothing but let me stop anyway. I worked as hard as any man in the fields, and no man could cut tobacco as fast as I could, or hang tobacco, split rails, plow corn, or do any other work better than me. My younger brother Bill was one of the faster men in the county cutting and hanging tobacco and bragged that nobody could beat him. My daddy reminded him that I could beat him, and he said that didn't count because I was his sister. My sister Nannie was much smarter than me because when they would send her to the fields to work she would plow through the corn and cut down the tobacco on purpose so our father would send her back to the house. My father made me share part of my money with my sister, which I totally disagreed with. But you didn't argue with your parents back then, not even when you were grown. Work on the farm was hard, but by the grace of God we made it. You had to set [plant] tobacco with a wooden peg and fertilize the fields. The work was never ending.

I remember when I saw a train for the first time when I went to the Cedar Hill train depot with my auntie. I was so scared that I jumped into her arms although I was nearly as tall as she was.

My family was very large—ten sisters and brothers—and all of them had large families except me. I was the only one without any children. I often sent money home from the North to help out my sisters and brothers with their families. Once my brother's tobacco barn burned down with his whole year's crop, and I sent enough money to keep things going.

There is not a building that could hold the Terrys if they all got together. When my father died in 1916, I counted seventy-six grandchildren and great-grandchildren.

I knew your great-great-grandfather Uncle Man, but not as well as I knew his wife, Aunt Henny, because he died several years earlier, before her. By the time I came to Washington when I married Henry Washington Sr., John Phillips was the cook. Aunt Henny was very sweet and loved to talk. Others who worked there at the time were Rachel Terry, Lady Terry, Caroline Dunn, and Belle Ayers. Aunt Henny had to pack water from the creek in the bottom to the Big House to do the laundry, and Aunt Sarah Jane Scott Harris used to work there too. Aunt Henny lived in the bottom in a log cabin near a stream, and my father-in-law,

Gabe Washington, lived next door. My husband was kin to Aunt Henny. They used to hold prayer meetings in Aunt Henny's house on Wednesdays, and her house was always very neat. I remember when she died. Her funeral was held in the front yard down there at Washington in front of the Big House. Hundreds of people were there. And I mean Reverend Stoner from Antioch Baptist Church really did preach that funeral. They then took her body to the old slave graveyard at Washington. I didn't go to the burial because I had to go back to work in the Big House. The Washingtons were very fond of Aunt Henny and always treated those older slave people with great respect.

When my aunt Isabella died, she was so large they could not get her body through the door, so they had to knock down part of the wall to get her out to bury her. You know that old Washington house is haunted. One time when I was working in the Big House all the doors started slamming and everyone said it was George A. Washington's ghost. Nobody else was in the house.

I worked for the Washington family most of my life and later moved with the Blagdens, around 1915 when they moved to the Northeast. Me and my husband couldn't make it, so I got a divorce and started back using my maiden name. A lot of people think I have never been married because I have always been called Terry, but I have been married three times in all—to a Washington, a Hardin, and a Lewis. I've had two presidents' names, Washington and Hardin. No one should think I've lived all these years without a man.

When I left to go up North, my father told me good-bye and "I have lived to see you get grown, but I will never see you again." I said, "Of course you will see me again because I'll come home as often as I can." His words came to mind when in 1916 I received a telegram that he had died and had to be buried before I could get back to Tennessee. I came back home later that year and did so just about every year.

During the days of segregation, whenever I rode the train I was allowed to ride in the front cars with the Washingtons or by myself when I came South to visit because of the Washingtons' connections with the L&N Railroad. The conductor didn't like it very much, but there was nothing he could do about it. [George A. Washington had served as a director of the railroad in the 1870s, so the family received special attention.]

When I moved from the South with the Blagdens, they lived near John D. Rockefeller and while playing with some of the children I was raising I threw a baseball through their kitchen window. Mrs. Rockefeller was very nice about it. I have traveled all over the country with the Blagdens and Kinsolvings and got to see many things and it never cost me a cent. When I saw an airplane for the first time, I was not as afraid of it as I was of the train.

I returned to Washington for visits often. One time I told Aunt Henny and Aunt Sarah Jane and the other laundresses that they should be getting more money than fifty cents a day for their work because people up North were paying lots more for domestic work. Mrs. Washington [Mary Kemp Washington] heard me and didn't like it very much, but she didn't say anything.

I was a member of the Antioch Baptist Church in Turnersville. Most of the black families in the area attended Antioch back then. We used to have joyous times at the services held there back then. I remember we would have revivals and it would be midnight when church was over. We would walk back home in the dark for miles, and we would be singing and shouting all the way. You could hear the singing echo through the woods. My brothers could really sing well, and we really had a good time. I got baptized in the creek in the wintertime and they had to break the ice to get in, but I was not cold because I was filled with the Holy Ghost. Many people who left the area, like I did, would come back each year for the church homecoming held on the fourth Sunday in May. Some of the former Washington slaves also attended Mount Herman Baptist Church and the Saint James Baptist Church in Cedar Hill.

Miss Matt and I remained very close until her death. I often ran errands for her, and she was always very thankful. She would remark, "You have been better to me than if you had been my own son, and I will always love you for it. You know you never know how the Good Lord will work things out. When I was young, I used to go up to the Big House at Washington and get things for your great-great-grandmother Aunt Henny, and now you're doing the same thing for me after all these years." As a token of her appreciation, she made me a quilt when she was in her nineties, and remarked, "When I'm dead and gone, you will always have this to keep you warm and remember me by."

After my first visit with Miss Matt Terry, she suggested that I contact Cousin Carrie Washington, since she had been at Wessyngton most of her life and had an extraordinary memory. Cousin Carrie then lived on Central Avenue, formerly known as Thirteenth, a five-minute walk from my house and two blocks over from Miss Matt. As I knocked on the door, Cousin Carrie came to the door and in a stern voice said, "What do you want and who are you?" I told her that my grandmother was Sallie Washington. She then said, "Well, you're my cousin then, come on in." She then asked if I knew we were cousins. I told her that I knew she and my grandmother were second cousins. "Well, then if you knew that I was your cousin, how come you haven't come to see me before now?" she replied. Before I could answer, she told me she was glad I came by, and I told her about my research.

Carrie Williams Washington, 1894–1993

My name is Carrie Williams Washington. I was born in 1894. Kinchem Williams was my father. My mother's name was Mary

Ellis; she died when I was young, when my brother Herschel was just a baby. My daddy moved to Washington when I was a young girl and I worked there most of my life until I retired. My father's daddy and mama was Wes and Fannie Williams. There's their picture hanging on the wall. They lived down at Washington and stayed with their son Uncle Robert Williams, my father's brother. After Uncle Robert got drowned going to Clarksville with a load of tobacco, they moved with my daddy. Look at Grandma Fannie's picture. She was an Injun woman, who came from across the big waters. Grandma Fannie could tell fortunes with a deck of cards. She was really mean and didn't take nothing off nobody, even back in slavery times.

I married Guss Washington Jr., who was born at Washington, he's kin to your grandmother too. Guss's father and mother, Guss and Jenny, were both Washingtons and came from that plantation. Nearly all his people going back five generations were born or lived at Washington. Guss was the first black school-bus

*Carrie Williams Washington (1894–1993)
and Guss Washington Jr. (1892–1976).*

*Fannie Ricks Keaton Garrison Williams (1836–1920) and
Wesley Williams (1838–1918), portrait.*

driver for the Robertson County school system. [My mother, who lived in Springfield at the time, recalled going to spend the night with her cousins who lived in the country just so she could ride the first school bus.]

I've got several things that came from Washington. This Lincoln rocker came from down there, and these marble-topped tables too, and I've got silver and crystal from there. [When Cousin Carrie needed to go to a local nursing home, I purchased some of the silver and my godmother purchased the Lincoln rocker, a curio, and other items.] I draw a pension from working down at Washington now. My husband, Lady Terry, Mattie Terry, and Mary Terry all get pensions from the Washingtons.

I listened to Cousin Carrie for an hour before I could ask a single question. "Now let me show you a picture of some of the slaves from down at Washington," she said, looking at the same photo of my ancestors that I brought along. Pointing to Allen Washington, she said, "This was my husband's grandfather. He was the dairyman at Washington. You know that you are kin to my husband too. I can remember everything and everybody and just how they are all kin. Your great-grandmother Cousin Callie Washington was my mother's first cousin. My husband's grandmother Clara Washington was Uncle Man Washington's sister, that's how you're kin to him."

Cousin Carrie, do you remember my great-great-grandparents Emanuel and Henny Washington who had been slaves on the Washington farm?

Of course I do, I've known them since I was a girl.

Do you know who their parents were?

Lord, child, I don't know nobody old enough to tell you that because they were real old people when I was just a child, and you know how old I am.

As I prepared to go, Cousin Carrie said, "Be sure to come back and see me, and let me know what you find out about our family. There's a whole lot of Washingtons and other families that came from down there at Washington. Some of them still carry the Washington name and some of them have other names too." Over the years I visited Cousin Carrie several times to share information, which often brought things back to her memory and provided me with additional leads.

Next I visited Miss Lady Terry. Several branches of her family spanning several generations also came from Wessyngton. Miss Lady worked at Wessyngton for years and knew many of the slaves who came from the plantation. She had known my grandmother all her life as well as her parents and grandparents (my great- and great-great-grandparents). My grandmother would visit her at the home of her daughter Idella Williams each year when she came to Tennessee to visit. At the time Miss Lady started working at

Wessyngton, my great-great-grandmother Henny Washington was still there, so she had many memories of her. Miss Lady possessed an extraordinary memory and was known throughout the area for the many beautiful poems she wrote. She died in 1981, one week before her one hundred third birthday.

Fortunately, when she was ninety-eight, she recorded some of her childhood memories in a small booklet called *Reflections of the Past and Present,* which featured the remembrances of some of the senior members of the Antioch Baptist Church and others who grew up in the Turnersville community near Wessyngton.

Lady Terry Williams, 1878–1981

From "Life Story of Lady Terry Williams," in *Reflections of the Past and Present,* August 1976:

In the year of 1878 on January 18th Lady Terry was born to Wiley Terry and Rachel Washington Terry. I had four broth-

Rachel Washington Terry (1854–1918) and Wiley Terry (1851–1931), portrait.

ers and three sisters. I was born at Mt. Herman, West Cedar Hill, Tennessee, on the farm of Bill Miles. I started to school at the age of six years old at Mt. Herman. My first teacher was Pet Johnson. My sister Fannie Lou died while we lived there. Later my daddy bought his own farm. The land belonged to Joe Washington and he built a five-room house. We went to Turnersville School; two of my teachers were Bessie Taylor and Mattie Harris. When my father got old after we all were grown and married, he built another house and married. The house had four rooms. When he died, he left all of us twenty-one acres of land.

My grandfather and grandmother were slaves, and my mother and father were slave children. My father said he used to go to the field when he was a little boy and he would get so tired he would fall and his master had a big whip and he would whack him across the back and cut his shirt half in two.

I went in church at an early age at Antioch Baptist Church at Turnersville. I have been writing poems and papers since I was young. I would often give concerts. I wrote all my plays and songs and drills. The white people would ask me to come and use their barns for concerts, but as I got older I stopped that and used my talent for God.

I had two accidents when I was a child and one after I got grown. My sister and I went to the spring and it had been raining and the creek was out of the banks and I climbed up in a tree over the creek and the limb broke and I fell in the creek and I almost drowned. I was going down the third time and my sister Geneva was holding to a tree root and she caught my dress tail and our dog named Mack caught her by her dress and he pulled both of us out and it was country talk. They put it in the paper: "Dog Saves Children's Lives." We got a paper once a week.

The next accident I had my father and I was crossing the

*Seated: Richard Terry (1880–1968), John Terry, (1877–1943),
Sellie Terry (1875–1946). Standing: Lady Terry Williams (1878–1981),
and Geneva Terry Williams (1882–1972).*

creek in a buggy and it turned over and he fell on me but I was soon alright, and the last accident I had I was grown and had been married. My sister and I went to Adams, Tennessee, to see my blind auntie and on the way back home a car came around the curve and the horse ran off and turned the buggy over and my sister fell on me and hurt my chest.

I married Wash Williams December 29, 1898, we had five children and he had two of his first wife; she died, and I raised them. Wash was the cousin of John Williams, Ed Williams, and Bell Williams Dunn. After we married we lived at Benny Farmer's and stayed there several years, then we moved to Clarksville, Tennessee. We lived there a while, then we moved to the country to a place called Sango. We lived there until the tobacco growers had trouble and the association was started. The Night Riders were then organized. The farm Wash was on was with the wrong man and one day I went out and it looked like a battle. It was so many horses lined up on the hill that

Wash, my stepson Jim, and their boss had to run and hide in the straw [hay] stack until the next morning. Then my husband left home and was going to send for me but never did. I went home and started to work for the Washingtons in 1912 and remained there until 1955. I moved to Springfield, Tennessee, in 1927 but still worked at Washington. The Washingtons moved to Florida in the winter and I would go to Nashville to work.

I joined the Church of God and worked there until my health failed me in 1963. I helped all the churches around everywhere that asked for help. I think that's what God wanted me to do. The song I love so well is, "I Thank You, Jesus, You Brought Me from a Mighty Long Way." I cannot tell my whole story of ninety-eight years. This is just some of it.

———•———

With the bits of information I had gathered from the interviews, I went back to the archives for further research. The Washington Family Papers contain approximately 11,200 items, covering the period 1796 to 1964, and are stored on sixty-nine reels of microfilm. It contains accounts (farm and household), bills of sale, correspondence, court records, diaries, financial records, genealogical data, inventories, journals, land records, military records, newspapers, photographs, tax lists, receipts, maps, and other items. Over the years, I have spent every free moment—incalculable hours—in front of the microfilm machine.

Documents in the collection relating to African Americans include: slave bills of sale where the Washingtons had purchased slaves from 1801 through the 1840s; slave birth registers, from 1795 to 1860; lists of males slaves raising their own tobacco on the plantation from the 1830s to 1850s; the names of all the males in 1838, 1850, 1856, and 1860; slave doctor bills, 1815 to 1863; bills for runaway slaves; lists of runaway slaves before the Civil War; men from the plantation who enlisted in the Union Army; sharecropper contracts; and Washington family wills, 1600s through the 1850s, giving information on slave ownership. Other documents catalogued slave food and clothing allocations.

I also studied many public records. The 1820–1930 United States Censuses for Robertson, Davidson, Montgomery, Dickson, and Cheatham counties of Tennessee; records of Southampton, Surry, and Sussex counties of Virginia; tax receipt records; death records; wills; and church records all added, little by little, to the wealth of data I discovered.

Daily correspondence in the Washington papers provided so much personal information about various slaves on the plantation and the Washington family, I felt as though I knew them personally. My mother has often said if you listen to me speak about my ancestors and all the others from Wessyngton you would think that I did. As I found information, I shared it with some of the older relatives and other families.

It was a giant jigsaw puzzle and I had to piece together who was related to whom and what life was like centuries ago.

When I first started my research, people asked why I wanted to undertake such a project. A number of them felt that it was too painful a subject to deal with, especially for someone as young as I was at the time. I suppose many African Americans felt the same way, as most of the time, until years later, I was the only black person in the archives and local library doing this type of research. I knew that our ancestors had experienced unimaginable indignities during slavery but felt that I had to continue my research to find out all I could. I examined anything available to uncover the past.

One thing that encouraged me to carry on my research was the wealth of information I found about my own ancestors and others that contradicted what I usually read or heard. Most compelling was that nearly every family on the plantation before and after emancipation was headed by a male. Then their endeavors and accomplishments were impressive for a newly freed people. Former slaves fought in the Union Army for their freedom. Every black male on the plantation twenty-one and older was registered to vote for the first election after emancipation. Former slaves purchased hundreds of acres of land, some of which they once had been enslaved on. They established their own churches and held meetings to decide for whom they would vote. Former slaves became educators and even had schools named in their honor. They operated successful businesses and made contributions to their communities. It made me very proud to know that I came from a people that could do all this in spite of seemingly insurmountable odds.

CHAPTER 3

We Walked Every Step of the Way from Virginia to Tennessee

————•◦•————

The early documents I found in the archives brought me face-to-face with the horrors of the slave trade. My ancestors were captured from their homeland, as were millions of others during the 1700s, and brought to America as slaves.

At the same time the farmers and planters were creating new opportunities for themselves, Africans were losing their freedom, culture, and families. They were first imported into Jamestown, Virginia, in 1619. Using DNA data, oral histories, and naming patterns, we can learn the origins of some of the Wessyngton slaves who began their lives in Africa in the eighteenth century before they were captured and taken to America. Virginia slaveholders preferred slaves from the region of eastern Nigeria. This has been corroborated by DNA tests of the Wessyngton slave descendants: the majority of the Wessyngton descendants tested descend from the Ibo and Yoruba of Nigeria. According to an anthropological analysis of photographs of Wessyngton slaves, most of them resembled people from the regions of Benin and Nigeria, particularly the Ibo or Igbo.[1] Other slaves were brought from Sierra Leone and were members of the Mende and Temne ethnic groups. Wessyngton slaves and their ancestors also came from Liberia, Angola, Cameroon, Ghana, Niger, and Morocco—members of the Kru, Mbundu, Ewondo, Ga, Fulbe, and Berber peoples.

DNA test results support the origins of some slave names as listed in a 1795–1860 Wessyngton birth register. Axum (born 1808) was given the name of an ancient city in Ghana and a kingdom in Ethiopia. As late as 1858, Olayinka, a Nigerian name of the Yoruba people, was recorded in birth records at Wessyngton.[2]

During the slave trade Africans were captured by raids on their towns and villages and taken to coastal forts where they were held until a shipload of slaves could be assembled. Most slaves were taken from the western coastal regions of Africa stretching from Senegambia to Angola, including the Windward Coast, Gold Coast, Slave Coast, Bight of Benin, Bight of Biafra, and the Congo. Other slaves were captured far in the interior of the continent and were marched several hundred miles to the west coast. The men were shackled to each other in groups of two and locked in the dark holds of the slave ships; the women and small children were kept in separate compartments on deck. Once the slaves were secured, they began their dreaded voyage to the Americas.

The journey to America was perilous. Maggie Polk Washington, a descendant of Wessyngton slaves, heard that when white slave traders came to Africa, they would drag brightly colored ribbons through an area where children were playing. The slave traders would lure them away, trap them, and put them on ships bound for America, where they were auctioned off.[3] August was a slave owned by Richard Blow, a neighbor of the Washingtons in Southampton, Sussex, and Surry counties. August told the Blow family that his father was an African king, and he was next in line to assume the throne. A jealous uncle who wanted to be king betrayed him. His uncle sold him to the slave traders; the heir apparent was condemned to a life of servitude.[4] Mattie Terry, also a descendant of Wessyngton slaves, heard some former slaves speak of their ancestors who had been captured and taken aboard ships to America.[5]

The five-week to three-month voyage came to be known as the Middle Passage. Under cramped conditions, lack of food, and no sanitation, as many as a third of the enslaved Africans died before reaching the Americas. Richard Blow (1746–1833) was a merchant involved in the slave trade as a partner in the firm of Blow & Milhaddo. The company owned a fleet of ships that sailed to Europe, the East and West Indies, South America, the Coast of Guinea, and the Barbary States. It operated stores in Jerusalem, Southampton County, and several other parts of Virginia and North Carolina. Most likely, the Washingtons purchased slaves from them.

In 1792 Blow & Milhaddo sent Secretary of State Thomas Jefferson a letter about the unacceptable treatment of its slave traders. Their complaint gives us insight into the process and the dangers of the slave trade. Their schooner the *David & George* sailed from Portsmouth, Virginia, "to all and every part of the coast of Africa which the Captain should judge proper to visit, from thence to the West Indies, and back" to Portsmouth. The slave traders wrote that the "exposure to a mortality in those unhealthful climates" and "the insurrection of nearly eighty slaves" was "often fatal to a third of the crew." Only in passing, they added, "the mortality among the slaves was greater, on account of the necessity of them being more closely confined."[6]

When the surviving Africans set foot on alien soil they were sold or traded; families were torn apart. They spoke no English and were at the mercy of the slave traders. Their exact birth dates were unknown. To establish the age of a child for future tax purposes, the owner brought the child before a judge who examined his teeth and size and arbitrarily established his or her age.

My ancestors were taken to Surry, Southampton, and Sussex counties, Virginia, and ended up on the plantations of the Blow family. The Blows were an old, prominent family in Sussex and Southampton counties, as well as very large slaveholders. Colonel

Slave bill of sale for Jenny and Sarah from Micajah Blow to Joseph Washington, 1802.

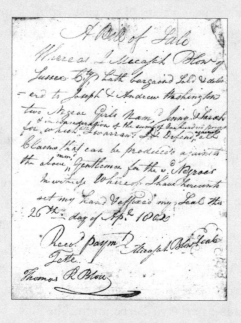

A Bill of Sale

Whereas I Micajah Blow of Sussex Cty hath bargained sold & delivered to Joseph & Andrew Washington two Negroe girls named Jenny & Sarah & in consideration of the sum of one hundred pounds for which title I warrant & defend against all claims that can be produced against the above named gentlemen for the said Negroes.

In witness whereof I have hereunto set my hand & affixed my seal this 26th day of April 1802.

Received payment   Micajah Blow [Seal]

Teste [Witness]

Thomas R. Blow

Michael Blow (1722–1799), who held several prestigious offices including justice for Sussex, deputy sheriff for Southampton County, member of the House of Burgesses (1774–1776), and colonel of the Continental Army in 1776, operated a large plantation with a labor force of fifty slaves. When his estate was divided in 1799, twelve slaves including Jenny Jr., or Little Jenny (b. 1792), Sarah (b. 1790), and their mother, Jenny Sr., and other immediate and extended family members were given to Michael's son Micajah Blow. The other slaves were divided among Colonel Blow's other children and grandchildren. In less than three years, financial difficulties forced Micajah to mortgage some of the land he had inherited and sell the two young girls, Jenny and Sarah, for 100 pounds English currency to Joseph Washington.[7]

This experience must have been traumatic for the two young girls. Although they managed to stay with their mother and other family members after the division of Colonel Blow's estate, they would now be taken hundreds of miles away and have all hopes of ever seeing their family again shattered.

The ten-year-old Jenny was my great-great-great-grandmother and the first of my ancestors brought to Wessyngton Plantation. She later became the matriarch of one of the largest families on the plantation and saw at least four generations of her family when she was finally freed after the Civil War.

Most of the slaves probably experienced a similar ordeal before their arrival at Wessyngton. Very few slaves were able to avoid sale, or being separated from family or friends their entire lives. Even if they were fortunate enough to escape it, there was always an ever-present fear that it could happen at any time.

———•·•———

After the American Revolution (1775–1783), white farmers and planters evicted the Shawnee, Choctaw, Creek, Chickasaw, and Cherokee Indians who for centuries had been living west of the

Allegheny and Appalachian mountains. The settlers poured into present-day Kentucky, Tennessee, Georgia, Mississippi, and Alabama during the generation following the signing of the Constitution. These new opportunities disrupted whatever security of family life slaves had established in their communities. Between 1790 and 1820, slave owners took nearly a quarter million slaves hundreds of miles from the worn-out lands in Virginia and the Carolinas to grow tobacco and cotton on the new frontier plantations.

———•——

Unlike so many writings about black history, I was able to research the history of the white Washington family over two centuries. The archives were a treasure trove of information, and Washington family descendants shared their photographs and their remembrances with me. Wessyngton slave descendants rounded out the picture with their memories.

The founder of Wessyngton Plantation was Joseph Washington. His parents, Joseph Washington and Zillah Branch, had eight children.[8] Joseph was born on July 8, 1770, in Jerusalem, Southampton County, Virginia. He worked with his father on their farm where they grew tobacco, the staple crop of Virginia. Joseph Sr. owned nineteen slaves in 1782.[9] He was not a large slaveholder, and he most likely worked with the slaves or supervised them closely.

Joseph Jr. became a slave owner at age twenty-three. He bought property in neighboring Sussex County and owned two slaves: "one above sixteen years and the other aged between twelve and sixteen."[10] Joseph returned to Southampton County in 1794. He owned five slaves—"three older than sixteen" and two between "ages twelve and sixteen"—from 1794 to 1798.[11]

In fall 1779, James Robertson led a group of several hundred men overland to prepare for the arrival by April 1780 of John Donelson's flotilla at French Lick on the Cumberland River. Donelson's party of 160 (120 women and children) traveled by thirty boats from the eastern border of present-day Tennessee. Their first settlement was located at the fort at French Lick, also known as Fort Nashborough; it was renamed Nashville in 1784. The Territory South of the River Ohio (the Southwest Territory) was established in which "slavery was sanctioned and emancipation outlawed: 'no regulation made or to be made by Congress, shall tend to emancipate slaves.'"[12]

The story of the founding of Wessyngton Plantation has been passed down through the family. In the Washington Family Papers I found a speech given by Joseph's grandson in 1915 on the occasion of commemorating his father's birth. By studying land deeds and books about the early days of Tennessee, I was able to amplify the stories that were part of the Washington family lore.

Tennessee achieved statehood seventeen years after the first settlement, in 1796. In that year Joseph was engaged to "his fair cousin" Rosanna Branch. He joined his uncle Benjamin Branch, his daughter Rosanna, and other family members on their three-month journey from Southampton County, Virginia, to Tennessee. He

Joseph Washington (1770–1848),
portrait by John C. Grimes, 1836.

made the journey on horseback (accompanied by his servant, also on horseback) and brought practically all of his worldly goods in a pair of cowskin saddlebags. He and his relatives moved westward with that restless tide of emigration ever seeking adventure and success in new fields, where good land was abundant and cheap.[13]

During the journey "a dashing young man who owned several race horses which he was taking to New Orleans" joined the party. "Rosanna fell in love and transferred her affections from her cousin to this young man. Her father seriously objected to the young man and got his gun and told him to go and he went. Joseph never renewed his affair with Rosanna," and she married someone else. The Branch family settled on a place on Whites Creek in Davidson County not far from Nashville, and Joseph set off to make his own way.[14]

Joseph reportedly "stopped over" to visit his friend Joseph Philips, whose parents were originally from Southampton County. He owned a farm outside of Nashville, three miles south of Mansker's Station. Joseph Washington felt that the area was too densely settled and continued thirty miles north of Nashville to what is now Robertson County.

Where the town of Springfield exists today, Joseph called upon his kinsman Colonel Archer Cheatham Jr. His grandson continued the story: "About 1790 [his father] Archer Cheatham Sr. from North Carolina [originally from Amelia County, Virginia] and his wife, Miss Anderson, had settled not far from the banks of Sulphur Fork Creek. They reared a family of eight sons, all of whom became men of power and influence." One son, Archer Jr., married Susan Long, a relative of Joseph; Archer Jr. was one of the founders of Springfield [and a very wealthy man].[15] "It was said that during his visit, Archer brought his newborn eldest daughter Mary and placed her in Joseph's arms with the remark, 'Here, Cousin Joseph, take her. She will make you a good wife someday.'"[16]

Joseph made his new home close to the Cheathams' property. There he found open, fertile land edged by a creek and heavily forested rolling hills. Game abounded, so there was no fear of starvation. He must have rented some land, because the founding of Wessyngton Plantation dated from 1796. "On July 10, 1784, the State of North Carolina, of which Tennessee was at that time a part, had granted 640 acres of land [for Revolutionary War service[17]] to Moses Winters Sr. [Moses and his son Caleb had come with Robertson's party in 1779, and his wife and their seven daughters were in the Donelson flotilla[18]]. [At first Caleb lived in a cave on Caleb's Creek and subsisted on the game which he killed.[19]] Caleb built his house at the bottom of a hill near a spring. His log cabin was one of the very first erected by a white man in Tennessee County. At that time and for several years later the area was infested by roving bands of hostile Indians.

"Moses and Caleb Winters, like their few and widely scattered neighbors, cultivated their crops with the trusty rifle close at hand. They never worked far from the house, which was both dwelling and fort. They lived in constant expectation of attack by a wily savage foe lurking in the bushes. Moses Winters made a small 'clearing' and planted an apple orchard, called the Winters' orchard. Caleb and Moses [d. 1798] and some members of their families, who may possibly have been killed by Indians, were buried near an ash tree on the lawn to the west of the dwelling [Wessyngton mansion]. Years later the rude headstone and sunken places were pointed out by the old Negroes as the Winters's graves."[20] Primitive stone arrowheads and a cemetery attested to the presence of Native Americans on the Wessyngton land centuries before the arrival of the first white settlers.[21]

Joseph's grandson continued the history that he had been told by his ancestors and that was confirmed by early land deeds and histories of Robertson County:

By a deed dated December 8, 1798, Joseph purchased sixty acres in the Horse Shoe Bend on the North side of Sulphur

Washington family crest.

Fork Creek from Hugh Lewis [for $360 [22]]. Lewis had pur-
chased the land from Benjamin Menees [Menees had bought
200 acres of the original land grant from Moses Winters Sr.[23]].

Joseph named his new home Wessyngton. The Washingtons
traced their ancestry back to William de Hertburn in twelfth-
century England where their family owned a manor estate called
Wessyngton—the Norman spelling of Washington. William de
Hertburn changed his name to William de Wessyngton.[24] The first
Washington to come to America in Joseph's line was John Washington, who immigrated to Surry County, Virginia, in 1658. One
of John's cousins also named John immigrated to Westmoreland
County, Virginia, in 1656. This John Washington was the great-

grandfather of President George Washington, thus making the Tennessee Washingtons close cousins of the president.

Joseph's grandson described those early days "when so many trials and dangers threatened the pioneer settlers, it was quite common for those who were friends and relatives to emigrate and settle in the same community near each other for mutual protection."[25] Joseph was not the only Washington to come to Robertson County. His younger brother Andrew (born 1775) and his family, and his sister Lucy Williams (born 1781) and her family migrated there during those years. Other relatives living near Joseph included the Thompson and Davis families.

According to his grandson in the 1915 speech, "Joseph made several trips back to his old home [in Virginia] and brought out a number of Negroes and other property." One of the pieces he brought was a wine chest that had a personalized inscription in a half-moon design: "1798, Joseph Washington, Virginia."[26] His grandson described the arduous journey:

> On a trip on horseback from Eastern Virginia to Nashville, the greater part of the way there was no road, which even a crude wagon could travel. There was only a trail blazed through the dense forest. These hardy pioneers on foot or on horseback crossed the Blue Ridge, the Allegany [as the Appalachian Mountains were called then] and the Cumberland Mountains; they forded or swam the rivers and raging torrents; they camped wherever night overtook them; they dared not have a fire after dark for fear of Indians.[27]

We can track the approximately 800-mile, three-month journey that Joseph and his slaves most likely took from Virginia to Wessyngton. By 1796 at least parts of the trail could accommodate small wagons, so it was probable that on later trips the group came by horseback, by foot, and by wagon. According to Mattie

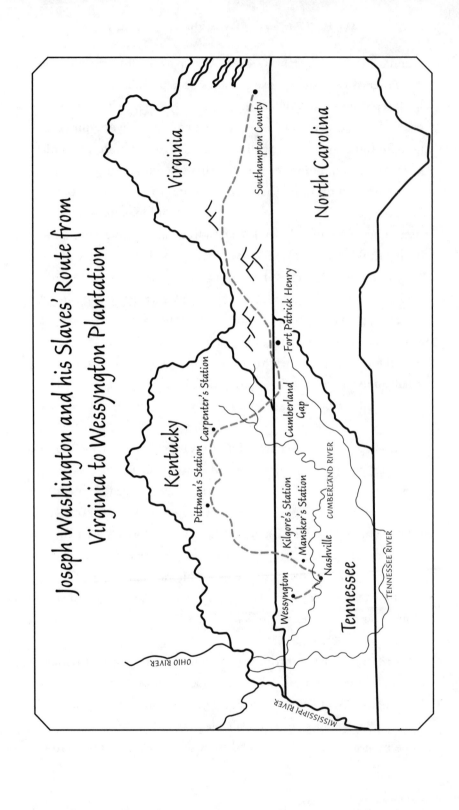

Joseph Washington and his Slaves' Route from Virginia to Wessyngton Plantation

Terry, some of the slaves walked every step of the way from Virginia to Tennessee.

They left Southampton County, sixty miles south of Petersburg. They traveled west to Big Lick (Roanoke) and, using roads and trails developed during and after the Revolutionary War, reached the Virginia frontier lying west of the Blue Ridge Mountains. They crossed the Appalachian Mountains and left the Great Wagon Road that travelers used to go from Pennsylvania to North Carolina. They connected with the Wilderness Road, which branched south. The Wilderness Road was first mapped out in the late 1760s by Daniel Boone who, on intelligence from peddlers who had contact with the Indians, discovered an east-west gap in the Appalachian Mountain range. On the Wilderness Road they entered the Shenandoah Valley, and then into the hilly areas of southwest Virginia.

They proceeded south past Abingdon, Virginia, branching in a westerly direction to pass through the point crossing the Cumberland Mountains at the Cumberland Gap and entered into the land that made up the future state of Kentucky. They then trekked partially northwest, following the route that James Robertson's men used (in their fifty-five-day overland trip from Fort Patrick Henry in East Tennessee to Nashville) to reach Carpenter's Station, about ten miles from Danville, Kentucky. They then turned south to Logan's Station (St. Asaph).

Once they turned west on this route, the Cumberland Trace, they crossed the Rolling Fork River and then reached Robinson Creek, passing near Buckhorn Creek, and wound down the south side of the Trace Fork of Sinking Creek (Pitman Creek). They crossed the Green River, a one-day journey past Pittman's Station, the Little Barren River at Elk Lick, and then the Barren River to reach Three Springs.

It would have taken five days to reach Mansker's Station in Tennessee. To reach Nashville, travelers would then cross the Cumberland River at the Bluffs.[28] Joseph and his slaves did not cross the river. Rather, they traveled northwest from the Cumberland River and journeyed over a winding hilly route for one more day, a distance of twenty-five miles, to reach the place that would become Wessyngton.

Joseph purchased more slaves in Virginia. Due to the scarcity of slaves in the newly settled Territory of Tennessee, it was probably not possible for him to buy them as cheaply as in Virginia. In 1801 he acquired two slaves: Juda, a part of his inheritance from the estate of Sarah Stephenson; and Samuel, purchased from his uncle, Newsom Branch, in Southampton County. Then Sam was purchased from Joseph Richardson of Edgefield, South Carolina.

Joseph most likely brought some of his brother Andrew's slaves with him to Tennessee or was left in charge of them when Andrew returned to Virginia. Joseph Sr. died in 1803 and named his son Edwin as executor of his estate. Edwin died on March 24, 1804, before settling his father's estate. Andrew wrote Joseph that their brother William planned to divide the land and slaves by Novem-

Andrew Washington (1775–1835),
portrait by John C. Grimes, 1836.

ber 4 and he should come back to Virginia by that time. Subsequently, Andrew, who was living with William and was about to get married, instructed Joseph to break open his trunk and collect as much money as he could from his notes, to sell his bed and wagon, to bring his slave Abraham and a horse with sixty or seventy dollars, and to take care of the rest of his Negroes as his own. He also told his brother to try to sell Easter and her children for $750 and to bring the money to Virginia. He subsequently advised him that she may not be worth so much and "$700 would do." Andrew continued, "If Easter and her children can't be sold, maybe we can make a trade when you come to Virginia."[29]

Easter and her two children, Britain and Nanny, were purchased by Joseph for $550. He returned to Tennessee with a number of slaves: Tom, a part of the division from his father's estate, and Jacob, received from his deceased brother Edwin. Joseph also inherited money and land from both estates.

Some of the slaves purchased by Joseph in these years were first-generation Americans whose parents had been captured in their native Africa and sold into the American slave system. We know very little about many of these early slaves—with the exception of the Blow family slaves—before they came to Wessyngton.

Joseph lived on his land at Horse Shoe Bend until 1802, when he purchased 204 acres from Moses Winters and his heirs for $816.[30] At the same time Joseph was to give "one Negroe between the age of eleven and sixteen years old, at the price of four hundred dollars to Winters and his heirs." In return Winters and his heirs promised to pay Joseph $99 "at the delivery of said Negroe," which was "the balance" that was due from the land purchase.[31] Although not named in the document, an oral agreement would have specified the (assumed to be male) slave involved. The slave's undetermined age meant that he most likely was born in Africa or was recently purchased. It was one of the few occasions that Joseph sold a slave.

The land Joseph purchased was located on the south side of Sulphur Fork Creek "beginning at a Sycamore tree in the mouth of Caleb's Creek where it empties into Sulphur Fork."[32] According to his grandson, "Joseph moved to a double log house with stone chimneys, which had been built by Moses Winters. It stood in what was called 'the Bottom Field,' about 150 yards of Caleb's Creek and nearly opposite 'Cave Spring,' out of which they used water."[33] Joseph became active in the community and held positions of responsibility. He served as county coroner from 1805 to 1814.[34] In 1807 he began an association with Robertson County's private school for higher education; he was a trustee of Liberty Academy for many years.[35]

———•••———

In the areas around Nashville, cotton was the major agricultural crop; it was easily shipped to market along the river routes.[36] Joseph, perhaps because of his upbringing in Virginia, chose a different path. According to local tradition, Joseph was the first settler in the Robertson County area to begin the cultivation of dark tobacco. He brought the first dark-fired tobacco seeds to the county. Dark tobacco was used for snuff, cigars, and chewing tobacco. Joseph and his slaves probably produced their first tobacco crop when he made his first purchase of sixty acres lying in the Horseshoe Bend of the Sulphur Fork Creek in 1798. By 1812 Joseph owned 1,037 acres of land and approximately twenty-five slaves. It was these slaves' labor, as well as the work of those who came later, that forged the Washington empire and the largest tobacco plantation in America.

CHAPTER 4

We Built That Big House Brick by Brick

L ocal and family lore had it that the Washingtons often purchased slaves in family units. They never sold any slaves
off the Wessyngton Home Place—and only two slaves
were ever sold from their other holdings.[1] This could be confirmed
by studying census data and documents in the archives.

Few slaveholders owned an entire family; at most, they owned
a mother and her smaller children. Male slaves were more likely to
be sold than females, and more often than not, alone. Slaves were
typically sold for several reasons: to satisfy debts, to settle estates,
and to be given as gifts or bequeathed.

Joseph lived on his plantation as a bachelor for more than a
decade. Then Archer Cheatham Jr.'s prediction on Joseph's visit
in 1796—that Joseph would marry his daughter—came true. On
March 12, 1812, forty-two-year-old Joseph married Mary who
was then sixteen. Mary, when not older than twelve, attended a
boarding school near Charlotte, North Carolina. A hearty frontier
girl, she made the journey of 450 miles by horseback, probably
on the new more direct route from Nashville through Knoxville
into North Carolina.[2] Joseph and Mary were second cousins once

Mary Cheatham Washington
(1796–1865), portrait by John C.
Grimes, 1836.

removed, so their descendants were related to President George Washington on both their maternal and paternal lines.

At the beginning of his marriage, Joseph had to deal with the consequences of a relationship he had when he was still single. At forty-one, Joseph fathered an illegitimate daughter who was born around the time of his marriage. The young mother was the daughter of Joseph's neighbor, Azariah Dunn, a farmer. Dunn sued Joseph for "the seduction of one of his daughters for which said Joseph Washington is charged of having begotten a child." The suit was settled in November 1812 with Joseph promising to pay a lump sum of $5,000 and seven notes valued at $15 due each year on November 9 for maintenance of the child unless the child died.[3] The child was not given the Washington name; the mother, a white and free person, married and moved out of Tennessee. Slave women who became pregnant by their masters, other whites, and even slaves had no such recourse under the law.

Joseph worked diligently to increase the size of his holdings. His strategy included the purchase of more land along water routes for transporting his crops. In 1814 and 1815 he received two land grants totaling 450 acres from the State of Tennessee. This land became known later as the present-day town of Orlinda and an area south of the town. Up to 1820 there were twenty-seven entries in the deed records in Robertson County: twenty-four of these were Joseph's land purchases. When his father-in-law Archer Cheatham died in 1823, Joseph and Mary inherited 615 acres from his extensive holdings.[4] By 1838 he had purchased thirty additional tracts of land.

With the increase in his property and land under cultivation, Joseph increased his workforce. This required the purchase of more slaves. In 1813 Joseph's tax records (the earliest yet found after his arrival in Tennessee) indicated that he owned thirteen slaves considered to be taxable.[5] Other records, such as slave bills of sale and recorded births for the plantation, showed that he owned at least twenty other slaves, thirteen of which were children under sixteen years of age.[6] In this group, only five families were discernible, consisting of sixteen slaves.

Many letters in the Washington papers discussed the purchase and sale of slaves. Mr. N. Minor wrote Joseph in 1814 regarding the purchase of a young girl:

> Mr. Middleton showed you a Negro girl yesterday, he will return with her to Kentucky this morning, probably to old Mr. Williams. When he has taken her back to Kentucky you may buy her there without any risk to either party, as there is a law in favor of purchasers residing in the state. Mr. Middleton will not sell in this state but when he returns to Kentucky his price will be $250.[7]

During this period Kentucky enacted a law to discourage slave trading within the state, requiring all purchasers to reside in the state and to sign an oath stating that the slave was for personal use and not for trade and that the slave had not been imported into the country from Africa after the 1808 ban on the transatlantic slave trade.

Joseph made his first purchase of a nuclear family in 1814 from his relative James Thompson: Tom, age thirty-two; his wife, Jenny, age twenty-nine; and their four children: Frank, age eight; Hannah, age six; Sarah, age four; and Henny, eleven months. The baby Henny was the mother of my great-great-grandmother, Henny Washington. In addition, Joseph purchased Jenny's mother, who was also named Jenny (born 1760).

Joseph obtained the last of the Virginia slaves in 1819 when he received four slaves from his brother William Washington's estate. At this time, Esther, her daughter Sally, Sam, and Simon were transported to Wessyngton. James Clayton of Southampton County, Virginia, informed Joseph at that time that the sale of slaves belonging to his brother had been completed. Clayton accounted for the high sale price: "Negroes continues to be high and horses low."[8]

Joseph and Mary lived in a double-log house opposite the Cave Spring[9] where Martha Susan was born in 1813 and George Augustine in 1815. From 1802 to 1815 Joseph continued buying land from Winters's heirs. In 1815 he purchased 211 acres for $600. On that land, on a high knoll overlooking the vast estate, Joseph and Mary immediately started the construction of the Wessyngton mansion. It took four years to complete. His grandson recalled, "When a very small boy, George Augustine used to ride behind his father up to where they [the slaves] were building the 'new house.'"[10]

The mansion was designed in the late Federal style, perhaps reminiscent of the architecture style in Joseph's native Virginia. The mansion as it stands now is much the same as when it was built. A center hall led to rooms on both sides. Off one of the large rooms was another room toward the rear of the house. The second floor with the bedrooms followed the same plan.

The bricks of burned local clay used to build the house were made by the slaves. The clay produced bricks in a warm salmon shade.[11] Each wall was four to five bricks thick. The lumber was grown on the estate and cut in a sawpit.[12] Sarah Washington Cheatham, born on the plantation in 1810, told her descendants that she remembered the construction of the mansion when she was a very young girl. With the other slaves, Sarah went to the banks of Caleb's Creek to collect clay. They carried the clay up the hill where the mansion now stands and baked it in a kiln. They built that Big House brick by brick.

Sarah recalled when the large front yard was sodded and the flower garden was landscaped.[13] The Washingtons added an historical touch to their mansion. At least one of the gutter downspouts was decorated with elements of the centuries-old Washington family crest.

Joseph and Mary's original double-log cabin was then used by his slaves.[14] To the rear of the main house was a row of cabins for the house servants. Down the steep slope behind the mansion to the south and west, toward the creek flat, stood other slave cabins. Some cabins were positioned on the hillside, leveled by the use of

Slave cabins on hillside behind Wessyngton mansion, ca. 1890s.

limestone piers, while others were located at the bottom of the hill where the land flattened out.

After the mansion was completed, Mary had a second son, Joseph Edwin, born in 1818, who died the same year. The Washington family cemetery was most likely started after their son's death. They chose a location close to the mansion, overlooking the hilly landscape.

In the early 1820s, Joseph and Mary sent their seven-year-old daughter Martha Susan to board at the newly established Nashville Female Academy.[15] There she took private piano classes and begged her mother to attend dancing school on Saturdays. On November 4, 1824, Martha Susan wrote her mother, "I am well except I have a very bad cold which I believe is very common."[16] Three days later (and certainly before her letter reached its destination), Martha Susan died. The story surrounding this tragedy was part of local lore:

> A remarkable vision experienced by Mrs. Washington just before the death of her only daughter . . . is one of those instances of forewarning. . . . From her sleep one morning, she started up with a cry of pain and told her husband of a distressing dream from which she had just awakened. In her vision, she was standing in the garden listening to rapidly approaching horses' hoofs. The hoof beats ceased at the gate leading to the house. Across the flowering shrubs presently came her husband's voice saying, "Mary, Mary, I have a message." A moment more and he was at her side reading aloud a letter that told them that their daughter was seriously ill in Nashville. Seeing the depressing effect of the dream on his wife, Mr. Washington decided that mother and daughter must no longer be kept apart. With the quickness of a dream, they were at once on their way to the sick child.
>
> Hasten as they would, over the ups and downs of the old dirt

road [about twenty miles], it was black night when they reached [what was later known as] Hyde's Ferry where the Cumberland must be crossed to get to the city. The ferryman, who was asleep, was aroused with difficulty and induced by more than a "silver crown to row them o'er the ferry." But all too late. When the parents reached the school, they were told at the door that their daughter was dead.

Every detail of the dream was fulfilled. The hoofbeats on the graveled road, the husband's call, the vain race to reach the ferry before dark, the delay occasioned there and the shock at the door of the school when they were told that their daughter had just died, all had come true.[17]

Joseph and Mary's sole surviving child was George Augustine. He "attended Liberty Academy in Springfield, then under the management of Professor Loring, one of the great characters in the educational world at that time."[18] His father had been a trustee of the

George Augustine Washington
(1815–1892), portrait, ca 1830.

academy for many years.[19] George graduated from the University of Nashville in 1832.[20]

Immediately upon leaving college George took up the life of a planter.[21] In the mid-1830s he took increasing control of the plantation's affairs. Correspondence between George and his parents detailed his travels to Canada, New York, Philadelphia, Baltimore, and New Orleans, where he made investments and purchased supplies for the plantation. He even traveled to Havana, Cuba, to study their techniques for the cultivation of dark tobacco.[22]

In 1836, while in Washington City, George visited President Andrew Jackson, who was from Tennessee. George wrote his mother, saying: "You know I always had an exalted opinion of him and I must say . . . it has increased. The old man was lively and animated, much more so than I had any idea he was, in fact I had formed an opinion that he was cold and morose; but I assure you this is not so."[23]

———•·•———

On January 17, 1831, Granville was born at Wessyngton. His mother, Fanny, born in 1815, was a Wessyngton slave, the daughter of Tom and Jenny, whom Joseph bought from his relative James Thompson in 1814. Both slave descendants and certain Washington descendants believed that his father was George Augustine, who was then fifteen. Photographs of Granville showed a marked family resemblance to George.

———•·•———

By 1820 the Wessyngton population had grown to forty-four blacks, consisting of at least seven families, thus making Joseph the second largest slaveholder in the county after his father-in-law Archer Cheatham, who owned seventy-seven slaves.

The slave market fluctuated with the prices of cotton, tobacco,

Granville Washington   *George A. Washington*
(1831–1898), ca. 1891.   *(1815–1892), ca. 1880s.*

sugar, and other plantation crops. The most expensive slave Joseph purchased was thirty-year-old Godfrey, bought for $800 in 1821.[24]

When Archer Cheatham Jr. died in 1823, Joseph and Mary inherited seven slaves.[25]

From 1832 through 1839, thirty-two slaves were purchased, mainly to work on the Kentucky plantation. Joe was purchased from Joseph's nephew Joseph George Washington in 1833. Joseph George sold three slaves to his brother Richard E. A. Washington in 1835. Harry was purchased in 1833 from the estate of Thomas Polk, President Polk's uncle. In 1835 the brothers Tony, John, David, Tom, and Edmund were purchased from Daniel White of Todd County, Kentucky.

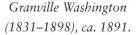

Isaac Franklin, along with John Armfield of Virginia, established the largest slave-trading firm in the United States. They were among the first professional traders to take advantage of the low prices for slaves in the worn-out lands of Virginia and Maryland, and transport them to the highly profitable slave markets of the Deep South. Their main office was in Alexandria, Virginia, and they had representatives in New Orleans, Louisiana; Natchez, Mississippi; Richmond and Warrenton, Virginia; Frederick and Baltimore, Maryland; and Boston, Massachusetts. By the 1830s the firm had transported more than one thousand men, women, and children from Alexandria to the Natchez and New Orleans markets to help meet the demand for slaves in the Deep South. While visiting Nashville in September 1833, George wrote his father: "Franklin the Negro trader passed through town today with 150 Negroes; he had something like 100 fellows chained together. They marched into town in a file of two with a large chain passing all along between them."[26] By the time Franklin and Armfield retired from business, each of them had accumulated over half a million dollars. Nathan Bedford Forrest was the largest slave trader in the Memphis area. He reportedly earned as much as $96,000 in 1850 in the trade. Although these enterprises yielded their owners enormous profits, they shattered the lives of countless men, women, and children as their family members were torn away from them and scattered throughout the country forever.

Being auctioned was terrifying and degrading for the slaves. They were paraded before large crowds of jeering spectators and treated with less dignity than animals. Often potential buyers examined the slave's teeth, limbs, and even their sexual organs to ensure they were making a sound purchase. Slaves lived in constant fear of being sold in this manner. They were well aware that they could be sold at any time to settle debts, be given as gifts, or inherited.

In an 1838 letter to his nephew George, Richard Cheatham recounted that he had dined with President Van Buren, and added:

"Negroes here in Maryland and Virginia are high. I learn but few are for sale. General Carter a few days since paid $870.00 for a likely yellow boy about twenty-two, a good servant."[27]

The Washingtons left thousands of documents that shed light on the lives of the African Americans on the plantation. During George's travels, he wrote many letters to his parents, his wife, and his overseers on various matters, including the slaves. They in turn informed him of events on the plantation: which slaves had run away, who was ill, who died, who was born. They told him about slaves that were available for sale in the neighborhood and the actions of other planters' slaves.

While traveling in the East in the late 1830s, George kept his parents abreast of the prospect of purchasing slaves there or possibly making other investments: "I shall leave this place sometime next week for Virginia and if Negroes are higher than I can afford to pay [,] I will return to this place and invest my funds in Tennessee bank stocks or Tennessee state bonds as both are quite low at this time."[28] Later, he wrote from Virginia:

> I arrived here on last Sunday evening, and have been engaged pretty much through the week attending auction sales of Negroes (of which there are more or less here everyday) and examining and pricing them in one of the principal establishments kept here for the sale and safe keeping of them (there are also some two or three of these in the city); but as yet find them selling too high for me to engage in purchasing, the market appears better stocked with women, children and boys than fellows, and commanding higher prices in proportion; women $700.00–$725.00, boys, from 12 to 14 $650.00–$700.00, girls the same age $550.00–$600.00, men although not so plentiful are lower say $800.00–$900.00 which prices are quite as high as at home. I shall remain here a few

days, and should there be no change for the better will return without buying and should I conclude to purchase will write for Mr. Simms to come on immediately.[29]

A small number of slaveholders made provisions for their slaves so they would not be sold at public auction. Jacob F. Young of Robertson County made an unusual provision in his will for his slaves: "I will that my three Negro boys: Colbert, Jerry and Moses have the right to choose their master and that he pay whatever he pleases and if they become dissatisfied that they have the right to choose again by the last master paying to the first whatever he paid to the estate and so on, and I request my executor to see to this as they have been faithful servants to me and desire that they shall be well treated." He made provisions for his other slaves that were to be sold that no Negro speculator (slave trader) be allowed to bid for them.[30]

When Henry Gardner died, his will stated that Aaron and Betty together with their increase (children) were to be sold at a private sale in one lot by his executors, and not to be sent to the lower country. Five slaves were bought from the estate for $2,270: Aaron, thirty-five, his wife Betty, twenty-five, and their three sons— Daniel, age ten, George, age nine, and Jackson, age eight. They were thereafter referred to as "Gardners" on all slave listings and in the Washington family correspondence.[31]

The plantation manager Benjamin Simms kept George updated while he was traveling:

> You state in yours that you wish my views as to the prospects of buying Negroes in this country, it is utterly impossible in my opinion for you to buy as many as you want here at any price for should there be a good crop, raised Negroes will bring I believe from $1,000.00 to $1,200.00 here. I wrote you last week informing you I had bought the Gardner Negroes for $2,270.00. $1,000.00 to

be paid the first of June and the balance the first of May
1840 and they are the only Negroes I know of for sale
anywhere. I will only say to you that my opinion is, was
I in your place I would buy while I was in that country
admitting you have to wait for me until the first of June.[32]

Despite Simms's advice, in view of the expensive prices for slaves
in Virginia, George informed his parents that he had decided to
rely on the markets in Tennessee and Kentucky to supply the labor
demands of the Washington plantations:

> I was very much pleased to learn from Mr. Simms he had
> purchased the Gardner Negroes, they were bought on
> very good terms much cheaper than such can be pur-
> chased in Virginia. I believe upon mature deliberation
> it will be better I should return without purchasing and
> depend upon picking them up about through Kentucky
> and Tennessee. In fact it would be better to pay one or
> two hundred more at home than it would in Virginia.[33]

We cannot determine from existing records exactly how much
tobacco Joseph and George planted each year, but family tradition
had it that they raised at least 250 acres each year after their holdings were extended. Barns that measured sixty feet by one hundred
feet and built of twenty-foot logs housed the tobacco. At one time,
there were nine tobacco barns on the plantation.

Tobacco production was and still is very labor intensive. We
can only imagine how difficult production was before the use of
modern machinery. The tobacco was hauled in wagons twenty-
five miles to the Cumberland River at Clarksville. Then it was sent
by flatboats six hundred miles down the Mississippi River to New
Orleans, where it was sold.[34]

Tobacco fields, Wessyngton Plantation.

With the free labor of scores of slaves Wessyngton became completely self-sufficient. The mansion was surrounded by a two-story brick smokehouse, blacksmith's shop, cooper's shop, nurseries, tobacco barns, great granaries, carriage house, poultry houses, milk room, stables, loom house, overseer's house, and slave quarters. Grist mills and a distillery were built on the plantation. Many of the slaves were trained as artisans, brick masons, carpenters, painters, blacksmiths, domestics, seamstresses, weavers, tailors, coopers, and stonemasons.[35] Their skilled labor was essential to all operations on the plantation.

All the corn not used for human or animal consumption was distilled into whisky. Joseph wrote down the instructions for distilling the finest quality whisky in an 1802 account book. Joseph must have brought the method of distilling whisky with him. There are many letters between his brothers and him about how much whisky was produced on their father's farm back in Southampton County, Virginia, in the early 1800s. In 1834 Washington built a still house, and the following year a doubling still was in operation.

There were vast peach and apple orchards at Wessyngton. The

fruit would be gathered into large wagons, and the mash was made and put into barrels and aged. The peaches and apples were converted into brandy and vinegar. As early as 1827 Joseph recorded the sale of 115 gallons of apple brandy and 32 gallons of vinegar. Between 1835 and 1836 he produced 3,560 gallons of brandy and 593 gallons of port.[36]

The plantation had a blacksmith shop located near the main house where horseshoes were made and iron work done. Recent archaeological investigations near the slave cabin site revealed that nails were manufactured on the estate during the early 1800s. Wagons, plows, barrels, and other farm instruments were made at the cooper's shop. A brick kiln was located on the property. In addition to producing bricks for the mansion and other buildings, Joseph sold finished brick. For example, he sold one thousand bricks to Jesse Darden in 1834.[37]

There was a sawmill on the property where lumber was manufactured for plantation use and for sale. Joseph sold wood, poplar planking, weatherboarding, oak plank, and hogshead staves to his neighbors Oliver Connell and William White in 1833. In their grist mills wheat was ground into flour for use on the plantation.[38]

The plantation had a major pork industry. Joseph and his slaves brought the method of curing hams from Virginia. In 1838 he recorded sending a slave Frank to Kentucky with 360 pounds of bacon, a one-month supply. Washington Hams were known for their superb taste throughout the South and were on the menus of the finest restaurants and hotels from as far south as New Orleans and as far north as Philadelphia during this period and later. Joseph operated a trading post on the estate. Account books from 1808 to 1839 listed the sale of large amounts of bacon, brandy, ham, lard, lumber, candy, coffee, salt, plows, beef, and mutton.

In 1836 tragedy struck the Washington family. Joseph's brother Andrew had a son, Joseph George. Joseph George was a striking, tall figure, "about six feet high, tolerably stout built, tolerably dark complexion dark eyes and black hair." He was a leader in the defense of the Alamo. He was killed in battle at the Alamo when he was just twenty-eight. Within the family, and in historical lore of the Alamo, he was thereafter known as "Alamo Joe." The Republic of Texas offered land to those men (or the heirs of those who were killed) who had helped it win its independence from Mexico. Joseph George's heirs requested his land grant.[39] A portrait of "Alamo Joe" was painted most probably by an itinerant painter who painted young George's. As was the style of many itinerant painters of the time, an individualized head was placed on a standard torso against a uniform background.

A few months later, Joseph commissioned the prominent portrait painter, John C. Grimes, to paint three portraits at a cost of

Joseph George Washington
"Alamo Joe" (1808–1836),
portrait.

$197—$150 for three portraits, $45 for three frames, and $2 for packing boxes.[40] By their similar styles, we believe that the portraits of Mary and Joseph were painted by Grimes. He was well known and painted such prominent people as John Price Buchanan, Phillip Lindsley (the founder of University of Nashville), Henry Clay, Felix Grundy, Lafayette, and Sam Houston.

Wessyngton and the Washingtons played a small part in the infamous forced relocation of Native Americans to the West in the fall of 1838, the "Trail of Tears." Thousands of Cherokees passed through Turnersville and Coopertown near Wessyngton. It took several weeks for all of the thirteen groups to pass through the area.[41] They carried the old and sick in wagons. Those Indians who walked usually crossed the Tennessee River in East Tennessee near Calhoun at the mouth of the Hiwassee River. They walked to McMinnville, Murfreesboro, Nashville, and crossed the Red River at Port Royal near Wessyngton. The Cherokees spent the winter of 1838–1839 in nearby Hopkinsville, Kentucky. After passing through Hopkinsville, they went through Kentucky, Illinois, Missouri, and Arkansas to Oklahoma.[42]

George wrote his mother in October 1838 from Nashville concerning the Cherokee removal: "[A] detachment of Indians came through here whilst Mr. Simms was in town. They left yesterday, and I will expect will reach Connell's tomorrow night. There is another detachment at Mill Creek, which will be here tomorrow, and I imagine will in like manner remain here some days. I think it likely if Mr. Simms would go over and see the agent who accompanied them, he might make arrangements for furnishing them provisions."[43] George's letter supports the local belief, and stories handed down by both African American and white descendants, that a group of Native Americans passed directly in front of the Wessyngton mansion and received food and water before continuing their perilous journey.

During the period between 1801 and 1843, Joseph and his son George acquired 141 slaves through gifts, inheritances, and purchases.[44] This involved forty-eight transactions: twenty-four single purchases, one purchase from the Union Bank of Nashville that included fourteen slaves, five purchases of mothers and their children, three purchases of nuclear families, four purchases of siblings, four purchases of slaves of unknown relationship, six instances of inheritances from estates involving seventeen slaves, and one gift of twenty-nine slaves consisting of seven interrelated families.[45] We should not forget, however, that these seemingly impersonal statistics do not reflect the real impact on the lives of hundreds of men, women, and children.

CHAPTER 5

By the Sweat of Their Brows: The Largest Tobacco Plantation in America

———————

S laves toiled endlessly, clearing land, plowing fields, raising livestock, erecting buildings, and planting crops to transform a pioneer wilderness into one of the largest farming operations in America. Tobacco cultivation is hard on soil because it uses up many of the nutrients over the course of a few seasons. The solutions, used even in the early nineteenth century, were a form of crop rotation or the opening of new fields by clearing hardwood forests. For that reason Joseph continued to increase the size of his holdings. By 1838 Wessyngton Plantation, with all of the Washington holdings, was 4,315 acres and held 86 slaves: 50 black men between the ages of one and sixty-one, 2 mulatto men aged seven to twenty-five, 33 black women aged one to sixty-three, and 1 mulatto girl age nine. Wessyngton was poised for the next stage of its expansion.

Joseph and his wife, Mary, created a typical Southern plantation. They furnished their mansion with exquisite antiques, ornate silverware, china, crystal, and other luxuries purchased in New Orleans, where the plantation crops were sold. The purchases were shipped back by flatboats on the Mississippi and Cumberland rivers to Clarksville. Portraits of early ancestors and prominent historical figures hung on the walls at Wessyngton. The Washingtons also had furniture crafted on the plantation by full-time or itinerant craftsmen as well as the slaves.

As Joseph's son, George, entered his thirties, he was very active in the plantation's business, and by the 1840s, he was in charge of most of the plantation operations, since his father was then in his seventies. In 1841 Joseph gave his son sixteen slaves and 750 acres of land in Todd County, Kentucky. Joseph had purchased several tracts of this farm during the 1820s and 1830s. In 1844 George purchased an additional 325 acres that adjoined the land given to him by his father. The land used for tobacco farming was located fifteen miles from the mansion. It had several buildings used for farming and cabins for the slaves living on the property.

George married Margaret Adelaide Lewis on September 15, 1842. His nineteen-year-old bride was born and brought up on the

Fairfield mansion, Nashville, Tennessee.

Fairfield Plantation near Nashville. She was the daughter of Major William Berkley Lewis, a longtime friend of Andrew Jackson from the Indian Wars and a member of the so-called Kitchen Cabinet during President Jackson's first term, from 1829 to 1833. Adelaide was educated in Philadelphia at a female academy under the supervision of a Madame Segoigue. She was considered to be the most beautiful young woman in Middle Tennessee. When George and Adelaide married, President Jackson sent his congratulations via Major Lewis:

> I received a letter from General Jackson who desires me to present his kind regards and salutations. He adds, "We all think here that your daughter Margaret is well married. Mr. Washington stands here as well in society as any young gentleman can in any society. He is respected by all who know him, and I am sure you will be pleased with him as an acquaintance." I quote his remarks to show that he has kind feelings for Mr. Washington and would, I am sure, be glad to see both of you at the Hermitage.[1]

President Jackson gave Major Lewis a gilt mirror and wall sconces that had once hung in the White House. Major Lewis presented these special pieces to his daughter as a wedding gift, and thereafter they hung in a place of honor at Wessyngton.

Major Lewis was with President Jackson when he died in 1845 at the Hermitage; he held Jackson's head in his hands and when the president expired, the major closed his eyes. He wrote George: "He died like a hero and a Christian."[2]

The Washingtons added to their mansion. They built a west wing addition that was used as a bedroom area with two bedrooms, a bath, and a small attic. They also added a large kitchen wing with servants' quarters on the second floor.[3]

Adelaide bore a son, William Lewis, on November 3, 1844; she died twenty-two days after his birth. George was absolutely devastated by the death of his young bride, whose health had always been somewhat frail. Major Lewis was also distraught; it was one more tragedy in his clearly unfortunate family history. Not surprisingly William (called Will or Willie) was the center of attention. There was a great deal of concern for his health. Lewis wrote his son-in-law, "I was truly relieved to hear that our dear little son was quite well and growing very fast—God grant that he may live."[4] Later when George returned from a business trip to New Orleans, Lewis wrote that he was happy that Will was "well and *healthy*. God grant that he may live."[5] Relatives also feared for George's emotional state. He had been counseled early by a Cheatham aunt: "All I can do is to pray with you . . . [Y]ou have her child left a part of her dear self and altho it now causes feelings of anguish to look at the dear little one, the time will come when he will be your greatest comfort . . . May God in Heaven help you my dear friend."[6]

One of George's grandsons told many relatives that as a young child in the early 1890s, he saw a very beautiful woman while he was sitting in a living room of the Wessyngton mansion. The woman was dressed in white. She walked over to—and passed through—the wall where a staircase had been located in the 1840s. The apparition was believed to be the ghost of Margaret Adelaide Lewis Washington, who often appeared in the living room dressed in her wedding gown.[7]

Joseph Washington died on November 28, 1848, at the age of seventy-eight. Fortunately, since George was his only surviving heir, the transition from one owner to another was simple and did not affect the Wessyngton slave community. Normally, the bankruptcy or death of a slave owner meant that there would be a disruption in the family life of the slaves who were often split up.

About five years after Adelaide's death, George met a student at the Nashville Female Academy. Jane Smith was born in 1830 in Florence, Alabama, located about 125 miles from Nashville. Her family's story and her story were complicated and quite difficult. Jane was the only surviving child of Joseph Lawrence Dawson Smith (1790–1837) and Mary Jackson Hanna (1798–1843). Jane's paternal ancestors came to Surry County, Virginia, in the early 1600s and then settled in Northampton County, North Carolina, where her grandfather owned the Bellview Plantation. Jane's father sold Bellview after his father died in 1811 and used the money to invest in the promising frontier areas of upper Alabama and Mississippi after the eviction of the local Native Americans. He had a vast estate by 1830, including a cotton plantation in Florence, Alabama, and one in Yalobusha County, Mississippi, worked by 120 slaves. His Alabama plantation was located across the creek from the Forks of Cypress Plantation owned by Jane's great-uncle on

*Jane Smith (1830–1894), future
bride of George A. Washington.*

Forks of the Cypress mansion, Florence, Alabama.

her maternal side, James Jackson. Jackson purchased the property from the Cherokee Chief Doublehead, maternal uncle of Sequoia, who invented the Cherokee alphabet. The Forks of Cypress was part of the family history of the author Alex Haley, who described it in his 1992 book *Queen* and a 1993 miniseries. Haley's maternal grandmother, Queen, was born a slave on the Forks of the Cypress; James Jackson's son was her father.

After Jane's father died in 1837, her mother remarried and then died in 1843. Jane was sent to Nashville to live with her Kirkman cousins and attend the Nashville Female Academy, a school founded in 1817 by a group that included several of Jane's relatives. The school was located on Church Street. The school offered education with an emphasis on music, art, and modern languages as well as social graces for several hundred young ladies each year.[8] After Jane's parents died, she was raised by her aunt Anne Hanna Pope, with whom she was very close.

We do not know exactly how George made the acquaintance of Jane when she was just eighteen and George thirty-three. George was absolutely "over his heels in love." He wrote Jane: "I fully realize the love I bear you; Here, I think of you by day, and dream of you at night, and happy, O! how happy in dreamland I am."[9] However, he cautioned Jane that he hoped and trusted that "you will love my mother, for in your loving her consists the probability of her loving you."[10]

George was aware of the potential problem with Jane's aunt Anne in Nashville. She had strong opinions as to where they and she would live after the wedding. Jane and Anne exchanged a series of heated letters on the subject. George's mother may have diagnosed the situation better than he did. She wrote George that she did not wish to live alone at Wessyngton, reacting to a proposal for all of them, or everyone except for her, to set up residence in Nashville. She observed:

> I thought the ties between me and you were as near as they were between Miss Smith and Ms. Pope, she knows as well as you do you are all the child I have, and that I am alone, what have I to live for but you, you are nearer and dearer to me than anything upon earth. Willie feels as near to me as he can because he was left a motherless babe with me and has been with me all the time . . . This is my home and your home. I think we both have an equal right if you will stay here with me there is no place upon Earth I had rather be at, but to live here by myself I cannot, I had rather die, than to give you up while I live and be left here all the time alone, you know that I wish you to manage the estate as you think best, let the farm be managed entirely by your directions at my death you know whose it will be. If you marry Miss Smith bring her home, I will receive her as a daughter and hope to love her as such. Invite Ms. Pope to be an inmate of our house. I hope we may all be a happy family and be united together as one family.[11]

Mary admitted that she was not favorably disposed to Jane's aunt, but she affirmed:

If you marry above all things give your wife and child
the uppermost seat in your heart and think of me as
a mother that is left with not one person upon Earth
to look to or advise with but you, no not so much as a
brother. If your wife loves you as she ought and is not
one of those fashionable women, and her aunt does not
have too much control over her she will be willing to
spend a good deal of her time out here or anywhere else
that you wish her.[12]

The question whether to stay at Wessyngton or go to Nashville
and leave the vast plantation to its manager and overseers or even
perhaps to sell out completely certainly went through George's
mind in 1849. Had he had decided not to continue at Wessyngton,
this would have proved catastrophic to the stable lives of his slaves
and the development of Robertson County. If he chose to stay in
Nashville, having seen the negative results of the absentee management of Major William B. Lewis's Fairfield, it would have been
quite possible that he would have sold out completely. He was very
successful at age thirty-four and had a five-year-old son and a new
young bride. He could have chosen the easy life in Nashville, but
he decided to remain at Wessyngton.

Even with all these potential problems, George and Jane married on the morning of June 21, 1849. Their wedding was held at
the elegant Nashville home of her cousin John Kirkman. After the
wedding, Jane's aunt came to Wessyngton to live, but she "was possessed of a very strong personality and very violent and ungovern-
able temper." Less than a month later, "Anne had made herself so
exceedingly disagreeable that Jane, George and Mary all agreed to
send Anne back to Nashville to live in a boardinghouse on Spruce
Street."[13] George signed a contract with Anne obligating himself to
pay her semiannually interest on a possible claim of $15,000 due
to her in Mississippi. The interest would be paid to her "so long as

she shall live separate and apart from me and my wife or so long as she shall not make my house her home and residence." These interest payments amounted to about $650 annually.[14]

These actions started an ongoing battle in which Anne wrote harsh letters to Jane, and evidently everyone else in her circle, commenting that she saw George as a "reserved, proud man, not very communicative, very close in money matters as well as other things . . . distrustful . . . too rich to be happy. . . ." She used harsh language to describe Jane's new in-laws: "the Cheathams are said to be proud and coldhearted."[15] She often complained to Jane that Jane's letters contained but one line of affection or remembrance towards her, and she only wrote of George and his endearments.[16] Jane ultimately told her that if she had to choose between her aunt and her husband, she would choose her husband.[17]

Even past the honeymoon period, George's letters to Jane were always filled with love and devotion, as well as attempts to bolster her trust and confidence in him, which could easily be shaken by the long, lonely absences of her husband on business and the continual onslaught of her aunty's venom. In his letters during his travels in these early years, George expressed his love for her and constantly asked for her help at Wessyngton and her trust in him. This surely won forever the heart of his nineteen-year-old bride and sealed a bond that would last in the hard times to come.

Anne became even more strident when she learned that Jane might be pregnant soon after their wedding, stating that she "despised the bestial appetites of men."[18] She also predicted her and Jane's complete separation. "I will write no more letters for a long time . . . If we should never meet again God bless you. Your Aunty."[19] Anne's accusations reached a low point in October-November 1849 when George reported to Jane that her aunt was continuing to write abusive letters and accusing him of treating her badly and claiming that Jane's ill health "has been the result of force upon [his] part."[20]

George always instructed her to take care of herself and her baby, and to give his love to his mother and son.[21]

Jane came from a family of major slave owners like the Washingtons; her family in some instances attempted to keep slave families together. The will of her father, Joseph L. D. Smith, stipulated that if any slaves from his plantation in Lauderdale County, Alabama, were sold, husbands, wives, and any children under two years old had to be sold together. His father, Lawrence Smith, provided in his will that two old slaves he owned, Jerry and his wife, Lucy, may make the choice to live with any member of his family should his estate be sold, and they were to be maintained comfortably. Jane's mother, Mary Jackson Hanna Smith, wanted to free her slaves after her husband's death, but Alabama law prohibited a woman from doing so. She thought there might be another way to accomplish her goal when a Presbyterian minister from the North, Samuel Hurd, appeared on the scene and claimed to be an abolitionist and representative of the Colonization Society. He promised if she married him, he would free her slaves. She did marry him. He not only reneged on his promise to free the slaves, but, according to Jane's descendants, he "very soon became a most zealous pro-slavery advocate and cruel taskmaster." She died a year later of a broken heart, according to her descendants. She left a will directing that her slaves be sent to Africa, but Hurd "ignored her wishes and his promises as to emancipation and claiming all the negroes as heir at law, held on to them."[22]

George received $60,000 from Jane's deceased father's estate when he married her. She had brought her childhood nursemaid Henny from Alabama when she moved to Nashville in the early 1840s. Henny was born around the 1790s and presumably grew up at Forks of the Cypress. She probably used the Jackson or Smith surname when she came to Wessyngton to distinguish her from the three other Hennys and one Henrietta on the plantation. On Wessyngton she worked as Jane's personal servant and probably never married. She died before 1860 and was buried in the slave cemetery.

After Joseph's death and George's marriage, Joseph's widow, Mary, ran the Home Place, the gardens, and the women's activities, and her daughter-in-law Jane ran the day nursery and visited and tended to the sick slaves. George and Jane had eight children over the next twelve years. Mary was born in 1850 and died when she was four from complications of the measles; Jane composed a long poem, "Lines on the Death of Little Mary," to express her grief, which read in part:

> I knew full well the loveliest are always the
>   first to go,
> Too finely wrought they sink beneath the
>   pressure here below.
> They mingle with us but to point to happier
>   realms than this,
> Where the pain of parting never comes to
>   mar its perfect bliss.[23]

Henny Jackson Smith at Wessyngton Plantation, 1849.

The five children born before the Civil War who survived their childhoods were Joseph Edwin (called Joe), born 1851; Martha Susan, 1854; Mary, named after her deceased sister, 1855; Bessie Adelaide, 1858; and Lucy Amelia, 1861. A son born in 1857 survived less than a week, and in 1860 a son was stillborn.[24]

Joseph and Mary had been members of the Harmony Baptist Church in Turnersville, and George was brought up as a Baptist. Jane was originally a Presbyterian and belonged to the First Presbyterian Church in Nashville. In 1852, upon the urging of her aunt Anne Pope, Jane was removed from the rolls of the church, and George, so angry about it, resigned from that church.[25] George became an Episcopalian by 1860, and their children were brought up Episcopalian.

Wessyngton was not like the fictional Tara in *Gone with the Wind*, with endless social events. In the hundreds of letters that have come down to us, we find no mention of holding a ball or even attending a social function. George and Jane's daughter Lucy Washington Helm later wrote that the plantation was so large and self-sufficient that the family left the place only twice a year, and that was to get shoes and Christmas gifts.[26] Jane did not seem to travel to Nashville for social events or visit with other local planters' wives.[27] Perhaps her higher educational and cultural level prevented her from socializing with her neighbors. Evidently reading was a favorite pastime as their "best books" numbered more than "150 volumes."[28]

Granville, George's unacknowledged son, became his personal valet and trusted servant. While George was traveling, Granville took on many responsibilities at Wessyngton. George's letters often assigned him tasks to complete, and Mary's and Jane's letters reported what he had accomplished.

The plantation produced 15,000 bushels of tobacco in 1850. Joseph's 1848 estate inventory listed that he owned approximately 3,700 acres of land and seventy-nine slaves at Wessyngton.

After George inherited Wessyngton, he increased the size of the estate tremendously. In 1853 George bought two tracts of land known as the Dortch Place for $16,680. The land was five miles from the mansion. It encompassed 1,667.5 acres of tobacco and agricultural land with several barns and outbuildings. Eighty-seven slaves worked the Dortch Place when he bought it, and there were slave cabins on the property. In the same year, George sold 1,329 acres in Todd County, Kentucky. The value of his real estate grew from $20,000 in 1850 to $250,000 by 1860. The 13,100 acres that made up Wessyngton consisted of 5,100 acres considered improved land and 8,000 acres considered unimproved (i.e., woodlands and rough pasture).

Wessyngton became one of the premier plantations in antebellum Tennessee with a reputation of producing only the finest crops and produce. One of George's daughters recalled: "I was told by an old cotton man in New Orleans, when I went there as a young woman, that when the word would go out that Washington's crops were in, everything and everybody rushed to the sales, knowing the goods were the best."[29] Potential buyers from all over the United States and Europe would be on hand to buy Wessyngton products. After the sales, the buyers would usually give a large banquet in George's honor.

George traveled often on business and carried considerable cash. He wrote his father in 1847 from New Orleans listing $22,600 in treasury notes of the United States in case he was in an accident and did not return home.[30] In December 1858 he deposited an even larger amount, $77,000, of Missouri State Bonds in Nashville Planter's State Bank at 6 percent interest. He used banks and credit houses in Nashville, New Orleans, New York, and Philadelphia. He also served as a banker for many of the smaller farmers around his plantation by offering them short-term credit. Sometimes he accepted repayment of a loan in work instead of money.[31]

Times were changing on the plantation. The authorities had

considered that a railroad might go through Wessyngton. There was a notation in an account book in 1854: "We the undersigned agree to buy stock in the Edgefield Railroad if it is run through the farm of Mary and George Washington as surveyed." However, the railroad never went through Wessyngton. When the railroad did come to the area in 1857, it went through the property of Edmond A. Fort and near some of the other Fort families. The Forts had subscribed substantially more stock in the railroad, and Edmond A. Fort was a member of the legislature at that time. This might have influenced the route selection. The railroad station was located in Cedar Hill, a few miles from the Wessyngton Plantation. To get from Wessyngton to the station in Cedar Hill, one needed to cross Sulphur Fork Creek. George proposed to the county that he would pay half the cost of a bridge crossing the creek near his home. Once the railroad was in place, his marketing changed. Most of his produce, especially tobacco, was then shipped by rail 170 miles to Louisville and from there 740 miles to New York City.

Covered bridge near Wessyngton Plantation.

The Washingtons had overseers on the different farms—the Home Place, the Dortch Place, and the property in Todd County, Kentucky—and one manager for the entire estate. It was likely that some of the most trusted slaves, or fastest workers, were used as drivers (slaves who worked under the overseers), for it would not have been possible for a few white overseers to efficiently manage such a large slave population.

In 1844 George recorded in his account book that he raised a total of 126,160 pounds of tobacco on his farms, and he listed the barns in which they were stored: 21,035 pounds in a barn up the creek, 35,945 pounds in the new barn, 41,560 pounds in another barn, and 27,620 pounds in the Cheatham barn. This would have required 180 acres of land based on a 716-pound-per-acre yield.[32] In 1856 George recorded 78,550 pounds of tobacco in barns on the Home Place.

George and his slaves increased the tobacco production to 250,000 pounds by 1860; this would have required nearly 350 acres of land.[33] This equaled one-ninth of America's total tobacco production and made Wessyngton America's largest, and the world's second largest, producer of dark-fired tobacco, second only to one of the khedives (viceroys of the Sultan of Turkey) in Egypt. The number of acres George planted in tobacco each year was greater than the size of most farms in Robertson County, which were on average only fifty-one to a hundred acres in 1860. In 1860 George at age forty-five was a millionaire.[34]

Apparently, George concluded that what we could call "the Washington Empire" had grown enough. By 1842 he discontinued the purchase of slaves altogether. Nevertheless, by 1860 the slave population had increased to 187 slaves on the Home Place, with 87 on the Dortch Place (including some slaves moved from the Todd County property to the Dortch Place when the Kentucky property was sold). With a total of 274 slaves, George was the largest slaveholder in the State of Tennessee.

The 1860 U.S. Agricultural Census listed Wessyngton as producing 50,000 bushels of wheat, 22,000 bushels of corn, 2,000 pounds of butter, 800 bushels of potatoes, 80 milk cows, 29 horses, 80 asses and mules, 4,000 bushels of oats, 1,000 bushels of rye, 500 pounds of wool, smaller amounts of peas, beans, Irish potatoes, and sweet potatoes, 50 work oxen, 230 other cattle, 275 sheep, and 1,200 hogs, $8,000 worth of slaughter animals, and $50,000 in livestock.

Wessyngton's pork industry was a good example of both self-sufficiency and a substantial source of income. Americans, especially in the South, ate more pork than beef or poultry. In 1850 a writer commented on the popularity of pork: "The people of the South would not think they could subsist without their [swine] flesh; bacon instead of bread, seems to be THEIR staff of life. Consequently, you see bacon upon the Southern table three times a day either boiled or fried."[35]

In 1844 George shipped 677 Washington Hams to New Orleans via Galbraith and Greenfield. In 1858, 446 hogs, weighing 90,854 pounds, were killed at Wessyngton, and 190 hogs, weighing 43,309 pounds, on the Dortch Place. The slave labor force at Wessyngton needed a massive supply of pork. Based on rations listed in account books, each adult consumed approximately a half pound of pork daily. Estimates based on the number of children and adults on the plantation indicated that in 1860, for example, they consumed approximately 42,000 pounds of pork each year, requiring the slaughter of more than 200 hogs.

When additional labor was needed, George hired slaves owned by other farmers, as well as white workers. Many slaveholders hired out their slaves when they did not have enough work to keep them occupied year round.

Slaves were hired out to support widows and minor children. A Robertson County resident, Ilai Metcalfe, stipulated in his will that his slave Major would be emancipated upon the death of his wife, Susannah. Until Susannah's death, Major was allowed to hire himself out in Robertson and surrounding counties as a stonemason and keep half the proceeds, with the other half being used for Susannah's support. George hired Major in 1848 and paid him more than $150.[36] Major built the original retaining wall in front of the Wessyngton mansion in the 1840s.

George hired out some of his slaves from the Todd County plantation to the ironworks furnaces. We do not know how much money the slaves earned for Washington, but we do know the work was extremely hard and dangerous, which led to some of them running away.

In the early 1840s George faced some obstacles in transporting slaves to his Kentucky plantation after the passage of a law requiring slaveholders to be residents of the state before relocating their slaves. This was an attempt to discourage the interstate slave trade. George was well connected and turned to his friends and relatives for help: In January 1843 his father-in-law, Major William B. Lewis, sent a letter to the governor of Kentucky asking a favor for George, "a very estimable young man" and "also very greatly oblige one who is very truly and sincerely your friend." Lewis explained the issue in which George "feels a very great interest. He wishes to get a law passed to enable him to transfer a few of his negroes in Tennessee to a tract of land he owns in Kentucky and for this purpose he has your Legislature."[37] Evidently the charges brought against George for violating the law were dropped. The governor wrote Major Lewis: "I am happy to inform you that James W. Irwin of the House introduced an amendment allowing your son-in-law George to bring five Negroes to his farm in Kentucky and it passed into a law. We are greatly indebted to the perseverance of Irwin for this success and as to the fine; the Governor will release it whenever application is made."[38]

During these years demand for slaves in Robertson County was so great that they brought unprecedented prices during peak seasons. The highest price George ever paid for a single slave was $875 for a twenty-five-year-old slave named Jim in 1840.[39]

Slave trading was a highly profitable business. Although George did not sell his slaves (except in two cases), he did sell slaves belonging to other slave owners. In 1841 he was in charge of selling a slave for Robert D. Carr.[40] George told Carr that his slave "goes up on the steamer James Woods free of charge, the charges for him I will keep an account of and give you when I come up. Since I came down here I've been at a boardinghouse at 37 1/2 cents per day, his suit of clothes cost $12.00. I believe I have charged him not to wear them on the way home."

Benjamin Simms, the plantation manager, purchased a slave locally and sent him to the New Orleans slave market to be sold, where he hoped to get $50 to $100 profit after owning the slave for less than a week. This was unfortunate for the slave Joe, who changed owners at least twice in less than a month's time:

> I send you on board of the Harry Hill my Negro boy Joe and if you can sell him for $750.00 or $800.00 either you will confer a favor on me, and if you can't get that price let him remain on the boat as I have hired him to Captain Lee. I bought him last week from Jack E. Turner for $700.00, which will pay me a fair profit knowing that the boat will stay but a few days in port if you think it best to keep the boy, do as you would with your own and I will be satisfied with anything you do.[41]

In addition to providing labor, slaves were often used to settle debts. George, through his connection with Major William B. Lewis, lent $15,000 to the late President Jackson's son. When Andrew Jackson Jr. was unable to repay the debt, he proposed to George that he take the slaves at the Hermitage as payment for the debt he owed him.

> I borrowed $15,000 of Mr. Washington in May 1853, and gave him bills on Buchanan at 6, 8 and 10 months. To settle this matter I am willing to allow Mr. Washington 8 percent interest on the $15,000 up to this time, I let him have the notes of Walker and Blood, and I am then willing to let him take the notes of Walker and Blood at ten percent discount per annum, and for the balance I am willing to let him have Negroes at a fair valuation or if he does not want the Negroes, to let the bill stand on the docket until May 1856 and then let a decree be entered for the balance that may be due according to this statement.
>
> May 24th, 1855,
(Signed) Andrew Jackson, [Jr.][42]

George refused the proposal. Within a year, the debt-ridden Hermitage was sold to the State of Tennessee. Major Lewis informed George that Jackson was selling some of his slaves to pay the debt:

> He sent some 12 or 14 of his negroes to Nashville to be sold, a part of which has been sold and the balance will be in a few days if not already done. P. S. My nephew James B. Lewis was in Nashville about the middle of last week and he told me that Mr. Jackson was selling his negroes and that they were going very low.[43]

An entry in George's diary on March 12, 1859, reported on the slave market in Springfield: "Mr. Epperson went to Springfield to buy a Negro but did not buy one. Edward Negroes sold high, fourteen Negroes and two children bringing $19,700."[44]

In 1850 the total United States slave population was approximately 3.2 million. Most planters listed slaves by gender or age, but in George's 1850 slave schedule slaves were listed in family groups. Although their names were not listed, his recordkeeping was so detailed that by comparing the list with other plantation documents, I could reconstruct the majority of these otherwise nameless slave families. The 1850 census for Robertson County listed George A. Washington with only seventy-nine slaves. I knew that this must have been an error on the microfilm I viewed because I could account for more than that number using other plantation records. So I hired a genealogist to do research at the National Archives in Washington, DC, and the true error was discovered. Some pages of the original census had fallen out of the book, were replaced out of order, and then microfilmed and listed under the Dardens, one of the Washingtons' neighbors. With the correct number of slaves listed, I could account for all the African American families at Wessyngton. The largest family group that I could reconstruct consisted of eleven individuals, ranging in age from one to sixty and included three generations. This family was headed by my own great-great-great-grandmother Jenny, her sons Alfred, Godfrey Jr., Bob, Emanuel, Willis, Felix, and Warrick, her daughter Clara, son-in-law Reuben, and a one-year-old grandson. Jenny was widowed by the time the 1850 slave schedule was completed. Emanuel lived with his mother until he married and then moved with his older brother Axum and his wife, Prudy. This find proved to be a genealogical gold mine for my family and the other Wessyngton descendants.

It must be noted that neither Joseph nor his son left any record regarding their sentiments on slaves being allowed to purchase their freedom or being emancipated outright. George, in an unsent letter to the editor of a Nashville newspaper in 1860, did refer to his slaves as his "property," which was what most slave owners believed.[45] Although the Washingtons were certainly aware that

over the decades some slave owners—even in Robertson County—
were freeing a number of their slaves, there is no record that the
Washingtons ever granted any slave his or her freedom.

Clearly, Montgomery Bell, the iron baron of Dickson County,
was the most outstanding of all the slaveholders to free blacks
in Tennessee. Bell emancipated fifty slaves in 1835 and paid for
their transportation to the newly created colony of Liberia on the
west coast of Africa. Bell sent fifty more blacks to Liberia in 1853.
Thirty-eight of them were members of one family. Bell brought a
teacher from Philadelphia to teach his slaves to read and write,
which was illegal in most states. In his lifetime he emancipated
nearly 250 slaves and sent them to Africa. This would have cost
him an estimated $100,000. Bell planned to emancipate some of
his other slaves who did not want to leave the country to a free
state, but he could not find a state that would permit it.

Robertson County had twenty-six free blacks in 1850; sixteen
of these, 61 percent, were mulatto. Twenty-five of the twenty-eight
free blacks in the county by 1860 were mulatto, 89.3 percent of
the total of free black population.[46] These numbers did not corre-
late with the black-to-mulatto ratio in the general population. The
larger percentage of mulatto free blacks indicated strongly that
their white fathers or other relatives freed these individuals.

As the Washingtons amassed a fortune through their business acumen, they profited greatly from the unpaid labor of its
hundreds of slaves. Their slaves were in bondage and not free to
have their own lives. Wessyngton was built by the sweat of their
brows. These African Americans could only imagine a life outside
of Wessyngton.

CHAPTER 6

It Takes a Whole Village

————•◦•————

The strength of the nuclear and extended families on Wessyngton made that plantation community quite unusual and had an impact on the generations to follow during slavery, emancipation, and up to modern times. The description of the community, family, daily life, and customs drawn from documents in the Washington Family Papers reveal the facts as do the memoirs of Lucy Washington Helm (1861–1955), one of George A. Washington's daughters. When I conducted interviews with descendants of former slaves, I always asked them specifically about the stories and details that were passed on to them; very often these remembrances supported the documentation.

While I would have loved to have found data about every facet of life on Wessyngton Plantation, that, of course, was not realistic. Nevertheless, I was amazed with the amount of information I gathered that shed light on how the slave community was organized and what daily life was like. I have assumed some facets of life did not change that much in the mid-nineteenth century. Therefore, I sometimes include information from immediately after the Civil War if I believed that it was applicable to the antebellum period.

Since I describe just Wessyngton and the area close to it, I include only a few generalizations about other plantations in the South to illustrate how Wessyngton was similar or was different. I based these assessments on the numerous books and articles I have read, but I cannot and do not claim to be an expert on all plantations. Within this framework, we can learn a great deal about life on Wessyngton Plantation.

The transatlantic slave trade had a devastating effect on the family unit. The slave trade at its peak tore millions of Africans from their homes and families and removed them as slaves to various parts of the world. Throughout the slave territories, households were large, and the typical slave cabin contained four to seven residents. Marriages, unless broken by sale, were usually long lasting. Families constituted a fundamental survival mechanism, enabling the slaves to resist the kind of dehumanization that many believed they underwent.[1]

Unlike the Washingtons, who did not sell members of families, in Robertson and Davidson counties, the majority of slave purchases were for a single person—meaning a family was torn apart. When George married Adelaide Lewis in 1842, her father, Major William B. Lewis, gave the couple twenty-nine slaves as a wedding gift. This gift caused the breakup of several families at the Lewis plantation.

After making the gift, Major Lewis wrote his son-in-law about some problems the arrangement caused the slave families:

> I hardly know what answer to make in relation to what you say about the Negro men and their wives. They ought not to be separated if it can be helped, and I would be very willing to make an exchange either temporarily or permanently, if it would not deprive me of hands indispensable for the cultivation of my farm. Of this, I cannot judge at present as you have not given me their names, and I do not myself know who they are. It is a problem;

however, that you can decide as well as I can and I am perfectly willing you shall do so. It is quite too far for the men to be traveling backward and forward to see their wives, and I think at all events a temporary arrangement had better be made.[2]

Major Lewis wrote Washington's overseer Benjamin Simms in December 1844 that he was going to let his son-in-law have a slave, Rachel, and her child, for Billico who had a wife at Fairfield. Two years later, however, Major Lewis appeared somewhat indifferent to the separation of his slave Bob from his wife as he wrote George on Christmas Day, a day when slaves were often allowed to visit relatives and friends on other plantations:

Bob is as much disappointed and perhaps more so than I am at your not coming. He has been here all day waiting for you and finding you did not come he begged me to write to you and ask you to say to his wife, should you visit your plantation before you go down the river, that he has been too sick and is still too unwell, to go to Kentucky this Christmas. The fellow has been very sick having had a severe attack of pleurisy, but he is now better and wished to go to see his wife, as if he cares anything about her, but he begged so hard that I would write to you to let his wife know the reason why he could not go to see her, I promised him to do so; and after all the fellow may be attached to her.[3]

In similar situations, the slave was expected to find a new wife or husband as if his or her feelings did not matter.

Few slaveholders owned enough unrelated slaves for them to marry on their own plantations and farms. In the early years on Wessyngton, males greatly outnumbered females (especially on the

Todd County, Kentucky, farm). Consequently, most slaves probably had wives and husbands on neighboring farms in arrangements known as off-plantation, or broad, marriages. Most slave
owners in the county owned fewer than three slaves, which would
have made it impossible for slaves to have families on their own
farms and plantations. This gave rise to off-plantation marriages.
In off-plantation marriages slaves married the slaves of other slave
owners and were allowed to visit on weekends or holidays such as
Christmas. Any children born to these unions would become the
property of the mother's owner. By law, a slave's status followed
that of his mother. Jenny, purchased in 1802, maintained a non-
legal broad marriage with a slave named Godfrey who lived in the
vicinity. Godfrey was not purchased and brought to Wessyngton
until 1821. Jenny had several children fathered by him before his
arrival on the plantation: Axum, born 1808; Alfred, born 1814;
Godfrey Jr., born 1816; and Susan, born 1821.

In West Africa marriage between certain relatives was forbidden as incestuous, and descent lines were traced in part to ensure
that no common relationship existed.[4] Continuing that custom,
the slave prohibition of marriage between close blood relations
greatly increased the number of off-plantation or broad marriages.
The strict taboo of marrying relatives existed among the Washington slaves and the slave community. For that reason even in later
years when Wessyngton's slave population was very large, many
off-plantation marriages existed. Although their white masters had
no such prohibition (and frequently married their first cousins),[5]
many of them seemed to have understood and accepted that their
slaves were upholding stringent rules of exclusion.[6] Several generations of marriages and procreation created intricate and complex
kinship ties that could have been discernible only to the slave community members themselves.

Although slavery made family life exceedingly difficult for African Americans, they tried to maintain close ties with one another,

and all members of the slave community were treated as family. In 1860 the Wessyngton Home Place consisted of 187 slaves housed in at least twenty-seven dwellings. At least nine families were direct descendants of Jenny, born 1792 (who came from Virginia with Joseph Washington), and at least six were descended from "Yellow" Jenny, who was purchased by Joseph along with her husband "Yellow" Tom and four children in 1814. Only four families are believed to have had no other relatives on the plantation. Individuals who were bought or inherited from other plantations headed fifteen of the households. Slaves of the first generation of the Wessyngton slave community headed the remaining twelve households. The slaves held on Wessyngton's Home Place had family and marital ties to slaves on the other Washington holdings—the Dortch Place and the Todd County, Kentucky, plantation.

Undoubtedly the males on George's Todd County plantation must have had spouses on neighboring farms; in 1850, there were a total of seventy-four slaves there consisting of thirty females (one aged sixty, eighteen aged from fifteen to thirty-five, eleven aged from two months to eight years old); forty-four males (thirty-eight aged from fourteen and forty and six aged from two months to eight years old). There were more than double the number of males aged fifteen to forty than females in the same age category, making it difficult, if not impossible to have maintained on-plantation marriages.

Like other slaveholding states, the State of Tennessee did not recognize slave marriages. Kenneth M. Stampp writes in his history of slavery: "Slave owners varied in their perceptions regarding slave marriages. Some required their slaves to get their permission before getting married. Other slave owners showed little regard at all, and allowed their slaves to change spouses at will, creating total chaos for the slave family once they were emancipated."[7] When spouses were sold, they generally remarried not expecting to see one another again and started a new family. This must have been very traumatic, especially for males who saw their wives and children sold like cattle while they were powerless to help them.

Slaves considered their marriages to be valid and honored them. Several former Wessyngton slaves indicated to census takers in 1900 that they had been married for more than forty years, proof that they regarded their marriages as valid prior to emancipation. In 1908 when Clara Washington (Emanuel Washington's sister) applied for pension benefits for services her husband Reuben Cheatham Washington had rendered during the Civil War, she declared that the black minister Reverend Horace Carr had married them in the 1840s. Clara stated that she was married without a license, as was the custom of the slaves.[8]

The earliest known record of a slave marriage at Wessyngton was from 1851 when George noted in his diary on December 27, "Tom asked for Olive for wife."[9] Although this was the first documented reference to slaves asking to marry, there were many other references to couples on the plantation as being married, and there were a number of slave bills of sale indicating that slaves were already married before coming to the estate. The first bill of sale listing a married couple was for Tom and Jenny, whom Joseph purchased in 1814.

Slave owners, local white ministers, or perhaps a slave acknowledged to be a minister among the black populace usually performed slave marriages. Marriage ceremonies included the African custom of jumping over a broom.

Many slaves felt that it was unnecessary to inform their masters of their marriage commitments to one another, since their owners really had little regard for them. Slaves maintained their own customs and beliefs outside the realm of their owners. It was likely that some of these marriage arrangements may have been without the permission of the owners, although they were recognized among the slave community. Davy, the most notorious of all the Wessyngton runaways, claimed a wife on the farm of J. W. Kendall, who lived near the Todd County, Kentucky, plantation. Kendall stated in a letter to George that he has "a girl born ours" whom Davy "calls his wife," indicating that their marriage was without his knowledge or consent.[10]

———•—•———

Although the Washingtons kept registers of births and deaths, many slaves did not know their date or year of birth. Some slaves calculated the months of their births by relating their births to various growing seasons on the plantation, such as tobacco cutting time, or special events, and holidays like Christmas. Based on the 1870 census for Robertson County, former Wessyngton slaves Allen Washington, Emanuel Washington, and Granville Washington and their families knew their exact ages according to what they reported to census takers. Their ages were in accordance to plantation birth records. Several other Wessyngton slaves in later census records reported the correct months in which they were born.

With the lack of birth documents, African Americans used their personal histories to determine their births, as we can see with former Wessyngton slave Otho Washington, who came from Fairfield Plantation when he was a young boy. He stated in his 1907 pension application for military service during the Civil War:

I am unable to furnish the evidence called for in the circular letter from the Commissioner of Pensions dated November 14, 1907, returned herewith for the reason that I was born a slave and there was no public records kept of births in Robertson County, Tennessee, where I was born, at that time; there was no baptismal record kept of my birth nor was there ever any family or Bible record kept so far as my knowledge goes. I had been chopping weeds, hoeing in the fields, and plowing about eight years when the war commenced. They usually put slave children to hoeing and chopping at ten years of age. From what my mother always told me, I was eighteen years of age when the war broke out from my own recollection, I was born in March 1843. This is my only means of arriving at my age except that when the war broke out, I was considered a man and doing a man's work on the plantation of Mr. George Washington to whom I belonged before the war.[11]

Otho probably never knew that the Washingtons kept very detailed records of all the slave births on the plantation.

The slave community was similar to an African village made up of several large families headed by an elder member. We cannot underestimate the importance of the older generation in the slave community.

Older slaves were commonly called uncle or aunt; they demanded and received respect and veneration. Frederick Douglass once remarked: "Strange, and even ridiculous as it may seem, there is not to be found, among any people, a more rigid enforcement of the law of respect to elders than the slaves maintain. A young slave must approach the company of the older with hat in hand and woe betide him, if he fails to acknowledge a favor, of any sort, with the accustomed 'tank'ee,' etc."[12]

George's 1860 tax list of twenty-seven families at the Home Place revealed that twenty-one households were headed by fathers; two were headed by elderly widows with children, grandchildren, and great-grandchildren; two were headed by mothers with children and grandchildren; one was headed by a sister and several brothers; and one was composed of a group of unrelated slaves. Five families included three generations, and two included four.

———•·•———

Slaves were usually known by their first names. Slaves on most plantations did not use surnames except to distinguish themselves from others who had the same given names. For that reason the use of surnames by slaves was more common on large plantations where more people would have the same given name. We have the first record of surnames used on Wessyngton in 1838. On an 1838 list of slaves, one slave was listed as Mose Terry and another as Mose Gardner.[13] In 1856 a similar list recording the names of men and boys included Sam Vanhook, Allen Holman, Henry Terry, Joe Lewis, Bob Price, John White, Jim Woodard, Dick Terry, Tom White, Mose Terry, George Gardner, George Fairfield, and Dick Fairfield.[14]

No slave at Wessyngton was listed as using the Washington surname on any records prior to emancipation. However, we could assume that most of the slaves who did not use other surnames were considered Washingtons as this was the most common surname among them (particularly the older families) after emancipation.

Prior to emancipation some slaves used their previous owner's surnames: the Lewis slaves, the Terrys, the Scotts, the Whites, and the Gardners. Most of the Lewis slaves, given to George in 1844, retained the Lewis surname with its association to Major William B. Lewis from Fairfield Plantation. Some of Lewis's former slaves used the surname Fairfield, the name of the Lewis plantation.

While African Americans were limited in their choice of surnames, they selected given or first names for their children from a wide spectrum. The origins of the given names of the slaves born on Wessyngton were indeed varied and creative. Many Southern slaves waited at least eight days before naming their babies. This was to ensure that the child would survive before naming. If the child died, no other sibling could be given the same name, as the slaves believed this was bad luck. However, it was common to give someone in the next generation the deceased person's name.

One important source was the slaves' African background. Although we do not know exactly how many slaves at Wessyngton were born in Africa, based on the names from a birth register from 1795–1860, we believe that there certainly was an African influence. True African names appear on the register as late as 1858. Few American-born slaves, if any, knew enough about Africa to pass on an African name to their children without the knowledge and influence of a native African parent, grandparent, or other relative. It was an African tradition in some tribes that grandparents named their grandchildren. In the seventeenth and eighteenth centuries, it was customary for slave children to receive African "day names" such as Cudjo, Mingo, and Cuffee, denoting the day of the week on which they were born.

The nineteenth century brought noticeable changes in naming practices.[15] Native Africans were often given English names when they arrived in America, although a small number were allowed to retain their original names. Although forced to accept new names upon arrival in America, many Africans passed on their names to their children. Too, when they were forbidden to use their African names in the presence of whites, many of them still used their African names among themselves in the slave community. With the 1808 prohibition of the transatlantic slave trade, the number of Africans and African names greatly decreased, and Biblical and European names replaced them. During the first quarter of the nineteenth century most American slaves had become anglicized to the extent that they were mainly giving their children English names, although some African names still prevailed. Although masters assigned names to newly imported slaves and sometimes intervened in the naming of slave babies, American-born slaves were able to name the majority of their babies.

Joseph and George allowed their slaves to give their offspring names of African origin. When the Washington's American-born slaves gave them the African names of their children to record on their "List of Negroes Ages," they certainly must have known they were of African origin. The African names included Olayinka, Luzinka, Dasha, Dinka, Alik, Axum, Vina, and Bena. Olayinka (born in 1858) was the last slave born on the plantation with a true African name. Olayinka's grandmother Saby (Sabra, born in 1802) was purchased by Joseph from Reuben Bowers in 1813, and her mother, Mahala, was born at Wessyngton in 1818. Olayinka's name traced directly to the Yoruba people of Nigeria, and DNA tests of Wessyngton slave descendants confirmed genetic ties to the Yoruba.

The African names used by the slaves at Wessyngton were too varied among African ethnic affiliations to have been a part of one family. Most of the families could be traced back before their arrival on the plantation through slave bills of sale, and they had no common connection. Some of the names could be associated with the parts of Africa from which the slaves originated. Axim (Axum) was born on the estate in 1808; his name corresponded to a city in Ghana and a kingdom in Ethiopia. Dinka had the name of an African tribe from which she likely descended. The slave Bena, one of the older slaves, bore an African name. No African day names were present among the slaves listed on the birth register although it was possible that some of the older slaves that were not listed on the birth register did have day names.[16]

The membership records of the Red River Baptist Church and estate records of some of the county's earliest settlers, such as John Bell and Elias Fort, showed that several of the first black settlers in Robertson County bore true African names. Some of the female African names were Abena, Anka, Annaca, Arrie, Bena, Cubena, Dasha, Dinka, Essi, Kora, Henna, Nanna, Layinka, Olayinka, Oda, Tenah, Jenne, Ludema, Lettice, Lettuce, and Luzinka. Male African names included Alik, Bela, Burrel, Cudjoe, Axum (Axim), Dinka, Juba, Mingo, Oba, Olif, and Samba. Many of these names are those used by African people today, such as the Ashanti (Ghana), Fanti (Ghana), Fulani (Niger), Ibo (Nigeria), Yoruba (Nigeria), Mende (Sierra Leone), and Grebo (Liberia).

Although there were several females at Wessyngton named for their mothers, in general fewer females were named for their mothers than for their grandmothers. "Black" Jenny, purchased by Joseph in 1802, was named for her mother. She did not have a daughter named for her but had two granddaughters named in her honor. "Yellow" Jenny's youngest daughter (born 1830) was named Jenny and nicknamed Jincy to distinguish her from all the others. Jincy had a daughter Jenny (born 1866) who also named her daughter Jenny in 1899, thus making four consecutive generations. "Yellow" Jenny's daughter Henny (born 1814) named her daughter Henny in 1839; that Henny named her daughter Henny in 1880, and had a granddaughter named Henrietta in 1905.

We could assume that Joseph or another Washington must have chosen or suggested the names derived from non-African sources. The names Madison, Jefferson, Monroe (named for presidents), and Gabriel, Emanuel, and Sampson (named for biblical figures) appeared on the registers. More than likely, the Washingtons chose the names Caesar and Augustus (named for famous Roman emperors).

Some of the slaves, especially house servants, carried given names that were common among the Washington family. All of Granville's children except his oldest daughter Fanny (his mother's name) and youngest son Grantz were named for members of the white Washington or Cheatham families: Foster, Hugh Lawson, Bessie, and Joyce. Emanuel's children were named for important Washington relatives. One had the name General for General Washington. Emanuel's daughter Martha was probably named for Martha Washington (Joseph Edwin's daughter). His son Grundy was most likely named for Felix Grundy, a famous Kentucky Supreme Court judge and senator who moved to Nashville and was President Van Buren's attorney general and a supporter of President Andrew Jackson.

Nicknames were common among the slave community and still prevalent in the African American community today. Nicknames are used so frequently in some small communities that many people are not known by their true given names. Under slavery, when there were several slaves with the same name, they were distinguished by height, color, size, place of origin, or other physical characteristics. Multiple names often arose from the purchase of other slaves and family names being passed down. "Dining Room" Mary was distinguished from the other Marys. There were several Toms on the plantation, so they were called "Black" Tom, "Yellow" Tom, Hezekiah Tom, and "Carolina" Tom (undoubtedly originally from North or South Carolina). Jenny appeared to be a very popular name; they were distinguished as "Yellow" Jenny, "Black" Jenny, "Old" Jenny, and Jincy. Henny was a common name; my great-great-great-grandmother was called Henny, and there were three others. There was Dick Scott, called Big Dick, Dick Terry, and Dick Fairfield (from the Lewis plantation) who was also called Dick Lewis. Those with Native American ancestry were called names such as "Creek" Betty, who was part Creek Indian, and "Yellow" Sarah (compared to "Black" Sarah). "No Leg" Jack was born with only one leg. Slaves on the plantation were named for their occupations. Bill "Sheep" was the shepherd, and Billy "the smith" was a blacksmith.

The merger of various cultural and ethnic backgrounds was evident in the Wessyngton slave community, as it was on other plantations. The community on Wessyngton Plantation was made up of slaves who were born in Africa, slaves of African origins who were born in America, and slaves of mixed African, European, and Native American ancestry.

Before modern times the word used for describing the offspring of a white (Caucasian) parent and a black (African American) parent was "mulatto." In some cases the term was used to define any person of mixed ancestry, whether black-white or Native American. Mulatto was used in official documents, censuses (until 1930), and in common speech. At present the correct terms in America are "mixed race" or "biracial," although "mulatto" is still used (without negative connotation) in many countries throughout the world. To maintain accuracy with the historical times, I have used "mulatto."

Miscegenation, or race mixing, occurred among Native Americans, Europeans, and Africans since they first encountered one another during America's earliest history. When white settlers first came to the Americas, intermingling occurred with Native Americans due to the scarcity of white females. Later, as Africans were imported to the colonies, they were added to the mix. During colonial times the ratio of male to female was far from equal. Among Africans there were at least three men for every two women, and among whites, men outnumbered women by three or four to one, especially in the South. African males also intermarried with Native American women, especially when white men reduced the already short supply of African females.[17] As the new settlers drove Native Americans from their lands and imported more Africans, interaction between the races was generally only between blacks and whites. This pattern continued as plantations were established throughout the South.

Laws from the mid-eighteenth century forbade intermarriage between blacks, whites, and Native Americans. Whites who fathered children by slaves took varying positions regarding their offspring. Few white men openly acknowledged their children by slave women. In some instances, they gave them minor preferential treatment or assigned them to positions as house servants, while others allowed them to learn a skilled trade. Others freed their children upon their deaths or during their lifetimes but did not recognize paternity. In contrast, some slaveholders preferred black domestics so they would not have to be constantly reminded of their indiscretions with the presence of their offspring, who often resembled white family members. Some slave owners sold their mulatto offspring in the domestic slave trade just as they would any other slave. Planters' wives had different views regarding this situation, often blaming slave women instead of their husbands. Fanny Kemble Butler, an English actress visiting the South during the 1830s, wrote, "Any lady is ready to tell you who is the father of all the mulatto children in everybody's household but her own. These, she seems to think, drop from the clouds. My disgust sometimes is boiling over."[18]

These issues existed at plantations like the Forks of the Cypress, where Jane Smith Washington's mother and Jane's maidservant Henny Jackson Smith had lived for years. Alex Haley's *Queen* makes clear that his grandmother was forced to leave the Forks after the Civil War even though she had been fathered by James Jackson's son and had worked in the Big House during the time of slavery.

From all records and interviews, we could conclude that only one Washington fathered a child by a slave, and on Wessyngton that situation was handled in a different manner than it was on many other plantations, including the Forks of the Cypress.

Granville (1831–1898) was believed to be the son of George A. Washington, according to some descendants of the Washington family. The Southern branch of the family had no knowledge of Granville's paternity, or at least they never spoke of the possibility.[19] There was no mention of the family connection in memoirs or in the family trees compiled meticulously by George's Southern descendants.[20] Family lore on the Southern side had it that Granville was purchased as a small child in the multiracial city of New Orleans, and that accounted for his extremely white features. The Northern branch of the family knew his paternity and thought everyone else did as well.[21] Among the slave community it was just accepted as the truth that he was fathered by a Washington.[22] While the Washington children addressed the other older slaves by "uncle" and "aunt," they always referred to Granville by his name, although they were very close to him.

George was believed to have fathered Granville when he was only fourteen years old. Granville's mother, Fanny, was also fourteen years old and grew up from childhood with George. Fanny's family had come to the plantation in 1814, and many of them worked as house servants. At the time the relationship was never acknowledged within the family or in public records. Even without any confirmation, the very strong physical resemblance between the two was undeniable to anyone who chose to see it. Granville was not sent away, sold, or banished to the fields. Granville was brought up in the mansion and served as George's valet and trusted family servant. Over the course of their lives a close relationship developed between George and Granville.

Many of the house servants of Richard Cheatham, Joseph's brother-in-law, were mulattoes, quadroons (persons of one quarter black ancestry), and octoroons (persons of one-eighth black ancestry) and maintained a close relationship with the family even after emancipation. They all bore names of the Cheatham family members. Many of these slaves descended from a slave Fanny, whom Cheatham inherited from his father-in law, Edward Saun-

Richard Cheatham   *Susan Saunders Cheatham*
(1799–1845), portrait.   *(1802–1864), portrait.*

Fanny Saunders Cheatham   *Harriet Cheatham Bowling*
(b. 1803), pre–Civil War portrait.   *Bransford (b. 1834), portrait.*

ders. Fanny had at least two daughters, Harriet and Clara, and possibly others fathered by Richard Cheatham's business partner Joseph A. Green. Green also fathered a son he named Joseph, by another one of Cheatham's slaves, Nicy. Fanny had a son named Anderson, named in honor of Richard Cheatham's son.

Benjamin Simms, the plantation manager, also fathered at least two mulatto children by a Wessyngton slave, Ary: Clinton (born 1837) and Marion (born 1838). Marion married Cheatham's slave Joseph who had been named for his white father Joseph A. Green. This union could have been arranged or encouraged by both slave owners because they were both mulattoes. Harriet Bowling Jones White, a granddaughter of Joseph Green's sister Harriet Cheatham, stated that she was told by family members that the Cheathams encouraged their fairer-skinned slaves, particularly among their house servants, to marry only others of light complexion.[23] Joseph Green was permitted to visit his family at Wessyngton.

A former female slave told Maggie Polk Washington that "if

Joseph Green (1834–1914) and Marion Simms Green
(1838–1919), portrait.

a white man told you to lay, you had to lay, like it or not." She
recalled one of her mother's first cousins, George Step Washington, had daughters with bright red hair; she supposed that they
had inherited it from two former Wessyngton slaves, Aunt Hannah
and Aunt Prudy, who were redheaded.[24] Hannah was George Step
Washington's paternal grandmother; she came to Wessyngton in
1814 with her parents and siblings. One of the Lewis slaves, Peggy,
was also a redhead. She was the sister of Gilly Lewis Washington,
who was a nursemaid to the Washington children.

While in the South miscegenation was part of life under slavery, whites from the North looked at the practice with abhorrence.
Edmund Kirk, serving in the 82nd Indiana Regiment in the Civil
War, expressed his sentiments and reactions to miscegenation and
the horrors of slavery when he wrote of his experience in Tennessee assisting a slave in relocating to a free state after he had provided information that his master was harboring a Confederate
captain:

The old Negro lived in a little log cabin near his master's house, and the day he was to leave, I rode out to see him safely off. His small amount of personal property was stowed away in an ambulance [covered wagon], which was to take him to Nashville; and his wife, a good-looking mulatto, had already mounted the wagon. A pretty quadroon woman of about thirty, who passed as his daughter—though she couldn't have been of his blood, was helping on to the seat one of the most beautiful white children I ever saw. She was well dressed, and had a fair, clear, rosy skin, and an eye as blue as indigo. Supposing she was the master's child, I asked her where she was going. "Way up North, Massa, long wid gran'dad," she answered. I was thunderstruck. She was the old woman's grandchild, the planter's own child, and a slave! I never till then realized what accursed thing slavery is.[25]

A small number of slaves on Wessyngton claimed to have some Native American ancestry, primarily Cherokee. Joseph purchased "Yellow" Tom and "Yellow" Jenny, along with their four children, Frank, Hannah, Sarah, and Henny, in 1814. They were said to be of Native American descent. Native American features were evident in photographs of some of their descendants. None of the Washington papers ever recorded any member of this family as being mulatto. Henny, born at Wessyngton in 1839, was believed to be the daughter of a Cherokee Indian by a slave, Henny, who came to Wessyngton with her family in 1814. DNA results indicate that I have traces of Native American/East Asian lineage, which is consistent with what I would have inherited from Granny Henny, my great-great-grandmother. Creek Betty (born 1797), was said to be part Creek Indian. Fannie Williams (1836–1920), who lived near Wessyngton and later moved to the plantation with her family, was said to be of Native American ancestry; this ancestry was confirmed by DNA tests on her descendants.

The slave community on Wessyngton was a microcosm of the slave communities throughout the South. Nevertheless, it had special characteristics that enabled it to be a vibrant community centered around family and kinship. The deep and significant meaning of the ancient African proverb "it takes a whole village" could indeed be found at Wessyngton.

CHAPTER 7

Working from Can't to Can't

———•◦•———

D ocuments from the Wessyngton Plantation indicate that the slaves worked under a task labor system. Joseph Washington could have learned that system in Virginia before he came to Tennessee, since the task system was common in that state. The slaves were assigned a particular job: some had to cut so much tobacco or perform various tasks or chores. On completion, the slave was allowed his own time to raise his own crops or to work for others. This system gave slaves some minor control over their lives and the ability to make purchases of items other than those provided by the owners. Some slave owners, however, assigned such difficult tasks that only a few slaves could ever accomplish them in time to work for themselves. They often required their slaves to strip and stem tobacco plants even after sunset. Punishment could be given out for those who did not complete assignments. A benefit of tasking was that it saved slave owners expenses related to the need for the numerous white overseers required by gang labor.

The tobacco growing season shaped the slaves' work routine at Wessyngton. The slaves were involved in every aspect of the process, and they were issued farm implements such as axes, hoes, and baskets to use for the various tasks.[1]

In the fall, they prepared beds of varying sizes. During the winter tiny tobacco seeds the size of ground pepper grains were sown in the beds. They covered the seeds with canvas to protect the young plants that sprouted and developed slowly during the next three months. They prepared the ground in April and May and used a plow to "check" or measure the fields into approximately one-yard squares. Hills were made with a hoe where the furrows crossed. In May or June six-inch-high seedlings were transplanted from the bed to the well-fertilized fields and set in rows, one plant in each hill. The slaves often used wooden pegs to make a hole to plant the seedlings.

Though the tobacco plant was generally hardy at this stage of development, it needed daily attention during the heat of June, July, and August: chopping out weeds from between rows with a hoe, removing suckers from the plant, plowing, topping, worming, and removing other insects.

Tobacco leaves ripened at different times during late August or September. The slaves split and cut the tobacco stalks with a tobacco knife or machete. The stalks were left in the fields to wilt. After the tobacco wilted the stalks were placed on sticks about four feet long. Each stick held five to six stalks of tobacco depending on its size and weight. The tobacco was placed on scaffolds in the fields until it was loaded on wagons and taken to the barn for hanging. The tobacco was hung and cured during the fall and winter. It was cured by firing: fires were set beneath the sticks holding the stalks, and the smoke and heat cured the leaves.

In November, December, or even early the next year, when work had already begun on the next crop, the tobacco was prepared for market. The slaves stripped the leaves from the stalks. Then they graded the tobacco into leaf, lugs, and trash. Leaf was the best grade and commanded the best price.

They arranged the leaves into hands (or bunches) of six to twelve leaves each and tied them into bundles. The tobacco was then "prized," or pressed, into hogsheads. Hogsheads were large barrels manufactured on the plantation—three feet five inches long and thirty-one inches across the head. Each hogshead held approximately five hundred pounds of tobacco. In later years George used hogsheads that held sixteen hundred to two thousand pounds of tobacco.

The tobacco was then stacked in storage barns until it was ready for shipment. The slaves loaded the hogsheads on wagons pulled by six mules with trappings and bells on the leaders. The wagons were driven to Clarksville, where they were loaded on flatboats for the six-hundred-mile trip down the Mississippi River to New Orleans, where it was sold.[2] After the mid-1850s, the tobacco was shipped by railroad to Louisville then to New York.

Initially Joseph had fewer slaves to manage and may not have felt it necessary to keep as detailed records as his son, George. Or perhaps those records he kept did not survive. Although his records are less numerous, we can conclude that he probably had a closer relationship with his slaves initially than he did later, after he became more prosperous and the number of slaves increased dramatically. In the early years, it is likely that he worked alongside his slaves, as did many small slaveholders on the new frontier. Most slave owners with labor forces of twenty or fewer slaves worked the fields with their slaves.

Slaves at Wessyngton typically worked Monday through Friday, from sunrise to sunset, and half a day on Saturday, with a break of one to two hours at noon. When not engaged in the production of tobacco, slaves were kept busy in the plantation's huge pork operations, as well as distilling whisky and brandy from the vast peach and apple orchards. Slaves were required to feed livestock, mend tools, erect buildings, clear fields, pick fruit, kill hogs, clean out fencerows, chop wood for winter, make clothing, do washing and cleaning, repair slave cabins, and a multitude of other tasks. As the saying goes, they worked from "can't see to can't see."

On most plantations, house servants generally acquired their position based on tenure and family connections. Mulatto slaves were often given positions as house servants. However, at Wessyngton most of these positions were based on the tenure of their families on the plantation or close connections with the family. With few exceptions, these positions usually passed from one generation to the next, some even after emancipation. Most of the house servants descended from the first families ("Black" Jenny and Godfrey, and "Yellow" Jenny and "Yellow" Tom), whom Joseph brought with him, or those he purchased in the early years after his arrival. The Washingtons may have felt that these families could be trusted most, since they had been there the longest. The only exceptions to this were when Joseph's and George's wives brought servants with them who worked in the mansion.

A tax list from 1860 details some of the domestics in the Wessyngton household: "Yellow" Joe, Amy, Betsy, and Turner (milk room), Felix and Nelson (kitchen), Henry and Susan (loom house). Granville stayed in the mansion. Other domestics included Marion and Clinton, the children of Benjamin Simms, the plantation manager, by a slave, Ary.

The number of domestics in a household depended on the number of slaves on the plantation, the size of the Big House, the number of members in the family, and how often the family entertained. Domestics at Wessyngton included a cook, a coachman, five gardeners, a valet, a dining room maid, a dining room man, a nurse for the children, chambermaids, a laundress, and a dairyman. They performed many tasks including cooking, cleaning, ironing, gardening, washing, sewing, milking cows, spinning, churning, running neighborhood errands, shopping, getting the mail, and delivering messages.

The house servants, artisans, nurses, and slave drivers clearly were the slave elite. However, they were not necessarily the leaders of the slave community. On most plantations, there were two or three slaves to whom the other slaves looked for guidance and direction. These natural leaders received their credentials from strength, age, practical wisdom, or religion. Many of these leaders were women.[3] Due to Wessyngton having such a large slave population, there were probably several slaves in various capacities considered leaders of the plantation. By the age of eighteen Granville was probably the head of the household staff at Wessyngton and probably placed in authority over the other slaves by the Washingtons, although the slaves may not have necessarily seen him as their leader. Dick Terry or Monroe Washington, who were generally rebellious and defiant, may have been looked to as leaders among the slaves, or the leaders could have possibly been some of the older male slaves who were the plantation's earliest residents. "Black" Jenny and "Yellow" Jenny, both matriarchs of the largest two families on the plantation and two of the oldest slaves on the estate in 1860, may have been considered leaders.

———•———

No work was required on Sunday. During this time, most slaves spent time with their families or visited other friends or relatives on neighboring farms. Some slaves chose to use their time off to cultivate their own crops. Slaves were paid for any work performed on the plantation during their time off. This same work pattern was maintained at Wessyngton after emancipation by both black and white sharecroppers.

Although no surviving record defining the terms of production for slaves who raised their own tobacco at Wessyngton has been found, the records do show as early as the 1830s the names of slaves who entered into agreements with the Washingtons. This practice probably existed on the plantation much earlier. If Joseph followed the same practices of his father and his brothers in Virginia, he could have allowed his slaves to raise their own crops when he first came to Tennessee. Estate records for Joseph Washington Sr. and his son Edwin mentioned money owed to slaves for crops and for work performed.[4]

The earliest existing records from Wessyngton indicating how much tobacco the slaves produced for their own use date from 1838. That year twelve slaves raised a combined total of 4,000 pounds of tobacco. Fifteen slaves (Britain, Axum, Eleck, Alfred, Sam, Umphrey, Joe, Dennis, Godfrey, Everett, Gilbert, Black Tom, Silva, Sam, and Hannah) raised 2,803 pounds of their own tobacco in 1840. In 1856 Axum, George Gardner, Munroe, Allen, Job, Bill, and Clinton had 1,840 pounds of their tobacco being cured in the barns.[5]

George kept a register in which he recorded the amount of tobacco raised by each slave or group that raised a crop together. He paid the slaves when he sold the produce in the New Orleans markets. The slaves received two cents per pound, which was about one-third of the price George received. The one-third was the same as most postemancipation sharecropper contracts. In addition to tobacco, the slaves raised chickens. George noted in an account book from the 1850s that he purchased eggs from Caroline Lewis, Nancy, and Lucy, and birds (possibly quail or other wild birds) from Leroy Lewis and "Carolina" Tom from his Dortch Place.

The records showed that most of the slaves who did raise their own tobacco at Wessyngton did so in family groups. Although women were not required to do hard labor on the plantation, it appeared that they assisted spouses and family members with the cultivation of their own crops. It was estimated during that time one adult made could cultivate four acres of tobacco.[6] Most men who raised crops together appear to have been brothers, and a smaller number of them fathers and sons. Some that were not related were close friends or shared the same living quarters. George noted on Sunday, September 26, 1852: "Negroes are cutting their own tobacco." After the crops were sold, he wrote: "Paid the Kentucky Negroes for tobacco; Edmund, Dick Terry, Jim, Sampson and Allen, West, Jesse, Green, Big Dick [Dick

Scott], Ea and Otho."[7] Although domestic work appeared to be easier than working in the fields, these occupations did not afford them as much an opportunity to earn additional money as field work.

George mentioned several slaves in his diary who worked for others on their time off. He paid the slaves for any work performed on their allotted time off and during the Christmas holidays, and recorded in his diary in February 1855: "Several Dortch Place Negroes here, I think I have finished paying them for Christmas work."[8]

Women and children worked under a different system than the male slaves on Wessyngton. According to Lucy Washington Helm, no mother with a young baby was expected to do any outside work until her baby was two years old. The new mother knitted and sewed for the community, worked the looms, and did the spinning. Lucy wrote: "The beginning of day nurseries must have been on large places like ours. My mother has told me that on our place there was a very long building, where the little children were taken, and two or three older women took care of them while the mothers worked. The other women only did light work in the fields and gardens."[9] Gabriel Washington (1857–1932), the last Washington slave to remain on the plantation after emancipation, told his children and grandchildren that the only work he did as a slave was to take water to the field hands, and on occasion go to the post office to collect the Washingtons' mail.[10]

This situation was unusual as most slave women throughout the South reported that they worked as hard as slave men did on most plantations. However, lighter workloads for slave women who had children created an incentive—rewarding them to continue having children—ultimately adding to the wealth of the owner.

Gabriel told his descendants that the slaves were always well treated and housed by the Washington family.[11] Lucy wrote, "The farm hands were always well treated and supplied with comfortable quarters."[12] These recollections were supported by many documents and archaeological digs on the plantation.

Based upon pottery fragments, dishes, and other household items found during an archaeological dig at a slave cabin site in 1993, this area was established in approximately 1830. Joseph owned eighty-six slaves in 1838. The increase in the number of slaves at Wessyngton during the first three decades of the nineteenth century corresponded to the expansion of the quarters (housing) in the area encompassing the hillside and creek flat below the main house.

Typically, slave housing at Wessyngton consisted of hand-hewn one-room log cabins measuring approximately 20 by 20 square feet with brick end chimneys. Some of the cabins were as large as 18 by 36 square feet. Each cabin had log flooring and a loft, where children normally slept. Some of the house servants also had quar-

Slave cabins on hillside behind Wessyngton mansion, ca. 1920.

Wessyngton Plantation slave cabin, ca. 1900s.

ters in the main house, in the basement of the mansion, rooms above the detached kitchen, the milk room, and in the loom house. Slave housing at Wessyngton was somewhat larger than typical slave dwellings, and at least the same as, if not better than, the homes of most whites of the period.

From postbellum pictures taken at Wessyngton (Emanuel and Henny Washington and their family), and several others in the late 1800s and early 1900s, we can conclude that some of the cabins had fences around the front yards and garden patches. The split-rail fences on the property had steps to prevent people from climbing over them.

John McCline, the only known Tennessee slave to have authored a book about slave life, described the cabins constructed in 1858 at the Clover Bottom Plantation in Davidson County:

They were good frame houses, of one room each, the lumber of which they were built having been taken from the forests on the place. Each house had one big wide door, which closed with a hook. The beds used in these houses were the regular four-

Emanuel, Henny Washington, and family at
Wessyngton Plantation, 1890s.

poster kind, and were made by the carpenters on the place. The
houses were whitewashed inside and out twice a year, and had
a neat and comfortable appearance. Each had its twenty-foot
front yard space, which was kept clean by sweeping. In some of
them, there was evidence of taste and means. The floors were
scrubbed with soft soap and water once a week, and were nice
and clean on Sunday. A large pothook hung in each fireplace
so that cooking could be done with some degree of conve-
nience. All had the usual Dutch oven with cover attached, for
baking purposes.[13]

Slave housing normally varied from plantation to plantation and
depended on the owners. Most slave quarters were arranged in
avenues or streets and located behind the mansion or great house.
They were strategically placed to give the owner or overseer a clear
view of the slaves, so their activities could be easily monitored.

The slave settlement at Wessyngton, however, did not fit this
pattern. The lack of a clustered settlement pattern at Wessyngton

was very unusual among antebellum plantations. We believe that this was primarily due to the hilly topography of the plantation. The scattered pattern may have given the slaves at Wessyngton more freedom and made it far more difficult to keep them under constant surveillance. The Washington Family Papers indicated that some of the trusted slaves were permitted to live in dwellings outside the general vicinity of the main slave quarters. George noted in his diary in 1851 that "the hands are working on the road by the hill by Yellow Jenny's house today."[14] Slaves at Wessyngton were housed according to their positions on the plantation and their tenure. The house servants generally resided in the cabins closest to the mansion. Some of the artisans and craftsmen lived in the next section, while field hands generally lived furthest away.

The furniture and furnishings used by the slaves on Wessyngton came from various sources: their masters gave them some items, they purchased some items themselves, and some were personal gifts they received from the Washington family. Most of the furniture used by the slaves—beds, benches, tables, chairs, and even utensils—were manufactured in one of the shops on the plantation. The slaves made water dippers, jugs, bowls, and other utensils out of dried gourds. Many of them made baskets woven from straw, an art brought from Africa. Wessyngton slaves probably made clay pots and other needed items in the kiln where they made bricks. Bedding usually consisted of mattresses filled with straw or feathers. Some slaves purchased luxury items not furnished by the plantation owners. One of George's slaves, Anderson, gave him money in 1850 to purchase a tin tub for his family, a cast-iron skillet for his wife, and a padlock, which would indicate that he had other valuables to protect.[15]

The house servants' quarters were probably better furnished than those of most field hands. Many of the slaves had store-bought furniture, dishes, and silverware, picture frames, portraits, clocks, statues, chests, and figurines. While looking for housing in New York in 1865, Jane wrote to her mother-in law: "the beds and bedroom furniture [are] not as good as Marion [a Wessyngton house servant and wife of Joseph Green, a Cheatham slave] or Irene [Granville's wife] still has in their houses."[16]

According to some former slave descendants, when the Washingtons broke a dish or a cup belonging to a set of china, they would give the set to the servants and purchase a brand-new one. Another way slaves acquired items from their owners was by inheritance. In some instances, owners bequeathed valuable items to their slaves. Some of these items were passed down to the descendants of the slaves and remain in their families. When David M. Wells of Robertson County died in 1856, for example, he willed to a slave Lewis "one cow and calf he now claims, one bay mare that he now claims, provided he pays the value to my heirs."[17] Mildred White provided in April 1864 "that my Negro man Henry be free at my death, and I do hereby free him at that time, and I will give him my wagon, two mules and harness, provided there is enough money to pay all the demands of this will. If not, Henry must pay the amount that will be lacking or sell enough of the property given to him to pay it."[18] Henry bought land and built a house by 1869 on seven acres.

Slave descendants said the Washingtons clothed their ancestors well, compared to slaves on most other plantations. In an 1858 account book entitled "Negro Clothes," Jane listed the amounts of clothing given to each slave as well as bedding, axes, and plant baskets. She mentioned giving yarn to several women, indicating that some of them made their own clothes. All slaves received articles of clothing and shoes even if they were not part of the plantation workforce. Women in their seventies and children as young as four received shoes. Jane gave them petticoats, stockings, shirts, breeches (pajamas) for bed (to a slave, Otho), and chemise for chil-

Wessyngton Plantation house
servant, ca. 1880s.

dren's clothing. Waistcoats were given to the slave men every year and to the women every third year.

Much of the clothing was made on Wessyngton. The plantation raised cotton solely for clothing, and sheep were raised for wool for knitting and weaving. Dyes for clothing were made from cedar berries and other colored wild plants and berries to achieve bright colors. There was a loom house with four large looms and three or four spinning wheels; the women did the carding and weaving to prepare cotton and wool for weaving yardage of cloth. Some of the women's dresses were solid white, and others were striped with various colors. The slave women sewed and knitted for the plantation community, making socks, stockings, shirts, pants, dresses, gowns, underclothes, and bed linens.[19] The 1850 census for Robertson County stated that there was a tailor at Wessyngton, Robert Hamey, who made some of the clothing for the Washington family and the slaves. A woman cut the women's clothing.

George often traveled to various cities on business and to purchase supplies for the plantation such as jeans, linsey (a coarse linen and wool blend fabric) for the slaves' clothing, blankets, caps, and hats. He bought materials in large quantities and shipped them back to the plantation to make clothing for the slaves. There were several notations in George's account books where he purchased shoes and other articles of clothing for the house servants. As early as 1839 he wrote his mother regarding items he had purchased: "On my return to Philadelphia I will have your shoes made and also buy the plaid domestic you say you should like for the house girls."[20] In the 1830s, Joseph paid Wilson Brantly $34.50 for making seventy-nine pairs of shoes. George had shoes made in 1849 and 1850 for the house servants (Henry, Granville, Clinton, Marion, Mary, "Yellow" Sarah, Eleck, and Violet). Some shoes were manufactured on the estate.

Wessyngton Plantation servant
stringing peppers, ca. 1880s.

Slave women on the plantation wore bonnets, handkerchiefs, and bright-colored bandannas tied in African style as headwear. Women wore varying hairstyles; some wore their hair which today would be termed an Afro, others wore simple plaits or braids, and some wrapped their hair with strings, stockings, or twine. Some of the slave men might have also worn their hair in short braids. A number of the men were clean-shaven, while others sported goatees or full beards. All the men received hats to protect them from the sun as they worked. Jane noted that a slave Bill returned a brown hat to get a black one. Some of the men wore a type of skullcap (resembling a Muslim fez).

On Sundays, the slaves wore their best clothing and visited other farms and plantations. The house servants wore the finest clothing among the slaves, often wearing cast-off clothes of their owners. Slaves prided themselves in how well they were dressed and groomed. In wealthy homes like Wessyngton, domestics such as butlers, coachmen, maids, valets, and cooks felt they had to uphold the prestige of their white families by dressing well. The Washington slaves, especially the house servants, considered them-

Wessyngton Plantation garden plots and storage buildings, ca. 1890s.

selves as the aristocracy among the slaves in the community. Some slaves earned extra money to purchase their "Sunday bests."

Male infants often wore their hair plaited as girls did until they were a year old. Some slaves believed that it was bad luck to cut a boy's hair before his first birthday because if it were cut, he would be unable to speak. Slave children wore gowns that came just below the knee until they were ten to twelve years old and started working on the farm. Amos Washington (1870–1955) told his son that when he was a child, he did not have to wear gowns like the other children because his father Emanuel was the cook, so he always had pants, shirts, and shoes to wear.[21]

Slaves who earned their own money often had members of the Washington family purchase clothes for them when they traveled to northern and eastern markets. George noted in his diary the names of several slaves who gave him money to purchase clothing for them: "Ea gave me $2.20 to buy a coat of jeans and armstick shirt, Big John $5.00 for a big overcoat, Claiborne $5.00 jean suit."[22] He mentioned that John's coat cost 75 cents more than he gave him, which probably had to be repaid later.[23] In 1850 a slave Joe purchased a razor. In 1864 Granville gave George $20.00 to purchase a gold watch in New York.

The slaves also manufactured starch, soap, and candles. As a child after the war, Lucy observed some of the women's activities on the plantation: "I well remember seeing the starch being made and the tallow melted and poured into molds to make candles. The lye was made in big hoppers behind the house from ashes from the fireplaces; soap was made from the waste fats with good strong lye."[24] Jane listed in her 1858 records that she gave out soap.[25]

Most Wessyngton slaves told their descendants that they were well fed on the plantation.[26] The slaves milked the cows, churned the milk into butter, and made cheese. To supplement their diets they planted their own gardens and raised domesticated animals, which they killed for meat. There was a garden on the estate for the white family as well as the slaves; they made preserves from fruits and pickled vegetables.

Each Saturday, the women assembled at the plantation smoke-house to receive their weekly allowances of oil, bacon, flour, molasses, lard, and meal for their families. Meat was issued for each household according to the number of family members. Jane recorded in her 1858 plantation daybook for slaves on the Dortch Place: "Caroline gets at her house 20 pounds of meat per week, Dicy 14 pounds, Nancy 14 pounds, and Lucy gets 7." Caroline's family consisted of six adults and five children, Dicy's four adults, Nancy's four adults, and Lucy's two, her and her husband. For one day's meat allowance, Jane gave Dick Terry seven pounds for him-self, his wife, seven children, and one other adult. Children were probably given small portions of meat, if at all. Many Southern blacks as late as the twentieth century believed it was unhealthy to give children excessive amounts of meat. This belief may have been African in origin, as many West Africans ate little meat. In 1838 Joseph noted in an account book that he sent Simon with 160 pounds of bacon to Todd County, Kentucky, for two weeks' allowance. Two weeks later, he sent Frank to Kentucky with 360 pounds of bacon to last one month.[27]

Most of the game that slaves ate was probably trapped. We have not found documentary evidence to support that Wessyngton slaves, with the exception of Granville, were allowed to carry guns, as this was illegal, especially after 1831. It was possible, however, that some of the most trusted slaves could have had weapons prior to the 1830s.

Hundreds of hogs were slaughtered each year on the plantation to produce the famous Washington Hams. Lesser choice cuts of pork products were used to feed the plantation labor force. These included the snout, feet, head, plucks, and ploos (a stew made of heart, liver, and lungs, highly seasoned with sage), liver, lungs, chitterlings, maws, tails, ribs, ears, and neck bones. They probably consumed some cuts of beef, especially ox tails.

The slaves cooked much of their food on outdoor hearths because most of their time was spent outside their houses, as it had been in Africa. The hoecake (later evolving into hot water cornbread) was commonly eaten by slaves. It received its name because they cooked them on their hoes over an open fire while in the fields far from their cabins. Postbellum photographs of Wessyngton slave cabins show kettles hanging over fires in the yards, which were used for cooking and for other tasks. The slaves at Wessyngton could have had a pit in a secret area in the woods on the plantation that they used. The popular Southern barbeque may have gotten its origins from the African custom of roasting pigs, beef, and chickens on an open pit with a pan of sauce for dipping the meat.

Slaves consumed a variety of greens such as collards, turnips, and mustard greens. Ann Nixon Cooper recalled as a child that her granny (Irene Lewis Washington), who was a former Wessyngton slave, could prepare greens like no one else. She could picture her with a large bushel of greens, and her washing them under the hydrant in the front yard, and how she could hardly wait for them to be prepared. At the age of one hundred six, Mrs. Cooper still could recall no one who cooked greens that could compete with Irene's.[28]

Emanuel, the cook before and after the Civil War, was famed for his cooking. Joseph E. Washington wrote to his mother, while attending Georgetown University after the Civil War, that he had been invited to the White House for Christmas, and related how splendid everything was decorated, and how beautiful the ladies were, and how elegant the food was, but it could not compare to Uncle Man's.

My grandmother Sallie Washington, the daughter of Amos

Washington, Emanuel's youngest son, said that her father could cook cornbread that was as good as cake. He must have learned this from his father. Even today, many of the Washingtons are known for their excellent cooking skills.

Family members recall an occasion when Amos Washington was working as a sharecropper during the tobacco-cutting season. The landowner's wife had cooked for all the workers. When the meal was served, she piled Amos's food on his plate in a very messy fashion, which insulted him greatly, and he refused to eat it. He stated that his father was Emanuel Washington, the cook at Washington, and he was raised at the mansion and always had the best food to eat, much better than what she was used to. He often boasted about how well his father could cook and the high esteem in which he was held by the Washingtons. Many house servants, especially cooks, ate the same food as the planter class.

The style of Southern cooking that later became known as soul food had its origins in slavery. Although whites generally gave their slaves the less desirable portions of meat, or things they felt unfit for their consumption, slave cooks, with the art of seasoning, transformed these dishes into delicacies. Many of these dishes now epitomize Southern hospitality.

CHAPTER 8

I Couldn't Hear Nobody Pray

———·•·———

I n general, the South was a deadly environment for everyone. Diseases present throughout the black population included dysentery, diarrhea, consumption, measles, mumps, influenza, whooping cough, dengue, scrofula, scarlet fever, rheumatism, typhoid, typhus, smallpox, diphtheria, dropsy, and tetanus.[1] The mortality rate from tuberculosis was very high. Many of these ailments were attributed to poor living conditions and diet. Although yellow fever and malaria were both serious killers throughout the general population, blacks usually contracted yellow fever in a milder form and suffered fewer fatalities than whites. Those from West Africa carried a resistance to some types of malaria. Work on plantations was dangerous, and it is no wonder that accidents frequently happened as a result. Workers were kicked by mules or horses, they fell off buildings, broke arms or legs, injured themselves using farm equipment, and received cuts from using saws and other tools.

Slave owners were concerned about their workers' health insomuch as it affected their ability to work and their value if they were to be sold. Hence, the health of slaves was mentioned in some bills of sale. When George A. Washington instructed his overseer, Benjamin Simms, to purchase a family of five slaves from the estate of Henry Gardner in 1839, a specific clause was included: "It is hereby indentured between the contracting parties that the Negro woman Betty is in a state of bad health and is not considered as forming any part of the consideration above specified."[2]

The medical treatment given to the Washingtons' slaves was ongoing and thorough. Wessyngton medical records, letters, and diaries detailed the physical condition and medical treatment of their slaves. On average, the Washingtons spent $100 to $300 each year in medical expenses. In the course of a year most slaves were treated only a few times, indicating that the slaves at Wessyngton were generally in a reasonable state of health. We find no mention of a hospital at Wessyngton for sick slaves. Most likely, they remained in their cabins after being visited by the plantation mistress, who would send for a doctor. George's daughter Lucy Washington Helm recalled, "My mother visited and looked after the sick on the place."[3]

Doctors A. W. Cheatham, P. F. Norfleet, R. Hobson, Newton Fox, James Thurston, C. H. Lockert, and John R. Dunn treated the Wessyngton slaves. The Washingtons paid the doctors fees generally ranging from $1.00 to as much as $25.00 per visit, depending on the severity of the illness. A notation in George's diary in 1855 mentioned having the "Spring Negroes" vaccinated.

On Wessyngton, even the elderly and the children not involved in plantation operations received the same medical attention accorded to those who worked.

In August 1851, George consulted Dr. R. W. January of Murfreesboro about treating a young house servant for breast cancer. January claimed to be able to cure cancer provided the disease had not spread to vital organs:

> You had best send your Girl by the stage to Nashville, and by the cam from that to this place, by doing this, I can have sufficient time to make the cure, as soon as the cancer is removed she can be sent home and nature will complete the work."[4]

Four months later January sent his regrets that the servant was "sinking under that most fearful disease."[5]

Several slaves were treated numerous times in the course of a year. There were a few instances that in the same year the number of treatments was quite high. In 1854 Jane sent for the doctor for "old Rachel," but she told him that she did not want him to visit Rachel "as a patient but merely to prescribe for her, and leave general directions." She "saw no use in his coming to see her every day, when probably she would be laid up for months."[6] Rachel was treated twenty-nine times in 1860, costing $15.25. Camilla, when she was just a girl, was treated twenty-two times, costing $75. In 1851 when she was seventeen, Camilla ran away from the plantation with her husband, Merideth. The next year Dr. Newton Fox attended to her for fifteen hours before she passed away from inflammation of the bowels.

Most babies were delivered by midwives. When complications arose, several slaves were seen by doctors during their pregnancies (for Sarah Jane, for example, eleven visits, and for Tempy, seven visits) and during deliveries. Ary needed a doctor's attention when her child died before birth and more than twelve times during her subsequent pregnancies. Other women used the services of a doctor for the removal of the placenta after delivery.

George made notations in his plantation diary about the health of his slaves and received letters from the plantation overseer, his mother, and his wife frequently regarding the health of particular slaves. Mary Washington informed her son: "All is well except Jim Ryan, and he has been of no service since you left, constantly coughing and sometimes spitting blood."[7] The plantation overseer Benjamin Simms wrote George: "Will dropped dead in perfect health,"[8] and in another letter informed George: "Some sickness since you left. Big Moses, Alack, Sarah and Mariah. Mariah had typhus fever and died on the thirteenth. She did not speak for three days before she died."[9] An entry in George's diary mentioned that a slave Otho was sick with measles. One month later he was sick with flux (excessive diarrhea), and Granville was sent to Kentucky to pick him up in a baggage wagon and bring him back to Wessyngton. The Washingtons may have felt that he could get better care at the Home Place, but he died anyway. Other correspondence reported Mose's death, "Dining Room" Mary's child dying of diphtheria, and Violet's Jack, born with no legs, dying early one Monday morning before breakfast.[10]

Medical records for Wessyngton from 1815 to 1865 listed information on the treatment of the slaves for various illnesses including pneumonia, flux, measles, bleeding children's gums, bilious fever, wounds, pulling teeth, fractures, tonsil removals, child vaccinations, wound dressing, cancer, and tumor removal.[11] The doctors prescribed medicines for the slaves (as well as for the Washington family), including cod liver oil, castor oil, iodine ointments, calomel, quinine, laudanum, burgundy plasters, paregoric (for stomach and intestinal ailments), and even cough drops.

In addition to being treated by white doctors, slaves used a variety of home remedies and herbs to cure many illnesses. This was common in most slave communities. Many of them believed that a daily dose of whisky would ward off many illnesses. Most large plantations had a slave who was known for treating various ills with natural herbs and potions. On Wessyngton the slave Jane Washington (1835–1916) had a vast knowledge of herbal medicine and took care of the sick. Jane was known to be very spiritual and was said to have had healing hands.[12]

Slaves learned how to cure some illnesses from Native Americans. Since several of the Wessyngton slave families had mixtures of Native American ancestry, particularly Cherokee, they would have known about these remedies. Several native Africans cured with roots and herbs many ailments that plagued colonial Americans. However, many of them were also notorious for poisoning their owners.

Jane Washington (1835–1916).

Although we do not have written records, oral tradition indicated that slaves used a number of plants and roots for medicinal properties. Whites and slaves used a local plant called mullein for aching joints and sores. Flag root was used for stomachaches. They used a plant called jimsonweed to cure some ills such as headaches and dropsy and a mixture of red oak bark, or pokeberry tea that did in fact possess medicinal properties.[13] Slaves applied a mixture of tobacco juice or soot on open cuts or to soothe bee stings; put lard on cuts and bruises; and a concoction called pizzle grease made from hog bladder. Some of these home remedies were used as a cure-all for every ailment.

Slaves used herbs and other precautions to preserve their health. Some wore pouches containing herbs such as garlic, believed to ward off illness. They had a number of beliefs that probably had little to no actual medicinal healing effect: tying a sock around the neck to cure a sore throat or walking barefoot in the first snowfall to prevent colds for the year. Some believed that tying a dime around the ankle prevented some illnesses and warded off evil forces.[14] Asafetida bags were used to ward off illness. Some believed in what was called black magic.

Several slaves at Wessyngton lived to advanced ages. In 1850 the 143 slaves included five men and five women who were between sixty and ninety years old. By 1860 this ratio declined as there were only two men and six women from ages sixty to eighty-five in a population of 187 on the Home Place.

———————

While literacy was not a skill that even most whites had, it was outright illegal for slaves to learn to read. The education of blacks challenged the institution of slavery and was a key factor in keeping them enslaved. Although we do not know how many Wessyngton slaves could read and write prior to emancipation, we can conclude that some of them could. At Andrew Jackson's Hermitage—a similar plantation, but smaller and with fewer slaves—an archaeological dig uncovered slates, chalk, and eyeglasses. Some slaves learned to read by eavesdropping on the white children when they studied their lessons. Most slaves could probably count to some degree, because this was a skill needed to keep up with livestock, fieldwork, and other tasks. Whites even taught some slaves to count for that purpose. John McCline, a slave at Clover Bottom Plantation in Davidson County, was taught to count from one to one hundred by the overseer's wife, so he could keep a count of the forty cows he had to drive to pasture after each morning's milking.[15] In addition to the more tangible reasons for becoming literate, learning to read and write was one way slaves could rebel against the system of slavery.

———————

Children often ran wild, swimming, picking berries, robbing orchards and melon patches. Joseph Washington (1895–2002) and other children of former slaves remembered spending time playing in the Indian graveyard where they often found centuries-old arrowheads.[16]

On isolated plantations like Wessyngton, the slave children were often accompanied by children of their masters. Adult house slaves spent some of their free time with the Washington children in the mansion or in their cabins or rooms. They probably spent less time with their own families on that account. Their influence on the master's children was exemplified by their baby talk as re-created by Jane in a letter to her husband:

> I asked Mary [age three and a half] yesterday where is Pa, she said "Done U Orleans, My Pa done down deep river, lef he chiluns all by da selves." . . . This evening Mary was sitting in my lap, when all at once without my saying a word she said "Mudder me do wish my Pa tome home. Me wish he tome home."[17]

Lucy wrote that as a child she often visited with Aunt Amy and Uncle Joe, two servants who lived in the basement of the mansion under the dining room.[18]

Singing and dancing—important elements of African culture that survived slavery—were prime pastimes in the slave community. They sang secular songs of the day as well as religious songs relating to every aspect of their lives: the daily trials and hardships of slave life. They sang during harvests and community get-togethers such as corn shuckings, parties, weddings, and funerals. Many of the songs were fashioned like African music. The songs were often accompanied by musical instruments; several slaves on Wessyngton played fiddles, banjos, and harmonicas. If no instruments were available, the hand-clapping and feet-patting provided the music and kept the rhythm.

Music was an emotional release from the injustices inflicted on them. The slaves comforted each other during their many trials and used music to communicate their feelings. The words of many of the songs longed for respite from labor, painful separations from loved ones, and troubles and heartaches. Slaves imitated the songs they heard whites singing and converted them to their own styles, which later gave birth to the blues and black gospel music.

One of the most pleasurable pastimes among the slaves was storytelling. They even shared these stories with the white children, according to Lucy, who wrote that they would sit by a big fire and were entertained by Uncle Joe and Aunt Amy.[19]

The slaves told chilling stories of ghosts, haunts, and other supernatural tales. George's children and grandchildren remembered the scary stories of Emanuel Washington.[20] The Washingtons had more than twenty grandchildren who would visit Wessyngton each summer. Uncle Man would be put in charge of the boys, and they would sleep in a separate building in front of the mansion that was also used as a law office. He would tell them such chilling ghost stories that they would be terrified. Uncle Man would be the highlight of their summer vacation each year. Emanuel kept strict discipline among the boys and they referred to him as "the police man." One of the stories they heard was Uncle Man's "The Graveyard Ghost":

Now you boys listen here to Uncle Man and I'm gonna tell you a story about the ghost that used to haunt the family graveyard. One stormy night when the moon was full I was comin' from the Big House going back down home and I saw this heavy fog over yonder in the graveyard. Then I heard a noise like somebody walking but I didn't pay it no mind. The next morning Granville, Irene, and some of the others around the house told me they saw this fog too and it seemed to be moving around the tombstones and thought they heard voices. The next night when I was going home I heard a voice as clear as day and it said, "You think, I am people, don't you?" It kept saying it over and over again. Then all of a sudden it started moaning, "Ohhh, ohhh, ohhh, ohhh." Of course y'all boys, know Uncle

Man ain't scared of nothing so I went over to that graveyard. As soon as I stepped up to the gate, there was this ghost that was just about ten feet tall! It said, "Think I am people, don't you?" I grabbed it from the bottom and said, "I know you are people, now get off of those stilts and get out of here!" Whoever it was fell off those stilts and ran away and we ain't seen no ghost in that graveyard since.[21]

The little boys were delighted at Uncle Man's bravery, and he became a hero in their eyes. One of George's descendants also recalled this story being told in the 1920s, and said one version of the story was that a gray horse had gotten out of the stable and was walking through the cemetery at night during heavy fog.[22]

The son of a Wessyngton slave, Joseph Washington (1895–2002) related one of Uncle Man's many ghost stories:

When we were children we used to go over to Uncle Man and Aunt Henny's house lots of times and wait for him to come from the Big House because he would bring us desserts he had cooked and would tell us stories. One night he came home and we didn't get anything and this is why according to what Uncle Man told us: "Chillun, Uncle Man ain't got nothing for y'all tonight. This is what happened. I had all kinds of cakes and pies I brought for y'all from the Big House in this nice basket. Well, when I came up to the gate out in my yard I saw a pair of big red eyes on the other side of the fence. At first, I thought it was an animal of some sort, but it wouldn't move and didn't make a sound either. Then I said, 'You're just trying to scare me, get away.' Well, it still didn't move. So I jabbed my fingers through the eyes and it went straight to them just like it was a ghost, and they still didn't move. So I dropped that basket and ran into the house. I guess that basket is still out there somewhere and if y'all chillun want to go look for it you can." Of course we children were too afraid to go out there and we all spent the night with Uncle Man and Aunt Henny.[23]

———•·•———

Though whites attended the same or similar churches as blacks, they had varying opinions about the religious beliefs of their slaves. Religious instruction served two related purposes on the Southern plantations: it was a means of teaching their slaves their view of morality and obedience, and consequently it enhanced the masters' social control. Owners felt religion was good if they could persuade slaves to be on their best behavior at all times, especially if they felt they were constantly being monitored by an all-seeing God. These owners never failed to quote Ephesians 6:5: "Servants be obedient to them that are your masters according to the flesh, with fear and trembling, in singleness of your heart, as unto Christ." On some plantations there were regularly scheduled services; on others, religion was left to the slaves alone. Some masters allowed religious instruction to be conducted only by trained ministers; others permitted the slaves to choose their own spiritual leaders.[24]

Some aspects of Christianity were important to the religious and social life of the plantation. Based on post–Civil War traditions at Wessyngton, we could assume that Christmas was always a great time of celebration. Slaves throughout the community visited each other. A wide array of foods was prepared. Family and friends of the owners came to share in the celebration. Since they brought their slaves with them, the Wessyngton slaves could meet with slaves from other plantations.

The Washington family attended the Harmony Baptist Church in nearby Turnersville. According to church records, Joseph and Mary became members (by being baptized in the church) the Saturday before the first Sunday in February 1836. According to oral tradition, during all-day church services and dinner on the grounds, the Washingtons would send some of their servants in ox-drawn carts laden with food. Later the family would arrive in one of their fine carriages.

Some slave owners would bring their slaves to church. Harmony Baptist Church permitted blacks to become members. The blacks sat in a separate section of the meeting hall or in the balcony. Although the Washingtons likely brought some of their slaves to church services, and some blacks were members, we have no records indicating that any of the Washington slaves belonged to that or to any other church.

Another Baptist church, the Red River Baptist Church, was located further from Wessyngton in Robertson County. Blacks and whites were members of that church as well. In 1805, a slave David attempted to join the church. He had been separated from his first wife due to his forced removal to Tennessee. The church members refused to accept him as a member because he had two living wives. Later they determined that his situation was beyond his control and could not be held against him. He was accepted into the congregation. The church members may have realized that if they had condemned David's actions, they would have had to acknowledge their guilt in placing slaves in these difficult positions.

In some instances slaves exercised more freedom than one might have thought existed before emancipation. At a service in 1820, church attendance was so large that the blacks were asked to leave the meeting house to make room for the white worshipers. The black members walked out during communion services. The white members later attempted to meet with the black leaders and members to resolve the matter.[25]

Although blacks were members, the church was an ally of the slave owners. In 1820, Josiah W. Fort reported to the Red River Baptist Church that two of his slaves, both named Hannah, had been quarreling, fighting, and using unbecoming language. The church took up the issue and expelled them.[26] From the minutes of the church, we learn that in some instances slaveholders did interfere with their slaves' marriages. As early as 1806 the members suspended a slave Bess from membership for marrying a man against his master's wishes and living in a disorderly way before marrying him. Later the majority of the church decided that she was justified. This incident also demonstrates that slaves did perform their own wedding ceremonies without the assistance or permission of their masters.[27]

Other slave owners in the area who could not control their slaves brought them before the church, often to no avail. Some of the charges included drinking, dancing, fighting, stealing, and cursing. Some slaves repented, while others blatantly stated that they did not care what the church thought and continued as before. Several slaves refused to be chastised by the church and resigned before they were expelled. Over the years, the church expelled several slaves as well as whites.

Some slaveholders allowed local African American ministers to preach to their slaves, mostly under white supervision. Around 1850 a slave Horace Carr of Port Royal (about ten miles from Wessyngton) was ordained by the Red River Baptist Church. Reverend Carr ministered to slaves in the Montgomery and Robertson county areas without white observation. He performed many wedding and funeral services for the African American community, including some at Wessyngton. One local plantation owner, Lawson Fort, was so impressed by Reverend Carr's preaching that he allowed him to come to his estate and preach any time he wished.[28] Fort did place one restriction on the meetings: he did not want slaves from other plantations on his grounds at night. He felt that his thirty to forty slaves were "first-class" and undoubtedly did not want them influenced by others; he may have worried about his and his family's security issues in the dark of night.

Since many Washington slave descendants have indicated that their ancestors were clothed, fed, and housed better than slaves belonging to other owners in the area, it is most surprising to learn that the Wessyngton slaves were not allowed to congregate in large numbers for church worship. Consequently they were forced to conduct their worship in secret. The Washingtons' prohibition on public meetings could have been a reaction to Nat Turner's insurrection in 1831, when several of Joseph's former neighbors in Jerusalem, Southampton County, Virginia, were killed. Tighter restrictions and the total ban on slave worship led to the creation of the "invisible church" on many plantations and farms.

Nevertheless, Wessyngton slaves did indeed worship. When praying or singing in their houses, they turned pots and kettles upside down and placed them at the door, believing that these items would absorb the sound to prevent them from being overheard by the whites. Blacks believed that this tradition went back to African customs to sanctify the ground, to ward off bad spirits, and to bring prosperity to the home. Gabriel Washington (1857–1932), born on Wessyngton, confirmed that worship was held in secret. Amos Washington (1870–1955) heard similar stories from his relatives and a former slave, Sarah Washington Cheatham.[29]

The slaves held secret meetings in the woods at night, sometimes attended by other slaves in the neighborhood. The meeting places for the slaves were often called "hush arbors," praying grounds where they expressed themselves freely away from the watchful eye of their masters. They informed each other of such meetings by using a secret code in the songs they sang as they worked in the fields. The songs such as "I Couldn't Hear Nobody Pray," "Steal Away to Jesus," and "Hush Somebody's Calling My Name" would indicate the location of the meeting and the time. Some of these songs later became known as Negro spirituals. Many of the songs were fashioned after the African call-and-response singing style. Slave owners felt that slaves were content when they were singing and did not realize that the songs carried secret communications.

Lay preachers led these secret meetings. Joe Scott (1843–1932), born a Wessyngton slave, said that he was called to preach at age fifteen, around 1858, seven years prior to his emancipation.[30] Edmund White Washington most likely began preaching in secret prior to his emancipation.

Olive Cheatham Bell told of a secret meeting once held on the plantation:

> A young girl became filled with the spirit and began shouting. The crowd tried to quiet her in vain, for fear of being heard. Shortly thereafter, the overseer did hear the girl as everyone suspected, and threatened to whip her. She told him that the Lord would protect her. As he attempted to grab her, there was an extremely loud burst of thunder followed by lightning, which hit a tree near the overseer. He then ran away and never attempted to bother her again.[31]

One Wessyngton slave, Sam Washington (1853–1930), became so overtaken with the spirit that he later became known to everyone in the community as "Shouting" Sam. When Sam died, the *Leaf Chronicle* of Clarksville, Tennessee, obituary read:

Olive Cheatham Bell (1833– 1928), portrait ca. 1870s.

"Shouting" Sam Washington, 83 Dies at Adams. The death of "Shouting" Sam Washington at Adams, Tennessee, last week has recalled to many who knew him, interesting incidents of "Shouting" Sam's life. Born in slavery, "Shouting" Sam went through the days of the Civil War and came forth a free citizen. Sam acquired his nickname from his intensely emotional religious nature. He professed religion at a revival held at Mt. Zion Missionary Baptist Church near here during the early seventies, and each year following his conversion, he grew more demonstrative in his religious activities, especially funerals and protracted meetings, till the sobriquet "Shouting" Sam was attached to his name. Ten days after his conversion he was baptized in Sulphur Fork Creek, near Port Royal, and he seemingly became overpowered by a shouting mood. The minister performing the ordinance, called assistants to prevent his drowning. "Shouting" Sam was born at Wessyngton, on the elder George Washington's plantation near Cedar Hill. . . . Little Sam was a great favorite with the Washington family.[32]

Joseph Washington (1895–2002) on his one hundred second birthday remembered vividly the prayer meetings they used to have at Wessyngton. Joe said they always had a joyous time singing and praying. "All those old folks back then could sing. I can remember as a child seeing Aunt Henny Washington sitting on the porch looking up into the heavens, and humming as if she was just waiting to go home to be with the Lord. I remember Aunt Sue from Topeka, Kansas, would say, 'My foot is on the Rock, that Rock that John talked about, and that rock is Jesus.'"[33]

Slaves often identified themselves with characters in the Bible, particularly to the children of Israel. Many of the songs slaves sang as spirituals told stories of events in the Bible. One expert on Negro spirituals suggested that if the Bible were destroyed, much of it could be reconstructed from the songs that slaves sang.[34] The slaves also sang many of the songs they learned from attending church services with whites and used their own musical styles. They substituted verses that applied to their daily lives.

My great-great-grandfather Emanuel "Uncle Man" Washington had a beautiful voice and led many of the songs. Joseph recalled Uncle Man: "I can see him now slapping his knees, with those big old hands as he sung his favorite song: 'I've Just Come from the Fountain His Name Is So Sweet.'"

Refrain
I've just come from the fountain; I've just come from the
    fountain, Lord,
I've just come from the fountain, His name's so sweet. O
    brothers
I love Jesus, O brothers, I love Jesus, O brothers, I love Jesus
His name's so sweet.
        Been drinking from the fountain, been drinking from
            the fountain
        Been drinking from the fountain, His name's so
            sweet.

[*Leader*]	[*Response*]
Oh sinner, do you love Jesus?	Yes, yes, I do love my Jesus.
Sinner, do you love Jesus?	His name so sweet.

Most slaves believed in some elements of the occult, superstitions, spirits, ghosts, haunts, omens, and various good and bad signs. Recent archaeological investigations of slave quarters on Southern plantations (including the Hermitage) have yielded charms, amulets, and bracelets made of coins believed to ward off evil spirits. Some, but not all, of these beliefs were of African origin.

Slave owners and whites perpetuated some superstitions. Local whites in the area held a strong belief in the occult. In 1868, Thomas Clinard and Richard Burgess were indicted for the murder of Charles Smith. Clinard felt that Smith had bewitched or put a hex on him. Clinard and Burgess attempted to arrest Smith and bring him before authorities to answer the charges. Smith then fired at the two. Clinard shot back and killed Smith. After deliberation, the jury returned a verdict of not guilty.[35]

Blacks learned from the whites of witches, ghosts, beliefs in talking with the dead, evil omens, and signs. Whites used superstitions to maintain control. They told house servants the common superstition that if a mirror broke, it would bring seven years of bad luck; this superstition would ensure the servant's care while cleaning expensive furnishings, many of them shipped from England. They taught slaves that it was bad luck to be outside at night, probably to prevent them from wandering about unsupervised after dark.

The slaves used some of their beliefs to frighten whites. House servants often taught the children of the plantation owners about ghosts, haunts, and other supernatural phenomena to amuse and frighten them. Some used the occult to gain special favors or privileges and avoid punishment. A slave named Jerry Fort (born 1847) was known throughout the Montgomery and Robertson county areas as a weather prophet. Many farmers prepared their lands and planted their crops according to his predictions.[36]

Jenny Washington Hayes (1855–1936), born at Wessyngton, was known throughout the area as a fortuneteller or reader. She was the daughter of Emanuel Washington's sister Clara Washington (1832–1925). Minnie Washington Ellis recalled as a young girl seeing Jenny grinding snakes and eels to make potions. Jenny was said to be a powerful psychic who could tell anyone's past or future. A local apparition known as Long Tall Fannie, who could been seen walking through various parts of Cedar Hill and suddenly disappearing, was said to have a connection to Jenny's sorcery. Fannie Ricks Keaton Garrison Williams (1836–1920), who was part Cherokee and a Wessyngton sharecropper after the Civil War, was known to read fortunes with the use of cards. According to the family, Fannie was really mean and poisoned her daughter-in-law Mary Ellis Williams to death. She was the wife of Kinchem Williams. No one knows what prompted the poisoning.

Psychic or portentous events had an impact on the slaves. A well-known psychic dream by Mary Cheatham Washington in 1824 foretelling her daughter's sudden death probably strengthened some of the slaves' beliefs in signs and omens.[37] A number of slaves in the area feared that the Judgment Day was at hand when stars fell (meteor shower) in Clarksville during the 1850s.

Whites and blacks alike around Wessyngton no doubt heard many mysterious tales of the infamous Bell Witch, who tormented the Bell family of the nearby Adams community. The Bell family came to Robertson County in the early 1800s and shortly thereafter were haunted by the mysterious being later called the Bell Witch. Dean, a slave owned by the Bells, had many hair-raising encounters with the witch. The Bell Witch is said to be the most documented case of the supernatural in the United States.

According to Mattie Terry, Margaret Fort Washington, who lived at Wessyngton (wife of Gabriel Washington), foretold her own death. At the Antioch Baptist Church one Sunday, Margaret sang "Sinner Don't Let the Harvest Pass Go to Hell and the Devil Laugh" and prayed a very beautiful prayer; she could always pray very well and was known as a prayer warrior. She then told the church members that they were seeing her for the last time because by the next Sunday she would be gone to Heaven to be with the Lord. As Margaret predicted, she died before the next Sunday's service.[38]

Minnie Washington Ellis recalled that the old covered bridge between Wessyngton and Washington Hall was said to be haunted by the ghost of a local slave who had been hanged.[39] Even at the turn of the century, Mattie Terry, while working in the Wessyngton mansion recalled hearing all the doors slamming shut. Everyone believed that it was the ghost of George A. Washington.[40]

————•·•————

Few records have survived regarding the burials or funeral services of slaves. One reason could be that the slaves performed these services in private. In some instances they held a slave's funeral weeks after the actual burial. This allowed other slaves time to come and pay their respects to the relatives of the deceased. Most large plantations owners designated land for use as a cemetery for the slaves, usually located in obscure, remote areas on the property unfit for any type of cultivation. Small slave owners often buried their slaves in their family cemeteries in segregated areas.

From 1818 to 1969 the Washington family members were buried in the family cemetery located near the mansion. On an 1860s map of Wessyngton, two tracts of land were designated as the Grave Yard Field and the Upper Grave Yard; this land on a hill was used as the slave cemetery. The earliest documented death of any of the Washington slaves was in the 1840s.

It was likely that some of the Washington slaves were buried in Todd County, Kentucky, where in 1850 there were a total of eighty-five slaves. Others slaves were buried on the Dortch Place. Another cemetery with approximately twenty-fives graves was located in a small cemetery on the farm on land that was part of Wessyngton, later called Glenraven. In that cemetery one tombstone had a date of 1861 and another was for a former Wessyngton slave Marina Washington (1812–1884) who was the mother of Granville's first wife, Malinda.

The Wessyngton slave cemetery was located a quarter mile from the slave cabin area. This site was likely selected for its closeness to the Washingtons' first home near Cave Spring before the purchase of land nearer to the mansion. It could have been that the slaves did not want to live close to the cemetery or they selected the best location. In many African societies, only a select group from the tribes buried or had anything at all to do with the dead. Others were strictly forbidden from even touching the dead. In some societies, only family members buried their loved ones. Many superstitions probably arose among American-born slaves due to the secrecy surrounding these rituals.

The customs surrounding death and burials centered around the community. When a slave passed away most often a designated person prepared and dressed the corpse in a white shroud. The deceased was placed on a "cooling board," a table covered with a white cloth, or in a coffin. A wake or "settin' up" lasted all night. Every member of the community came to "set up" with the deceased. They sang gospel songs and prayed for the soul of the one who had passed to the other side.[41] The body of the deceased was always carried from the house feet first because a superstition existed that if the head faced backward, the dead person might summon others to follow him.[42]

There is no record from Wessyngton stating the manner in which slaves were buried. Some of the first slaves may have been buried in a sheet wound around the body; later others were buried in wooden coffins or pine boxes made in one of the shops on the plantation. George sold coffins to his neighbors. He sold a coffin to Catherine Black for one of her male slaves for $3.00 in 1855.[43]

The slaves performed their burials in a fashion similar to those in Africa. Members of the Washington family probably attended the funerals of their slaves, especially the house servants or others with whom they had close relations. If the slave belonged to a local church, a white minister may have conducted the service. In some cases, black ministers on the plantations or in the community performed the services.

Slaves incorporated some of their funeral practices, such as singing, into the funeral services of whites. When George A. Washington died in 1892, the plantation was still occupied by several former slaves. At the grave, the services were concluded by a song from twenty or more of the family servants. The *Nashville American* reported that their "melodious voices touched all hearts."[44] This was probably requested by the Washington family, since there was also a white choir there from Springfield.

In the Wessyngton slave cemetery, corpses were oriented in an east-to-west direction. We do not know if this burial pattern was symbolic of Christian beliefs, because many African groups are buried in this manner. No tombstones have survived, so we do not know if any graves had headstones. Only a stack of rocks marked some of the graves; others had flowers such as wild roses planted at the head of a grave. A few graves seemed to have rocks marking the head and foot of the grave. The cemetery at Wessyngton contains approximately two hundred graves and is likely the largest slave cemetery in Tennessee.

The Wessyngton slave cemetery was used for burials of the slaves and later for them and their descendants until 1928. Maggie Polk Washington (1904–2003) recalled her mother, Mary Lewis Polk, attending funerals and burials there when she was a small girl. Members of the Washington family often attended the services. In the 1890s, one of the Washington children wrote that she, her cousins, and her aunt "went to old Aunt Prudy's funeral and they wanted me to look at her but I would not do it, the funeral was very sad."

African American funeral rites and services had their origins in Africa. These rituals were then molded by their experiences in America and the influence of Christianity. Many of these customs are practiced even to present times.

CHAPTER 9

Wessyngton Rebels

W hen asked his opinion of slavery by a visitor to the Hermitage, Alfred, the favorite slave of President Andrew Jackson, responded with his own question: "How would you like to be a slave?"

No matter how slaves were treated—good, bad, or indifferent— they all detested the institution. In the case of Wessyngton, the Dortch and Todd County, Kentucky, properties were more distant from the Home Place and had newly acquired slaves. Either the slaves on these properties displayed more defiance or that rebellious acts on the Home Place were not recorded.

Slave owners often threatened to put unruly slaves in their "pockets" for bad conduct, meaning they would sell them to the Deep South or to the islands. Slavery in the Deep South was known to be far worse than in the border states of Delaware, Kentucky, Tennessee, Missouri, and West Virginia. Slaves in the Caribbean islands had a life expectancy of only seven years after their arrival because of the harsh working conditions; they were literally worked to death. Prior to the ban on the transatlantic slave trade, slave owners in the islands considered it simply more economical to buy a slave and work him to death in three to seven years rather than raise one from infancy. On some of these plantations, the male population outnumbered women nearly eighteen to one, which made it impossible for most slaves to maintain a family life.

In the mid-1800s, Billie Villines was a Robertson County slave trader and mill owner. Captain Villines bought many of the "most vicious and unruly Negroes in Robertson County" and took them further south to work in the cotton fields. A large stone block was used as an auction block to transact slave sales; it still stands today near Villines's house.[1]

In 1856 Daniel G. Baird of Robertson County died, leaving a large plantation and about fifty slaves (some of whom had been purchased from the Cheathams) to be divided between his ten minor children. His wife, Mary, petitioned the courts to keep the plantation intact until the children reached adulthood; that petition was granted. Mary Baird later returned to court to get permission to sell a slave named Rose to the Deep South, because she was so unruly and could not be controlled. Rose was allowed to stay in the area once she promised that she would behave.[2]

In contrast, some slave owners offered their slaves rewards for "good behavior" by giving extra food rations, passes to visit other plantations, liquor, gifts, additional clothing, and better housing. These petty offers, however, still did not give slave owners the total control they desired.

The overseer was in the middle of two separate worlds. According to John W. Blassingame: "The overseer often came into conflict with the plantation owner. If the overseer used unusual force in driving the slaves, he incurred the wrath of the owner for damaging his property. On the other hand, if he were easygoing, the planter might dismiss him for producing a small crop. The disciplining of slaves was the major factor in the success or failure of an overseer. In fact, planters often dismissed overseers for cruelty, drunkenness, absenteeism, and lax discipline."[3]

Most slaves received the greatest amount of abuse at the hands of overzealous white overseers and black drivers. Usually the situation was made more difficult in the absence of plantation owners who traveled extensively for business. During the time George

A. Washington's father-in-law, Major William B. Lewis, resided in Washington, DC, as part of President Andrew Jackson's Kitchen Cabinet, he suffered large losses at his Fairfield Plantation under the management of a Mr. Berkley. He asked George to check on his affairs at the plantation because, from all reports, Berkley had taken over the plantation and the slaves as if they were his own and cheated Major Lewis out of thousands of dollars.

To retain his job, the overseer had to be adept at managing slaves. There were many pitfalls in the endeavor. If the overseer became too familiar with slaves or had sexual relations with black women, the slaves extracted favors from him and did little work. If the overseer was too cruel and hard-driving, the slaves did everything in their power to discredit him. It was often impossible for the overseer to find a happy medium between these two extremes. Slaves dissatisfied with the overseer informed the owner of his transgressions or ran away to escape heavy work or avoid punishment. Often the slaves refused to return to work until they had spoken to their masters about their treatment.[4]

Punishment varied according to the offense. Offenses ranged from minor actions such as refusing to hold a bag for another slave while picking fruit to those as serious as running away or striking an overseer. Notations in George's diary indicated that during the 1850s on his Dortch Place and Todd County, Kentucky, holdings overseers could not punish slaves without first getting his permission. He probably implemented this system to protect his interest against slaves being maimed or killed by overseers. Several drunken overseers had made threats against his slaves' lives and were quickly fired.

Slaves had disputes with overseers for various reasons. Some may have felt that overseers gave them too much work or not enough food, or they could have been competing for the same women. One overseer, later the plantation manager, Benjamin

Simms, fathered children by at least one slave woman Ary, and possibly others. Since there were few women on the Dortch Place, and even fewer on the plantation in Kentucky, this competition for partners was likely to have created problems.

We do not know if there was ever an actual jail building on the Wessyngton property as existed on some large plantations. The "jail" could have been some building on the property. Felix "Ditt" Terry recalled seeing whips, chains, and iron collars in a basement room of the Wessyngton mansion; it was referred to as the "white room."[5] Other members of the Terry family recalled seeing similar items.

George's diaries and correspondence from 1841 to 1863 indicated that at least some twenty-one slaves, including five women, were whipped for various reasons. These slaves mainly worked on the Dortch Place and Todd County, Kentucky, properties.[6] George noted in his diary that he had several slaves from the Todd County plantation whipped for going to Eleck Robertson's plantation without permission to attend the wedding of a slave Jeff.[7] Slaves were held accountable for implements and other articles left in their care. Jane noted that Warrick was to be whipped for the poor condition of his basket or he had the option to pay for it. She had the same complaint about two other slaves, Reuben and Willis. In a postscript to a letter to George in 1852, she matter-of-factly described a whipping:

> P.S. Since I finished my letter there has been a general fuss among the negroes, arising out of some lie Emily said Lavinia had told upon Joe. Not content with quarreling at Lavinia's house, they came on the hill where Mama getting hold of the story began prosecuting inquiries which ended in Jim, Lavinia, Joe & Emily being whipped, the chastisement brought down their tempers, and all is now calm.[8]

Wiley Terry (1851–1931) lived most his childhood on the Dortch Place. He related a harsh description of his early life on the plantation. One day when he was a young boy working in the fields, only wearing a gown as most children did, he was sick to his stomach, could not keep up with the others, and got so tired he fell. The overseer whacked him across the back with a whip and tore his gown to shreds. He remembered crying, but his parents were unable to help him. This was the only time he mentioned getting whipped.[9]

We can assume that there were probably many more incidents of punishment than those recorded. No records survived from the period 1795 to 1841. On the other hand, since slaves on the Home Place could have worked with less white supervision or under the direction of black drivers and lived under a strong family structure, this could have led to fewer violations of plantation rules. Cruel punishment was not restricted to slaves. Up to 1829 whipping, maiming, chaining, and the use of stocks was legal in Tennessee and used to punish whites also.[10]

Some slaves took matters into their own hands and retaliated against the overseers. The plantation owners had to walk a delicate balance: they supported the authority of their overseers, but they sometimes had to back their slaves against them. George's diary indicated that his relationship with his slaves was such that they could inform him of any abuse from overseers. His position was somewhat unusual, as most plantation owners would automatically side with white overseers.

Mary informed George of an incident while he was in Philadelphia. Jack nearly killed the overseer William Ogg, and the overseer injured Jack badly. George responded:

> Yours of the 16th was received yesterday and I was as much annoyed as surprised when I read the contents. It certainly is a bad business; but nevertheless, if the Negro is not dead, Mr. Ogg must be gotten back, if possible, and

if he will not return, I think Wimms will be the best
manager that can be had, as he is resolute and determined and you know it is necessary a man of such
character should be on the place.[11]

A few months later overseer Ogg fought with another slave, Jacob.
The plantation manager, Benjamin Simms, reported to George:
"Ogg says he never intends drinking another drop of liquor while
he lives on the place. I could not get him to say anything about the
fuss with him and Jacob."[12]

Major Lewis in one instance interceded on behalf of one of
his former slaves, Washington, to prevent him from being punished when he attacked an overseer. Major Lewis knew him well
as Washington and another slave Jacob had been purchased from
Thomas Crutcher when they were small boys; Washington had
then been given to George.[13] Major Lewis wrote George:

> Simms [the overseer] has been almost killed. If he be still
> living please remember me kindly to him, and I should
> like also to know how he is. I send you this note by
> Washington [the slave], who I fear has been acting badly.
> He tells me the overseer and he had a difficulty, and as
> he threatened to punish him severely, he determined to
> go to see you and started for your father's, but got lost
> and found when he learned where he was, that he was so
> near Nashville that he determined to come here to see
> his wife before he returned. This may or may not be true,
> but as he promised faithfully never to do the like again,
> and as I have a hope that he will comply with his prom-
> ise, I by that, ask that he may be forgiven this offense. I
> really think he will do better in the future and I should
> like you, therefore, to give him an opportunity to redeem
> his character.[14]

More than a decade later, overseer Ogg was still having problems. George noted in his diary: "Mr. Ogg came home quite drunk about dark and threatened to shoot Allen and drew his pistol on him." A few years later, Henton and George ran away from Ogg and refused to be punished by him.

Ogg was not the only overseer to have problems. An overseer Wimms hit Axum in the head with an iron pin to prevent Axum from killing him. George Harriett struck the overseer Epperson on the Dortch Place, and then went back to the Home Place and reported his own actions.[15] Allen and one of his brothers waited until overseer Easley got drunk and then nearly beat him to death. Allen informed George that Easley had gotten drunk, threatened to whip him, and then drew a pistol on him. George fired the overseer immediately.[16]

As a general rule, both the slaves and the elite class of plantation owners looked down on the overseers. We do not have much information about the Wessyngton overseers from 1855 to 1865. Simms died in 1854; descendants of his siblings still live in Todd County, Kentucky. Many of Simms's black descendants still reside in Nashville.

———•◦•———

Some Wessyngton slaves used passive forms of resistance to slavery such as feigning illness and secretly destroying tools. George noted: "Josh sick, Bob and Miles pretending to be, sent to work." Apparently Bob and Miles decided that they were not going to work in spite of George's orders, as he later recorded: "Bob and Miles did not go to work. Laid out all day." Several years later George wrote: "Josh and another slave Reuben pretending to be sick and nothing the matter with them." The next day, he mentioned that they were absent from work for the second day pretending to be sick.[17] Many slave owners were often astonished by the number of slaves who seemed to be sick for an entire week but recovered miraculously by the weekend when they were given time off. This type of defiance could result in a twofold loss to the plantation owner: lost labor and unnecessary doctor's expenses.

Slaves broke farm implements and rode draft animals (mules, horses, oxen) at night, making the animals too tired for work. George received many complaints that his slaves on his Kentucky plantation were riding the mules and horses of neighboring planters. George had several slaves whipped for running about at night: "Dick up from Dortch Place indicated and reports one of the mules having been ridden last night. Anderson and Henton suspected. They both are here and had them handcuffed."[18] Two days later they discovered that Anderson was the guilty party, and he was whipped.

Other slaves participated in higher levels of resistance, including stealing and damaging the property of others, purchasing stolen whisky from other slaves, stealing bacon and wheat, and fighting each other. Henry, whom George A. Washington purchased from Thomas Williamson in 1838 for $700, was accused of breaking into his former owner's house and stealing $50 and clothing. Evidently, the sixteen-year-old Henry had permission to visit his former home, because after this incident George told his overseer to keep Henry close to the plantation. The sheriff came with a warrant to search the slave quarters, but he did not find the money.[19] Henry probably felt he was entitled to part of the $700 his former owner received for his sale.

Slaves felt it was morally wrong to steal from another slave. When slaves took the property of their owners, however, they did not consider this stealing in view of all that had been taken from them, and the fact that their unpaid labor created the wealth their owners enjoyed. John Brown, a slave on another plantation, explained that slaves recognized that they were operating under an alternative morality, one suited for the special conditions of being defined as property itself. Brown recalled that slaves did not "see the wrong" of stealing from the slave owner. As long as "we were not acting against one another," the ethic against theft did not apply. "I am sure that, as a rule, any one of us who would have thought nothing of stealing a hog, or a sack of corn, from our master, would have allowed himself to be cut to pieces rather than betray the confidence of his fellow slave."[20] Some slave owners fed their slaves so poorly that they were forced to steal food to survive. Others took items from their masters to barter with slaves on other plantations. Presidents George Washington and Thomas Jefferson, who each owned hundreds of slaves, experienced rampant slave theft. Whereas Jefferson was able to comprehend why the slaves he owned stole from him, Washington was dumbfounded. Jefferson reasoned that men "in whose favour no laws of property exist, probably feels himself less bound to respect those laws made in favour of others;" therefore, could not the slave "justifiably take a little from one, who has taken all from him?"[21] Slaves had a common saying conveying their attitude towards stealing:

> Our Father, who art in Heaven
> White man owe me eleven, and pay me seven,
> Thy kingdom come, Thy will be done,
> And if I hadn't took that, I wouldn't have none.

The Washingtons did not experience major problems with slaves stealing or taking what they felt they were entitled to from the plantation. However, former slaves recounted one occurrence at the Home Place when a group of slaves stole a pig and barbequed it in the woods. They later brought the pig to one of the slave's cabins, where they planned to feast on it. As the feast was getting under way, one of the overseers headed toward the gathering. To alert the others that the overseer was coming, one of the slaves starting playing a banjo and broke into song with:

> Johnny kick the hog foot a little further
> under the bed,
> Johnny kick that hog foot a little further
> under the bed,
> Johnny kick that hog foot a little further
> under the bed,
> Ole Massa catch you stealing, kill a po'
> Negro dead!

As the overseer arrived at the crowd, he began to clap his hands with the slaves and exclaimed, "Sang, niggers, sang!" The overseer never learned that there was actually a whole hog, not just the foot, under the bed. The slaves joked about their close call many years later and passed the story on to their descendants.[22] Acts of defiance also included slaves going without permission to visit family and friends on other farms and meeting in the woods to gamble and play cards.

Some slaves had disagreements among themselves that led to bloodshed. J. W. Kendall of Todd County wrote George regarding a fight to the death between one of his slaves and one of George's: "Some four weeks ago a difficulty occurred between my Negroes and yours and both parties used threats. And one of mine had an axe as he said to defend himself. And after much trouble I found where they got the whisky from, for it was this that excited them to bloodshed."[23] They discovered that Dack, belonging to Solomon James, had been stealing his owner's whisky and selling it to slaves in the neighborhood. After interviewing witnesses to find out exactly what happened, Washington insisted that Kendall's slave be prosecuted.

Washington had several slaves on the Dortch Place and in Todd County whipped for fighting each other. One Saturday in the middle of the night, overseer Ogg had to send a slave Claiborne from Todd County to Wessyngton because so many slaves were fighting that he could not control them.[24]

With the blacks' lack of freedom and self-determination, it is not surprising that slaves had disputes with local whites. One of Washington's slaves, Granville from the Dortch Place, was shot in the leg by Will Carr in Turnersville, five miles away. Another slave, Anderson, reported the incident. It appeared that some of the slaves had been wandering around the neighborhood at night, and Granville had a dispute with Carr. George went to speak to Will Carr's father. He told George he did not approve of his son's conduct, but he could not control him.[25] It appears that the slaves in Todd County, Kentucky, as well as Washington's slaves there had a reputation for violence. A local doctor, Newton Fox, was ambushed and murdered by a group of blacks in 1854. Jane wrote her husband about the crime and their slaves' possible connection to it:

> Two of Dr. Fox's own Negroes and one of Wiley Yarboro has been arrested for the murder. Yarboro's was subsequently discharged as innocent; but from confessions made by his own there are others concerned who had not at the last advice been taken. The negroes say they murdered him for money, he having upwards of $500 about his person, but if they did, they must in some way been frightened off before the robbery was completed, as nearly that amount was found on and about the body. There is a boy formerly belonging to Dr. Grady, who is missing, and is supposed to belong to the gang, indeed one of Fox's negroes said this boy had the money that they got. I almost expected to hear of some of your negroes being implicated as every mean thing is generally laid to them but as yet they are clear.[26]

Robertson County court records include three cases where slaves were indicted for murder or attempted murder of whites. "Mahalah, a slave" was indicted for the murder of Nancy Newton in 1836. Mahalah endured three trials before being found guilty and sentenced to hang. Her attorney appealed the case to the Tennessee Supreme Court based on a procedural error. The court heard the case, reversed the judgment of the previous trial, and cleared her of all charges.[27]

In another case, in 1845, the Robertson County court indicted the slave Ned for the murder of his owner, David J. Walton, by hitting him in the head with an axe. It also charged the slave Peter with aiding and abetting Ned's act. There was no doubt that Ned killed his owner, but lawyers contended that Peter did not help in the crime. The all-white jury found Ned guilty and Peter not. While the jurors certainly could have found Peter guilty just because he was a slave, he was cleared of all charges. Ned was the first black person hanged in Robertson County. Gallows were constructed about one-half mile from Springfield, and Ned rode in a wagon sitting in his coffin from the jail to the scaffold. Local authorities allowed the gallows to stand for several years as a warning to potential evildoers.[28]

The third case involved a slave named Angeline, indicted on February 16, 1853, for the attempted murder of her owner, Mary E. Pennington. The indictment charged that Angeline choked, kicked, and beat Pennington with her fists and sticks. According to Arthur Howlington, "Both times the jury failed to agree and mistrials were declared. The attorney general refused to prosecute a third time. However, Angeline was not released. In an extraordinary procedure, 'all the parties' agreed that she 'should be further punished.' To 'avoid the trouble and expense of assigning her to another tribunal for that purpose,' the 'parties' submitted her to the circuit judge for punishment."[29] The judge sentenced her to receive, in the words of the court record, "on her bare skin one hundred lashes or blows . . . publicly at the Court house." The whipping was "to be inflicted with a paddle or some instrument other than a cowskin, so as not to break or lacerate the person." Angeline was to receive ten "lashes or blows each day" with the exception of Sunday "unless said Angeline shall elect to receive more or less per day." She was allowed to post bond "that she make her appearance every day to receive her lashes." The court further recommended to the slave's owner that, "Angeline within a reasonable time be sold."[30]

Many slaves refused to meekly submit. They found various avenues—from breaking tools and work slow downs, to violence—to protest their slavery. I thought of them as early Wessyngton rebels fighting for their rights. On the other side, the white judicial system in Tennessee was open to, and in some cases, worked in the favor of the slaves.[31]

CHAPTER 10

Follow the North Star

———— ·•·• ————

Running away was not taken lightly. It was a precarious undertaking, and failure resulted in severe repercussions, even death. To date, no evidence documents that an "underground railroad" operated in Robertson County to help fugitive slaves escape to freedom. Usually a runaway slave was on his own. Although most slaves who ran away had never before left the region in which they were born, according to correspondence and advertisements, most runaways knew to follow the constellations such as the North Star or the Big Dipper for direction. Despite the formidable obstacles, many chose the risk rather than live under the harsh conditions of slavery. Some slaves armed themselves with sharpened sickles, scythes, axes, and other homemade weapons. Runaway slaves faced many dangers: starvation, exposure to the elements, and attacks by vicious bloodhounds trained for the purpose of tracking them.

As John Hope Franklin and Loren Schweninger write: "Whether alone or with others, those who challenged the system paid a heavy price. The argument that slaves were not treated harshly because they were valuable property ignores the conviction among most slave owners and many other whites that it was often more important to them to deter slaves from revolting by issuing severe punishment to those who did. Those who openly defied the owner, plantation manager, or overseer were usually dealt with quickly and ruthlessly. They were whipped, beaten, had their ears cropped, branded, and had limbs amputated. They were sold away from their families or watched as their children were turned over to slave traders."[1]

When slaves ran away, their owners sometimes put notices in newspapers offering rewards for their capture. The headlines read "Runaway" or "Reward." Rewards ranged from five dollars to several hundred dollars, depending on the skills and value of the slave. Full pages of these advertisements were often illustrated by stereotypical caricatures. Slave owners could not always afford the cost of advertising or a reward, so the number of advertisements are not a reliable indication of the frequency of running away.

Joseph Washington's father-in-law, Archer Cheatham Jr., experienced problems with runaways as early as 1814. He offered a $20 reward for the return of thirty-five-year-old Lewis who had been purchased in Murfreesborough, North Carolina. The advertisement described Lewis as "5 feet 7 inches, stout made, and bow legged, a tolerable cooper, shoemaker and carpenter." He had been at large for at least a month when the reward was posted in *The Nashville Whig*.[2] Lewis was captured before 1823 (as he was listed in Archer Cheatham Jr.'s estate records). Some of Lewis's children were slaves on Wessyngton. George's father-in-law, Major William B. Lewis, advertised in 1819 that twenty-seven-year-old Paris had run away and had been spotted in Glasgow, Kentucky (80 miles from Springfield), and would probably head toward free territory in Ohio.[3]

Slave owners generally thought that free blacks living in the proximity of slaves would pose a threat to the institution of slavery and could lead to insurrections. This was especially true after a successful revolt led by Toussaint-Louverture in Saint-Domingue (later Haiti) in 1791 that freed the entire slave population. Free blacks had migrated to Tennessee due to the enactment of strict laws governing their activity in some eastern states such as Virginia and North Carolina. Many of these laws required an African American to leave the state within one year after emancipation or be forced to return to slavery.

The Nat Turner insurrection of 1831 in Southampton County, Virginia, frightened slaveholders throughout the South. The Turner revolt influenced the Tennessee legislature to pass laws in 1831 that prevented more free blacks from entering the state. Any person emancipating a slave had to send him out of the state. When the new constitution in Tennessee was written in 1834, free blacks were denied voting privileges.[4] Tennessee passed new laws prohibiting free blacks from entering the state, and those emancipated within the state had to leave or a white person would have to sign a bond stating they would be responsible for their actions.

Nat Turner's insurrection certainly must have had a great impact on Joseph Washington as it did on slaveholders throughout the South—perhaps even more so. The uprising involved a band of some sixty or seventy slaves. The massacre lasted about forty-eight hours and claimed the lives of fifty-one whites including Turner's owner, Joseph Travis, and his family. It was the largest slave rebellion in American history.

Slaves often ran away when they learned or suspected they had been sold far away from their relatives and friends. In 1839 J. B. Hall of Hendersonville, Kentucky, wrote George about the purchase of two slaves who ran away, fearing they had been sold to the Deep South. The slaves returned when they were informed they were sold to a nearby planter.

Slaves who ran away often presented their owners with problems even when they tried to sell them. In 1841, George decided to sell Henry (who was accused of breaking into his former owner's house); perhaps he had run away or was a threat to run away. Robert D. Carr sent Jim to the New Orleans slave market with George. George found that he could not sell the slaves without guaranteeing the purchaser that they would not run away. George informed Carr that the slave Jim was too sickly to fetch a good price. Then he explained:

> The highest offer I have had for Henry since I have been here is $800.00 on six months credit and the purchaser refused to take him because I would not guarantee him against running away. I shall keep him here until I leave and if I cannot sell him will take him to Nashville and sell him at auction, which in my opinion is the best thing you can do with yours. I not only take this cause in relation to your boy from my own judgment but also from that of Mr. Rayburn of the house to whom he was consigned, and you may suppose he would not advise that cause unless he thought it greatly to your interest, as he would be entitled to 2½% for selling him.[5]

Two months later twenty-six-year-old Jim and twenty-year-old Henry were sold for $800 each to the slave-trading firm of Joseph M. Irwin and Galbraith Logan and Company in New Orleans. The bill of sale guaranteed them to be slaves for life and free of all maladies prescribed by law—except against running away.[6] Henry (purchased in 1838) was one of the two Washington slaves who were sold away from the plantation.

———•◦•———

Although we have no documentation of any slave resistance at Wessyngton prior to the late 1830s, we can assume that it existed on some scale. We can conjecture about Joseph's possible reaction to the Turner revolt. Joseph and Nat Turner came from the same small community of Jerusalem. A number of the people murdered were his and his parents' neighbors. He might have known some of the slaves involved. At the time of the rebellion, the majority of the slaves on Wessyngton came from Southampton County and could have known or been related to Nat Turner or some of the other ringleaders.

In 1833 Tennesseans were alarmed when a slave Wiley clubbed a slaveholder and a patroller to death. A month later Wiley was captured and executed in Dickson County. In 1835 there were rumors that slaves working at the ironworks furnaces of Dickson County had plotted a small uprising. In 1849 George's widowed mother wrote him a letter lamenting her loneliness when he was away from the plantation. She pointedly added, "I really do not feel safe where there are so many Negroes left entirely alone."[7]

Joseph certainly must have curtailed at least some of the slaves' activities on the plantation. State law and local patrols mandated some changes. In George's diary he mentioned giving several slaves written passes to travel from his Todd County, Kentucky, plantation to Wessyngton; he often sent Frank with food supplies such as bacon to the other farms. If slaves were caught by a patroller when they were not carrying passes, they could be brutally beaten and taken to jail, and their owners fined. Those slaves would then be punished by their owners for leaving the premises without permission.

In 1838 Jack escaped from Wessyngton. He was on the run for at least nine days before he was captured and jailed in Cadiz, Kentucky, in Christian County, nearly sixty miles from the plantation. Joseph paid $30 including jail fees for his return. Three years later Jack made another escape and was again returned to the plantation.[8]

We have no evidence that any Washington slave made it to free territory and remained free. Nevertheless, there was always a risk of any slave running given the opportunity. George shared his concerns with his mother in 1839 regarding a house servant, Green, who had been inherited by his mother in 1823:

> After leaving Nashville I have come to the conclusion to
> send Green home, as I intend going directly on through

the state of Ohio to Niagara Falls, thence to New York and be in Philadelphia by the time Uncle Richard and Aunt Susan arrive there, and even after going to Washington city, I shall be in Philadelphia and other free cities so much that I would lose his services, a great part of the time I should be absent and the risk that would be run in carrying him through these states would be so great that I have determined as the best course to send him back, although thus far he has conducted himself very well.[9]

Several Wessyngton slaves made escape attempts between 1838 and 1865, especially from the Todd County, Kentucky, and Dortch Place properties. Most of the slaves on the Kentucky holdings were unattached single men in their twenties and thirties who had been recently brought to the area. They could have had more exposure to other slaves who had attempted to escape before or were familiar with what routes to take to freedom. There also could have been more runaways on the Kentucky property due to it being closer to free territory. The closest route to free territory from the Wessyngton Home Place was to Evansville, Indiana, to the north and Metropolis, Illinois, to the west. Both routes were approximately 120 miles from the plantation. The Ohio River had to be crossed on both routes; this was a dangerous undertaking. Some slaves escaped during the winter months so they could walk across the frozen Ohio River into free territory. Once reaching free territory, slaves were often assisted by conductors of the Underground Railroad. The conductors gave the slaves food, clothing, and information on how to reach Canada.

Lewis, a Washington slave from the Todd County property, came closest to obtaining his freedom. At the time there were thirteen other slaves in the area close to the Washington holdings who had run away. In June 1840 the plantation manager Benjamin Simms captured Lewis some thirty miles into Indiana. Lewis was in the company of another slave from Russellville, Kentucky, who was said to be a first-rate blacksmith. Their plans were to escape to Canada and go into business as partners.[10] Lewis was promised that he would not be punished or sent back to the ironworks furnaces if he told who prompted him to run away. In offering Lewis an escape from punishment, Simms probably wanted to ensure that he had run away of his own accord and was not prompted by anyone else who might incite discontent among the other slaves on the plantation or a possible mass rebellion. Lewis revealed the plot for escape. Simms knew that Frank and Bob knew about Lewis's plans. Frank, at age eight, had been purchased with his parents and sisters in 1814, and Bob had been bought in 1832 when he was eighteen. Simms reneged on his promise, and Lewis was severely whipped, as were Frank and Bob.

Simms wrote George of Lewis's escape and subsequent punishment:

> I promised you in my last letter that as soon as I got Lewis home, I would give you a detail of his travels. He states he was prevailed to go on by a Negro from Russellville belonging to Robert Bell. Frank and Bob knew where he had started to, and I have no doubt had Lewis not have been caught, that both of them would have been gone before this time. I have had Frank and Bob flogged well and whipped Lewis myself and collared him. He is now getting on well.[11]

In 1842 the plantation manager, Simms, wrote George that Big Allen (from the Todd County property) was caught in Trenton, Kentucky (twenty miles from Wessyngton) and was carried home. Simms reported, "I gave the gentleman a genteel flogging myself and I think he will stay at home."[12] In 1846 Jesse ran away from Wessyngton. Plantation medical records noted that he was whipped as a punishment.[13] Mary reported in 1853, "Daniel [Gardner] not been heard of since you left, taking pretty good holiday to himself."[14]

The most notorious of all the Wessyngton runaways was David (Davy) who worked on the Todd County plantation. Davy was purchased in 1835 at age eleven, along with his four brothers, Tony, John, Tom, and Edmund, from Daniel White of Todd County. In 1854 Davy ran away at least four times and was on the run for more than two months. On a cold snowy day, fellow slaves hid Davy in a barn to prevent his detection. Jane wrote to George:

> Davy has not been heard from away from home and no wonder. Morrow and Simms have discovered that on Saturday before you left, he was all day in the barn. You remember it snowed hard all day. George Harriet saw him there and I have no doubt Humphrey and Bob both had helped to hide him there more days than one, but he might walk into the kitchen in broad day and not a negro would report.[15]

The fact that while Davy was hidden right under the noses of the Washingtons not one of the hundreds of slaves reported it demonstrates how close knit the Wessyngton slave community was.

On August 2, 1854, George offered a $50 reward in Kentucky for the apprehension of Davy or information leading to his capture.[16] Davy may have inspired his brother as well as some of the other slaves. His brother Tom ran away on August 4 and was captured the next day. On August 8 Simms went to Clarksville to post a reward for Davy's capture. Davy must have been captured and escaped again because there was a notation in George's diary that he ran off again on August 14. Fearing the overseer Williams would whip him, Tom ran away again on August 13. The next day George recorded that there was a disturbance with his overseer Epperson and the Negroes, and that Israel was brought to the house and Daniel Gardner ran off.

During another of Davy's escapes at the end of August, the neighboring plantation owner Kendall wrote George:

> If you think of keeping your man, Davie after you get him home, I will sell or exchange with you the girl, he calls his wife; the girl has done us no good for two years and has excited my wife's sympathies so much as to agree to her being sold although she was born ours. We are looking everyday for Mr. King and his dogs from Logan County. If his dogs are well trained he can be caught.[17]

One week later Kendall wrote Washington:

> I learn that the dogs caught a boy of Mr. Brown's near Hadensville on yesterday. The boy was hired to Gillman's Iron Works and this boy, to induce his master not to let him go back to the iron works, has told who fed him and who was with him and what their plans were, and I am informed that it can under circumstances that may be regarded as facts. This boy says Davie is now lurking about your Home Place or the Dortch place and is to return to this neighborhood the coming week to meet a Negro man belonging to Mr. Hillman and they are to start for a free state.
>
> D.B. Smith, Colonel Duffey and John Moore have just gotten home from Indiana. Duffey had two out, Orly got one. Moore and Smith got both their men. Neither of them was caught until they crossed the Ohio River. I write you that you may take such steps as you may think proper. I think there is a man in the neighborhood with dogs and has gone to the iron works and will

be back next week. P.S. It is said that there is now out ten or eleven Negro men runaways in our region and Davie may have company with them. A boy of Mr. Norsorthey's was surprised and dropped his scythe blade a few days ago, it was rasped halfway down the balance of the blade was as sharp as it could be.[18]

On September 25 Davy was only a few miles from the free territory of Indiana and just about to ford the Ohio River when he was captured, with a sharp hatchet in his hand. The jailer advertised his capture, and he remained in jail for twelve days. The Henderson, Kentucky, jailer wrote George about Davy's capture:

Dear Sir: there was a Negro man committed to our jail last evening he calls himself Dave. The said boy is of dark complexion, about five feet six or seven inches high, well built, he has thick lips. He says he has been out about six weeks: I would take him to be about twenty-six years of age. He was taken up just below our town.[19]

Receipt for Davy's return to Wessyngton Plantation, 1854.

Davy proved that he could not be controlled regardless of the consequences. George concluded to sell Davy. He probably felt that he would be even more determined to run away than ever since he managed to get so close to freedom, or perhaps he would inspire others that it was possible to escape the bonds of slavery. Archer Cheatham wrote his cousin George regarding Davy's sale:

> I received your letter through the post office this evening, and went immediately to Porter's where I found your boy; I think he is at the best place you could have sent him, though all of these houses need some watching. I learn there are very few men in the market wishing to purchase Negroes, but it seems to me the boy ought to be sold for the money you ask for him, I am not now posted as to the price of Negroes as it has been more than six months since I purchased one, or had anything to do with the Negro market. I will with pleasure see to the selling of the boy and hope to be able to do it in a very short time. Porter is perfectly good and you will have no difficulty in getting the money as soon as the sale is made. P.S. I think your Negro ought to bring what you ask for him, if he was mine I would try him at that price for few days before I would take less.[20]

Davy was sold in 1855 for $925 in the New Orleans slave market two months after his final escape. Davy could have made escape attempts even after he was sold in New Orleans. He was the second Washington slave who was sold.

Some slaves who left the plantation without permission did not always leave with the intention of permanently escaping. In 1851 two slaves, Merideth and Camilla, the only known Wessyngton couple to run away together, escaped. They later returned of their

Rebellious Slaves on Wessyngton, 1838 to 1860

Name	Age	Residence	Date	Acts of Rebellion
Jack	18	Home Place	Sept. 24, 1838	Ran away, reached Cadiz, Ky., when captured.
Henry	17	Todd Cty, Ky.	Feb. 26, 1839	Accused of stealing money and clothes from previous owner.
Unnamed slave		Home Place	Mar. 31, 1839	"Nearly" killed overseer William Ogg.
Jacob	28	Todd Cty, Ky.	Dec. 12, 1839	Got into argument with overseer William Ogg.
Lewis	22	Todd Cty, Ky.	June 8, 1840	Ran away, reached Evansville, Ind., when captured.
Frank	34	Todd Cty, Ky.	June 8, 1840	Assisted Lewis in running away.
Bob	18	Todd Cty, Ky.	June 8, 1840	Assisted Lewis in running away.
Axum	33	Home Place	Sept. 1841	"Nearly" killed overseer Wimms.
Allen	39	Todd Cty, Ky.	Jan. 16, 1842	Ran away, reached Trenton, Ky., when captured.
Jack	22	Home Place	Oct. 20, 1842	Ran away, reached Springfield when captured.
Anderson	19	Todd Cty, Ky.	Feb. 13, 1845	Ran away, captured in Ky.
Washington	35	Todd Cty, Ky.	June 1, 1845	Beat overseer Benjamin Simms "nearly" to death.
Washington	35	Todd Cty, Ky.	June 1, 1845	Ran away, reached Fairfield in Nashville, returned on his own.
Unnamed		Home Place	Sept. 8, 1846	Ran away, reached Nashville when captured.
Jesse	33	Todd Cty, Ky.	Aug. 2, 1847	Ran away, captured, and jailed nine days.
Jesse	34	Todd Cty, Ky.	Aug. 14, 1848	Ran away, reached Clarksville when captured.
Unnamed slave		Todd Cty, Ky.	Sept. 27, 1850	Ran away.
Henry	31	Todd Cty, Ky.	Jan. 23, 1851	Purchased stolen whisky from a slave from another plantation.
Henry	31	Todd Cty, Ky.	Jan. 24, 1851	Ran away after getting whipped, returned after five days.
George Harriet	19	Home Place	Jan. 24, 1851	Ran away, came back the next day.
Bob	29	Home Place	Apr. 25, 1851	Refused to go to work as told; pretended to be sick.

Name	Age	Location	Date	Notes
Miles	18	Home Place	Apr. 25, 1851	Refused to go to work as told; pretended to be sick.
Jefferson	22	Home Place	May 3, 1851	Ran away, returned nine days later at 11 p.m.
Daniel Gardner	22	Home Place	May 3, 1851	Ran away, returned nine days later at 11 p.m.
Miles	18	Home Place	May 5, 1851	Ran away, caught by Mr. Neil one day later.
Miles	18	Home Place	May 22, 1851	Ran away, returned two days later.
Merideth	26	Todd Cty, Ky.	Sept. 6, 1851	Ran away with wife Camilla.
Camilla	17	Todd Cty, Ky.	Sept. 6, 1851	Ran away with husband Merideth.
Frank	45	Todd Cty, Ky.	Oct. 29, 1851	Ran away.
Aggy	27	Todd Cty, Ky.	Nov. 1, 1851	Ran away from Todd and went to Home Place.
Morris		Todd Cty, Ky.	Mar. 15, 1852	Ran away from Todd and went to Home Place.
Unnamed slaves		Todd Cty, Ky.	Apr. 4, 1852	Stole bacon.
Allen	31	Todd Cty, Ky.	Apr. 29, 1852	William Ogg got drunk and threatened to whip him and drew pistol.
Davy	30	Todd Cty, Ky.	Feb.14, 1854	Ran away.
Henry	34	Todd Cty, Ky.	Mar. 12, 1854	Had disturbance with overseer Williams.
Amy		Todd Cty, Ky.	Mar. 12, 1854	Refused to work.
Unnamed slaves		Todd Cty, Ky.	Apr. 22, 1854	Fought each other.
Unnamed slaves		Todd Cty, Ky.	May 4, 1854	Rode Mr. Hitern's [neighboring farmer] horses at night.
Ea		Todd Cty, Ky.	May 9, 1854	Rode Mr. Hitern's horse.
Davy	30	Todd Cty, Ky.	May 12, 1854	Rode Mr. Hitern's horse.
Moses	42	Todd Cty, Ky.	May 24, 1854	Ran away from Todd and went to Home Place.
Unnamed slaves		Todd Cty, Ky.	May 24, 1854	Bad conduct in general.
Unnamed slave		Todd Cty, Ky.	June 16, 1854	Attacked slave of J. W. Kendall with axe, killed by Kendall's slave.
Unnamed slaves		Todd Cty, Ky.	June 19, 1854	Went to Eleck Robertson's to Jeff's wedding without permission.
Henrietta	30	Todd Cty, Ky.	July 8, 1854	Went to Dortch mill without permission.

Rebellious Slaves on Wessyngton, 1838 to 1860 (*continued*)

Name	Age	Residence	Date	Acts of Rebellion
Leroy Lewis	19	Todd Cty, Ky.	July 21, 1854	Ran away from Todd and went to Home Place.
Allen	41	Todd Cty, Ky.	July 25, 1854	Refused to hold Old Smith's bag in apple orchard.
Davy	30	Todd Cty, Ky.	July 31, 1854	Ran away.
Henton	29	Todd Cty, Ky.	July 31, 1854	Ran away.
Tom White	28	Dortch Place	July 31, 1854	Ran away.
Tom White	28	Dortch Place	Aug. 13, 1854	Ran away from Dortch Place and went to Home Place.
Israel	28	Dortch Place	Aug. 14, 1854	Had disturbance with overseer Epperson.
Daniel Gardner	25	Home Place	Aug. 14, 1854	Ran away, had disturbance with overseer Epperson.
Turner	17	Home Place	Aug. 15, 1854	Constable came with search warrant but found nothing.
Tom White	28	Dortch Place	Aug. 26, 1854	Ran away, caught by overseer Williams one day later.
Davy	30	Dortch Place	Oct. 2, 1854	Ran away, jailed in Henderson, Ky.
Frank	48	Dortch Place	Dec. 2, 1854	Played cards with Trotter slaves.
Tom White	29	Dortch Place	Feb. 19, 1855	Captured by Williams and handcuffed.
George Harriet	23	Home Place	Mar. 1, 1855	Struck overseer Epperson and went to Home Place.
Granville	21	Dortch Place	June 2, 1855	Ran away.
Unnamed slaves		Dortch Place	June 3, 1855	Quarrelled and joyed [teased] each other.
Ea		Dortch Place	Nov. 19, 1855	Rode mules.
Mario		Dortch Place	Nov. 19, 1855	Rode mules.
Unnamed slaves		Dortch Place	Nov. 19, 1855	Acted badly, some stole wheat, rode mules at night.
Sylvester	46	Dortch Place	Mar. 4, 1856	Ran away, returned eleven days later.

Name	Age	Place	Date	Note
Granville	22	Dortch Place	Mar. 24, 1856	Ran around at night.
Unnamed slaves		Dortch Place	June 15, 1856	Six or seven slaves absent on Sunday morning per overseer Ogg.
Henton	31	Dortch Place	Aug. 21, 1856	Ran away from overseer William Ogg.
George	24	Home Place	Aug. 21, 1856	Ran away from overseer William Ogg.
Israel	27	Home Place	Feb. 23, 1859	Went to Mr. White's farm without permission.
Wiley	31	Home Place	Feb. 23, 1859	Went to Mr. White's farm without permission.
Hampton Lewis		Dortch Place	May 3, 1859	Had disturbance with overseer.
Hannah	39	Dortch Place	May 3, 1859	Had disturbance with overseer.
Jane	40	Dortch Place	May 3, 1859	Had disturbance with overseer.
Martha Lina	23	Dortch Place	May 3, 1859	Had disturbance with overseer.
Jesse	42	Dortch Place	May 3, 1859	Had disturbance with overseer.
Ea		Dortch Place	Dec. 12, 1859	Bit Alfred's finger.
Jackson Gardner	28	Home Place	Dec. 13, 1859	Went to Dortch Place without permission; bad conduct in general.
Anderson	34	Dortch Place	Mar. 7, 1860	Got stolen whisky from Solomon James's slave Dack.
Henton	35	Home Place	Mar. 7, 1860	Got stolen whisky from Solomon James's slave Dack.
Ea		Dortch Place	Apr. 27, 1860	Ran away.
Anderson	34	Dortch Place	Apr. 28, 1860	Quit plowing and ran away, caught the same day by Mr. Jordan's dogs.
Granville	26	Dortch Place	June 16, 1860	Wrestled Allen.
Anderson	34	Dortch Place	June 21, 1860	Nearly killed slave Allen.
Ea		Dortch Place	June 21, 1860	Nearly killed slave Allen.
Joshua	29	Home Place	Aug. 18, 1860	Refused to work for two days, pretended to be sick.
Reuben	35	Home Place	Aug. 18, 1860	Refused to work for two days, pretended to be sick.

Compiled from George A. Washington's diary 1850 to 1860 and Washington family correspondence, Washington Family Papers.

own accord. George also noted on May 12, 1851, "Jeff and Daniel [Gardner] came home about 11 p.m. had them chained."[21]

Slaves often helped other slaves who ran away, even if they were not willing to take the risk themselves. They provided food, clothes, and information despite the severe punishment if exposed for doing so. Miles, Jeff, and Daniel ran away from the Home Place on May 5, 1851. Miles was caught the next day and was whipped. Miles claimed that a slave Dan, who belonged to the Ayers, and Dick, who belonged to the Trotter family, had fed him. George noted in his diary the next day that he went to Trotter's to inform him that Dick had fed Miles. Dick probably received a whipping from his master as a consequence.

In March 1861, Granville from the Dortch Place ran away and was spotted in Graysville, Kentucky, twenty miles away. William F. Taylor wrote George and informed him that they were trying to catch Granville, but some of the slaves had warned him of the trap:

> I had known he was in the neighborhood and had made
> arrangements to catch him that night and would have
> done so, if you had not written Mr. Kendall. His boys
> went to Williamses and let some of the Negroes see them
> and they informed Granville of it before he went in the
> cabin. I know he was there and waited until 2 o'clock for
> him to go in a cabin but he is very sly, and since that time
> has been suspicious of our boy who we have to detect
> him, which is the only way to get him. He is now about
> Sandy Johnson's and makes his headquarters there, one
> at Lee Taliaferros and Williams' at the latter place mostly,
> where he can be kept well posted. I think you have
> another boy with him; one of D. B. Smith's is also with
> him. We are making all the effort we can to get them but
> there is no chance only to have them betrayed: he seldom
> goes in a cabin at all. If you could station a pack of good

dogs anywhere in five or six miles of here and let us know it. We can get him in two or three days from his lurking place and perhaps could get him in that way. But we will do all we can to get him otherwise.[22]

In a sad irony of the plight of the slaves, blacks were forced to assist in the recapture of their fellow slaves. An entry in George's diary stated, "Carr's Manuel was at Dortch Place last night, sent Carr word by Sampson."[23]

In addition to running away to escape slavery, some slaves were organizing rebellions. In December 1856 rumors circulated that an insurrection was brewing in Springfield. This alarmed the entire white community, but nothing happened in Springfield. There was a planned insurrection in the iron districts of Tennessee. It became known as the Slave Panic of 1856. It was on a much larger scale than the one of 1835 and included states from Delaware to Texas. Newspapers reported that the Tennessee counties of Montgomery and Stewart were then the most terror-stricken areas of the entire South. Newspapers, such as the *New York Journal*, the *New York Tribune*, and the *Evansville (Indiana) Journal*, published reports of the problems. It even made headlines in an English newspaper, the *Manchester Guardian*.[24]

Most of the iron furnaces were several miles apart, and in some areas the black population greatly outnumbered the whites. The leaders organized in military structures as generals and captains and planned the attack for Christmas Day 1856. They planned to march on Clarksville, capture the town, plunder its banks, and flee to free territory in the North. During the same period, a revolt was underway in Dover, Tennessee. The slaves of the Eclipse, Clark, and Lagrange furnaces planned to relieve the workers at Dover, then march to the Rolling Mill, then to Bellwood furnace, through

Lafayette, Kentucky, and on to Hopkinsville to the Ohio River. Apparently this planned revolt struck fear in local residents near Wessyngton. George noted in his diary on December 10: "Went to Springfield, they have eight or six Negroes in jail for a supposed knowledge of insurrection." The next day he went to Turnersville where "the Negro insurrection was the all absorbing topic of conversation."[25]

A slave employed at Montgomery Bell's Cumberland Iron Works, who had escaped in order to avoid participation in the conspiracy, revealed the plot to his owner. After the plot's failure, blacks involved in the proposed insurrection filled the jails of middle Tennessee. Nineteen slaves were hanged in Dover. Sixty slaves at the Cumberland Iron Works of Dickson County were implicated. Of those sixty slaves, a mob executed five and four others were hanged.

CHAPTER 11

On the Road to Freedom: Wessyngton Under Siege

————— —•—•— —————

The outbreak of the Civil War brought drastic changes to the lives of the African Americans at Wessyngton and the Washingtons. Although the war started on April 12, 1861, we do not know exactly when the slaves realized that the war could lead to their ultimate freedom. This was a time for which the slaves had secretly prayed for generations. Those slaves who were born in Africa had taught their children how precious freedom was; those born in slavery assured their children that one day the Lord would deliver them from slavery's bonds.

As early as the 1840s, George A. Washington was a member of the Whig Party, which supported slavery but opposed secession.[1] After the Republican candidate Abraham Lincoln won the election in November 1860, George wrote a letter to the editor for publication in the Democratic-leaning Nashville *Union and American* newspaper opening with the statement, "I take the liberty of addressing you although I have heretofore differed from you honestly in politics." In the very contentious presidential campaign of 1860, George had supported a large slaveholder, antisecession Tennessee senator John Bell, who was the candidate of the Constitutional Union ticket. In his letter, George explained his beliefs prior to Lincoln's election:

> I supported Mr. Bell during the last presidential cam-
> paign on his platform of the Union, the Constitution and
> the Enforcement of the Laws. I am still on that platform.
>
> 1st—In Union: I consider an equality in all that
> belongs to that union necessary.
>
> 2nd—Under the Constitution which was formed by
> its framers to carry out the objects and designs of the
> copartnership, I find that object is expressed in the head-
> ing of the instrument in the following language.
>
> "We the people of the United States in order to form
> a more perfect union, establish Justice, insure domes-
> tic tranquility, provide for the common defense, promote
> the general welfare, and secure the blessings of Liberty to
> ourselves and our posterity, do ordain and establish this
> Constitution for the United States of America."[2]

Senator Bell carried Virginia, Kentucky, and Tennessee. When Lincoln called for troops, however, Bell openly advocated secession and resistance. George too underwent a change of heart as he wrote in the letter:

> These being the express objects of the Constitution how
> can Mr. Lincoln take an oath to support the Constitu-
> tion while he maintains at the same time that we have no
> right to go into the territories with our property?
>
> I do not wish to argue with the Republican party or
> their Southern allies, but Sir I have felt humiliated to see
> Tennesseans from the rostrum, through the press, and in
> our National halls, apologizing for, and defending Lin-
> coln and Seward.

Sir have we not a branch of the Republican party in our midst? And is it not time to bury party and as one man strike for our rights, families, and our homes, before Tennessee freemen have been made slaves by Lincoln, Seward and their Tennessee Apologist. "Oh shame where is thy blush, that we are so degraded."

With all these lights before us we are told to Wait— Wait—and see what Lincoln will do. Did not Mr. Bell say Seward's appointment was the harbinger of Peace? Will it be Peace when our negroes are our equals and our territories filled with European serfs who regard a slave owner as worse than a murderer or thief?

I hope the people will take this into their own hands and demand their rights in the Union.

We believe that this letter was never sent to the newspaper.

The potential disruption of secession and war was a concern within the Washington family; George and Jane were considering moving to the North. This caused friction among their friends. Jane's friend in Nashville accused her of abandoning the South:

I am surprised that you accuse us of turning our backs upon the South, when our interests and feeling have ever been with her, & you upon the contrary have always expressed a strong desire to go & live at the North & educate your children there when you knew too the feelings of the North towards the South, & the South has ever suffered the comparisons which you drew between the two sections. How does this look Jane?[3]

In January 1861 several Southern states seceded from the Union. George and Jane were strongly pro-secession. Jane wrote her husband in New Orleans, "I suppose you find everywhere the wildest excitement, and all you meet must have the same feelings as your-self."[4] On June 8, 1861, Tennessee was the last state to secede. Jane noted her anger that Tennessee's early refusal to secede had pre-vented a peaceable secession to occur:

> Civil War in all its horrors. If Tennessee had taken that
> position [to secede earlier] there would have been a peace-able Secession for the North would have seen the utter
> fallacy of coercion, but now her people have almost as
> one man said come on, we will help whip in the Southern
> States and soon with scornful lips and dividing tongues
> our Northern masters will say Prove your devotion and
> turn your bayonets against the hearts of those who stood
> shoulder to shoulder on many a well won field. With her
> Republican confederates, I hope to see the day when I
> shall cease to call such a recreant state my home. I used to
> be ashamed of Alabama [her birthplace] but I imprint her
> name on my heart and am proud to call her Mother.[5]

George even armed and equipped a voluntary company for ser-vice with the Confederate Army.[6] Unlike families living in Nash-ville, the Washingtons, Cheathams, and Lewises were not divided by the issues of slavery or secession. Brother did not fight against brother, nor did cousin take up arms against cousin. They all sup-ported slavery wholeheartedly.

The slaves' road to freedom started in February 1862 when General U. S. Grant's Union Army defeated the Confederate forces at Fort Henry and Fort Donelson near Memphis.

From 1860 on, the mayor of Nashville was Richard Boone Cheatham.[7] He was one of Mary Cheatham Washington's neph-ews, originally from Robertson County. Both he and Mary were close cousins of the Confederate general Benjamin Franklin Cheatham. Richard Boone Cheatham surrendered Nashville to the

Union Army on February 25, 1862. It was the first Confederate capital to fall to the Union.

From that time, Nashville and the Robertson County area, including Clarksville and Springfield, were occupied by Union troops. The Union Army pushed the Confederates from Shiloh into Mississippi and occupied all of Tennessee by late 1863. Wessyngton slaves knew that a regiment of black troops from the North was stationed in Springfield. Still the Confederate Army was requisitioning war materials from property owners. On September 1, 1862, a Confederate captain took one horse and two mules worth $130 from Wessyngton and issued George an official document stating that "this receipt will be respected by all paymasters in the Confederate army."[8]

With all these events, operations at Wessyngton came to a halt. Life was in tumult. Rumors abounded. At one point, the slaves heard a rumor that the plantation would be divided among them, and they each would receive a forty-acre tract and a mule. Some slaves refused to work. Some demanded that George pay them for their crops they had growing in his fields.

Slave owners feared that their slaves would be emancipated, and their investment would be lost. A Robertson County slave owner Solomon Cobb (who lived near Wessyngton) sold his most valuable slave, Stevan, around 1862. Cobb sent Stevan in care of his eldest son Wesley down the Natchez Trace to the New Orleans slave market. After receiving $2,400 in Confederate money from the sale of Stevan, Wesley returned to Robertson County. Weeks later the Cobb family heard a knock at their cabin door. Stevan had escaped and traveled six hundred miles on foot to be reunited with his wife, Tennessee, and their children. Stevan and his family remained with and worked for the Cobb family after emancipation. My great-great-grandfather Thomas Black Cobbs had been sold to the Cobb family in 1854 when he was ten years old and lived in a cabin with Stevan and his family.

Tax records for 1862 listed ninety-eight slaves on the Home Place and forty-nine on the Dortch Place.

As late as 1862 slaves who left the plantation were still considered runaways by the slave owners. George paid $25 for the capture of John in May. In August, Matt, Jefferson, and Wiley were jailed as runaways.[9]

———•◦•———

Many slaves in the Robertson County area took advantage of the Union Army's presence to leave the plantations and farms. Some were so elated to be emancipated they walked off the plantations as soon as they received word that they had been freed. Some left alone, while others left in family groups.

Wessyngton was so large, it is likely that many of the slaves born on the plantation had never left the land in their entire lives. The men at Wessyngton were the first to leave the plantation. They did not abandon their families. Rather, they went in search of new jobs and homes and later returned for them. Since George allowed his slaves to farm land for their own benefit, his slaves had possessions. Consequently, they left behind their crops in the fields, farm equipment, farm animals, and household goods. Rumors abounded that they would lose everything, and those who left carried that fear with them. Just leaving the plantation was an arduous and dangerous undertaking.

Jane Washington (1835–1916) attempted to escape from the plantation during the war and took her children and hid in the woods one night. They were forced by cold and hunger to return to Wessyngton the next morning.[10]

Wessyngton slaves went to Nashville, enlisted in the Union Army, or ran away with federal troops. Slaves who left the plantations and crossed into areas controlled by the Northern troops were referred to as contrabands and lived in contraband camps.[11] By fall 1862, the flood of fugitive slaves caused the federal government to open a contraband camp at Grand Junction, Tennessee, sixty miles east of Memphis. There were other camps like this. Several Wessyngton slaves went to live in the contraband camps in Nashville (thirty-five miles away) and Gallatin (forty-five miles).

Throughout Tennessee, the tens of thousands of contraband camp dwellers became an essential labor force for the Union Army. The refugees were provided with army rations (pork, cornmeal, flour, beans, sugar, coffee, vinegar, salt, candles, and potatoes), clothing, medical supplies, military and agricultural jobs, and wages. They were also supplied with shelter (tents, log cabins, and plank houses). The refugees built military fortifications, repaired roads, bridges, and railroads, served as teamsters, common laborers, blacksmiths, military hospital workers, and surgeon assistants. Army officials employed them at a rate of $10 per month for women and $10 to $30 a month for men and boys. Some were servants to officers, cooks, and laundresses. Even a few were military spies.[12]

President Lincoln's Emancipation Proclamation, issued September 22, 1862, declared freedom to slaves in the Confederate states that did not return to the control of the Union by January 1, 1863. It did not free slaves from the border states Kentucky, Maryland, Missouri, and Tennessee. Many slaves from these states, however, were already free by this time due to self-emancipation—running away or being abandoned by their owners.

On March 11, 1862, General Buell had issued an order safeguarding George and his family and their property: all persons were "ordered not to molest or in any way interfere with or trespass upon the property of *Mr. George A. Washington,* nor to annoy him or his family in person."[13] Nevertheless, the Washingtons experienced a major scare in early 1863 when straw was stacked up high in the mansion's cellar and set on fire. Dr. John R. Dunn, the

Washingtons' family doctor, and George's son William put out the fire just in time. No one was caught in the act, but it was probably set by Union soldiers. The worries the slaves felt about their possessions proved valid. A number of them had their property taken for use by the Union Army.

————•◦•————

Family problems persisted for the Washingtons. In August 1863, Jane bore another stillborn son.[14] Perhaps as early as April 1863 and certainly by October, the family had to face a difficult dilemma.[15] Nineteen-year-old William was of draft age and in good health, but the family had other plans for him. It could be that his grandmother Mary, who had raised him after his mother's death, felt strongly that he should be sent to safety. So William was sent to school in Toronto, Canada. George's business associate in Louisville sent his son to study at the same school. It is ironic that even then, the wealthiest among us dodged the draft in favor of education. William came back to Wessyngton occasionally and met his father for these journeys. He wrote his stepmother Jane in September 1864 that their train from Louisville was so full of Union soldiers from Sherman's army, that neither he nor George could get a seat.[16] Jane wrote William often about the realities at home and concerns for the future:

> You must apply yourself diligently to your studies and
> be able to do a man's work at any business by the end
> of the next ten months. You will then be almost twenty,
> and if you will ever be able to help your father and sup-
> port yourself, you ought to be able to do so by that time.
> Learn bookkeeping and arithmetic thoroughly, for you
> may have to make your living by some such occupation.
> Our hopes have been very heavy and your father is verg-
> ing on fifty and has a large family of dependent children

to support, so that your own good sense will show you
that your future position in society depends upon your-
self. A good name your father can give you, your fortune
depends on yourself.[17]

We do not know how many wealthy or influential plantation owners and businessmen chose that route for their sons. William was
not the only young man from the area to be sent to school out
of harm's way. Eugene Castner Lewis, whose father managed the
Cumberland Iron Works in Dickson County (the site of the Slave
Panic in 1856), was sent after the fall of Fort Donelson in 1862
to the Pennsylvania Military Academy for the duration of the war
as his family feared for his life because he was high tempered and
prone to attack the Northern soldiers. When Eugene returned to
Tennessee, he reintegrated into Southern society and became a
community leader.

By spring 1863, the Union Army began to recruit and organize
black soldiers. The army found these recruits in the contraband
camps or on the plantations. By that time several slaves had already
left Wessyngton and set out on the road to freedom. Madison and
Jesse had left in December 1862. Gilbert, Amos, Daniel, Jeff, and
Ea had left in February 1863. Granville, a Dortch Place slave, left
in March 1863, and Alfred Washington and George Lewis left in
April 1863. In May the remaining men from the Dortch Place—
Dick Lewis, Joe Lewis, Little Sam, Leroy Lewis, Mario, Joe Davis,
Henton, and Nathaniel—left. Some slaves even took their own
beds, tables, chairs, wagons, and livestock with them.

During the Civil War, 20,133 black Union Army soldiers served
in Tennessee with the United States Colored Troops (USCT). The
troops were used for guarding garrisons and the Nashville &
Northwestern Railroad. All the Colored Regiments were com-

manded by white Union officers. The 40th U.S. Colored Infantry Regiment was organized in 1863.

The 15th U.S. Colored Infantry Regiment, formed in Shelbyville in September 1863, was stationed in Springfield by August 1864, where it remained until April 1865. The regiment was stationed at a fort in Springfield with headquarters in a building in the town. The regiment did guard duty on the Edgefield & Kentucky [now Louisville & Nashville] Railroad.[18] The regiment was in part made up of local black men. Colonel Thomas Jefferson Downey, a white officer, commanded the regiment in 1864.

George realized that his slaves would soon be tempted to leave Wessyngton. At the same time the Union Army was recruiting black soldiers, George made an offer to hire some of his male slaves for a rate of $10 per month. From February through May 1863, twenty-four men agreed to stay on the plantation and work for the offered $10 per month. Of those twenty-four, however, eighteen left within a few months.[19] The men had worked at Wessyngton all their lives and no doubt wanted to see what the outside world had to offer and to taste freedom. Although they were offered wages, they must have seen this as just a ploy to keep them on the plantation.

In these chaotic times, some members of the Washington family did not know how to deal with the slaves who remained on the plantation. The elderly Mary on several occasions instructed Granville to have those slaves who refused to work put off the plantation. The slaves ignored the orders, refused to leave, and threatened Granville and Mary.

George was concerned about losing those slaves who had left the plantation. He requested Major Lewis to ask what recourse he had regarding those who had left. Major Lewis advised George "to look closely after the slaves who were still on the plantation and to direct his overseers to abstain, as far as possible, from giving them any excuse for leaving you," hoping that some of them "might return of their own accord." Lewis had one of his slaves on the lookout for any of the Lewis slaves from Wessyngton. Lewis advised his slaves at Fairfield "to remain quietly at home and attend to their work, and wait until it is known what disposition is to be made of the negroes generally . . . any attempt to free themselves would endanger their lives, as well as the lives of all other negroes." His slaves felt that this was reasonable advice at the time. He further stated if they were not satisfied to stay, he would hire them out to the engineer superintending the erection of the fortifications in Nashville [Fort Negley], "which is a thing they really dread, as the work is very laborious, and disagreeable."[20]

Lewis indicated that the contraband camps were not as the blacks had anticipated when they moved there, and said that his slaves had seen enough of camp life when federal troops, "their northern friends" were camped close to their houses for six weeks. Major Lewis wrote George:

> The negroes in camp have fared so badly & are treated so badly, many of them have left of their own free will, and many more would go, if they could slip thro' the pickets. [The tollgate operator] tells me that there is not a day that he does not see some of them at the gate who express a strong desire to get back to their masters, but as they are looked upon, at least many of them, as spies, they can't get thro' the lines, without running the risk of being shot.[21]
>
> Most of the negroes in camp, on my land, were the most miserable wretched looking creatures I ever saw, lousy, ragged, dirty, half-starved devils that are anywhere to be found. And what is still worse when sick, no more attention was paid to them than if they were so many dogs, and in fact, five of them died in camp, while the troops were around my negroes' houses and were left to be buried by them (my own negroes), if buried at all. This

has been a good lesson to my own negroes, and I hope they will profit by it.[22]

Although conditions in the camps were not as many of the slaves had hoped, they were still preferred over enslavement.

———•·•———

In September 1863, Union troops came to Wessyngton and seized twenty-four slaves, including Bill Henry Scott Washington, Ike Washington, Alfred Washington, Horris Washington, Archer Washington, Joe Washington, Allen Washington, Axum Washington, Godfrey Washington, and Clinton Washington (who also used the surname Simms), and a few teenage boys. The slaves were to work on the Nashville & Northwestern Railroad. Others were conscripted by the Union Army to work at the military fortification, Fort Negley, in Nashville. While several blacks joined the troops, others ran away from them and hid in the woods.

When Jane protested the seizures to the commanding officer who was "very insolent," the soldiers would only agree to release two elderly slaves, Abraham Washington and Sam Vanhook. After leaving Wessyngton, the troops went to the farms of the Washingtons' neighbors and took all the slaves who were not too old to work. As Jane wrote: "they [the Union soldiers] had all Trotters' slaves but, Dempsey and Dick, and all of Old Dick Stone's, some from the Gunns, Bartletts, Burns, and I don't know how many more and even, Jake Ellis, poor Mrs. Ellis' only man."[23]

An 1863 tax return listed the number of slaves on the Home Place as thirty-two men and boys and thirty-three women and girls. Thirty-one slaves, including fifteen men and boys and sixteen women and girls, were on the Dortch Place.

Miles Washington, Frank Washington, Otho Washington, Carey Washington, Jake Washington, and Bill Henry Scott Washington enlisted in the Union Army in the 40th, 41st, and 42nd Colored Infantry Regiments stationed in Gallatin in November 1863.[24]

Otho Washington (1843–1920) served in the 40th USCT, Company B organized in 1863. Its soldiers guarded garrisons and the Nashville & Northwestern Railroad. Otho recalled his mother told him that he was about eighteen years old when he went to the war. Otho said he was considered a man and doing a man's work of hoeing and chopping on the plantation of George Washington when he enlisted.[25] In 1901, to assist in obtaining his military pension for service during the Civil War, Foster Washington and Sam Washington, who then lived at the nearby Glenraven Plantation, signed depositions stating that they were raised on the Washington plantation with Otho Washington and recalled when Union troops took him away. They further stated that they had always lived near Otho when he returned from the war, and he was of good character.

Frank Washington also enlisted in the 40th USCT, Company B. He remembered well when federal soldiers came to Wessyngton Plantation and took men and boys to work on the railroad and military fortifications in Nashville. He recalled his mother telling the soldiers he was only twelve years old, but they took him anyway.[26] He worked with the Union troops doing odd jobs for about a year and a half before enlisting.[27]

My great-great-grandfather Emanuel Washington ran away with federal troops. Several others ran away with Union troops, but we do not know if they actually fought in the war. Most did guard duty and odd jobs. Some slaves from other states were in black units used in combat toward the end of the war.

———•◦•———

The Confederates faced a dilemma: should they take the oath of allegiance to the U.S. government or remain true to the South? In October 1862, a rumor circulated that George's name was seen in the "Book in which the names of persons taking the oath of Allegiance are registered." One individual then certified that he had never seen George's name "in any such Book in Nashville or elsewhere and further that I never told any person that I had. And I denounce the whole thing as utterly false."[28]

By May 1863 Major Lewis reported that Tennesseans were "rushing into Nashville by thousands to take the oath of allegiance to the U. States, and seem to do it with pleasure, and to feel as if they were relieving themselves of a burden too heavy to be longer borne."[29] He advised George to do so:

> My dear George, I do really think that this is the best
> thing that can be done under all the circumstances of the
> case. The Federals are in possession here, strongly forti-
> fied, supported by an army that is abundantly able to sus-
> tain them, and will in all probability, overrun the greater
> part of the Southern country in a few months more. I
> have no doubt that every prominent man who refuses to
> give in his adhesion to the constitution and the U. States
> will be arrested and sent South or to prison. I assure you,
> that almost every man of wealth and character, has in this
> county [Davidson], taken the oath, and the few that have
> not, are still coming in.[30]

George A. Washington took the Oath of Allegiance to the United States Government on May 6, 1863, and filed with the Provost Marshal's Office "Bond for the faithful observance of the same."[31] He was one of the first men in Robertson County to make that decision.

Based on this oath, the military issued George passes so that he could go through military lines to the North.[32] In July 1863, Nashville's former mayor Richard Boone Cheatham asked a "personal favor" of a Union captain and Conductor of the Louisville

& Nashville Railroad for his relative George "to make room in the baggage or mail car" for him to reach Louisville, Kentucky, "without delay."[33]

A few months later George took a long trip to New York with Major Lewis. His letters home spoke of his concerns. Although the white overseer Edward Epperson was still working on the plantation, George turned to Granville and Monroe to protect his family:

> Should the place be visited by Robbers during my
> absence I trust to your courage & judgment; but have all
> the Negroes blow and ring up [have all guns prepared
> for firing] & I think it must be a pretty large or coura-
> geous band that will not decamp. [Two days later.] Have
> the guns kept in good condition and should the Robbers
> make their appearance do note hesitate to make Monroe
> & Granville use them . . . make a show of courage if you
> have it not.[34]

Washington was desperate and in fear for his family's safety, demonstrated by his arming slaves and giving them free reign to kill white men: bushwhackers, robbers, Confederate or Union soldiers, and anyone else who posed a threat to Wessyngton.

With the seizures of slaves and their voluntary departures, at the end of 1863 only three elderly male slaves (Britain Washington, Abraham Washington, and Sam Vanhook) and Granville and Monroe remained on Wessyngton. Some of the women and children were still at the Home Place. Jane was concerned about the women and children: "Heaven knows what will become of the women and children, if it was not for the expense of supporting them, I would not care so much."[35] The Washingtons still paid the medical treatments for the slaves who were on the plantation or came back for short periods of time from 1863 through 1865. In 1863 Granville was quite ill with a very high fever, which affected his mind until he recovered a few days later; the doctor's fees for his treatment during that year were $22.50 for fifteen visits.[36, 37] The number of medical visits and expenses decreased annually ($79, $31, and $24 respectively) as fewer people remained on the plantation.[38] The Washingtons' motivation certainly was to keep the plantation functioning, and they likely hoped that some of the slaves would return to the plantation after the war ended.

George wrote Major Lewis of his dire situation:

> My farming operations are about brought to a close and if I could get my corn in which is now in the fields I should be more than willing they should at once cease. The field men I have left have continued to go until I have but three left at home, the women have also commenced going off in the last five weeks. I have lost eighteen men and women. I wish to do nothing offensive to the authorities, but I desire permission to send a portion of the women and children inside the lines [contraband camps] to be taken care of. I do not like to do it unless I can get written permission to do so. You will therefore much oblige me by obtaining the permission to do so. Of the Fairfield Negroes [Lewis slaves], the last male has left. I desired a portion of the men back; I now do not ask that, but merely permission to send the children and some of the women where they can be kept from suffering for I have not the means to supply them with firewood.[39]

In December 1863 George requested and received permission from a Union Major R. S. Granger to send a portion of the women and children inside Union lines in Nashville.

In January 1864 General Rousseau issued Washington permission for additional firearms: four shotguns and four revolving pistols. In February another seizure of slaves occurred but in that case, former Wessyngton slaves—Little Sam, Leroy Lewis, Mario, and Simpson—probably met four Union soldiers in Nashville and brought them back to the plantation to get their families in case there was any trouble. The federal soldiers and the former Wessyngton slaves rode in a wagon to the Dortch Place, where they picked up Sarah Jane, Fanny, Isabella and her child, Allen Holman, Martha Lewis, Austin B., Harrison, Little Joe, Meredith, Big John White, and Tom White. The soldiers had guns, and the slaves had pistols. They took their bedding in a wagon and took Sampson's wheel mule, Joe, with them. They also took their dinner from the kitchen and a shoulder of meat. They announced that everyone who wished to was free to go. Jane feared that Simpson would bring them to the Home Place. Another Wessyngton slave Bob Price, who was at a shop in Turnersville, spotted the group as they went up the Nashville road.[40]

Less than a week later, when George was in Nashville, he went to General Rousseau's headquarters. The general ordered his soldiers to send the "17 Runaway Negroes . . . back home." With all the comings and goings, we do not know if they all returned to the Dortch Place.[41]

In August 1864 George obtained protection papers from the provost marshall's office, granting protection for his farm, timber, forage, stock, buildings, provisions, wagons, horses, and all other personal property. The protection papers also prohibited the impressments of his slaves, taking them from the plantation for army use. At the same time George obtained a permit to own a gun and ammunition to protect himself and his family. Major General Rosencrans signed the orders and charged all officers and soldiers in the United States service to respect and, if necessary, to enforce the protection. (In one of those ironic twists of history, Rosencrans's headquarters in Nashville was located at the home of Jane Smith Washington's cousin Hugh Kirkman. The mansion had cost over $125,000 to build and furnish in the 1830s, but the Kirkmans never reoccupied the house after the war; they considered it tainted by the presence of the Union Army).

The federal protection documents proved as worthless as the paper they were written on. Union soldiers made a number of visits to the plantation, taking provisions and slaves as they pleased and paid little to no attention to the orders. On August 8, 1864, a lieutenant from the Union Army came to Wessyngton to impress more slaves. Jane informed him she had only three or four left on the place and had General Rousseau's protection papers for them. The elderly Britain mounted one of the soldiers' horses and led them directly to the Fiser Field, where Granville thought he had safely hidden their horses. Another elderly slave, Humphrey, had told the soldiers where the horses were hidden. Humphrey walked off the farm after they took the horses and was not seen until after the war. Jane was enraged at the slaves informing the soldiers about the horses. She complained to George about all the slaves:

> I've heard nothing of Abraham since he left on the train, Munroe did not take his family and Gilly [his wife] swears he did not come home, but I do not believe her as he was seen on the road coming from Springfield. Godfrey was here last week, but we never heard of it until today. Saturday he left Lavinia [his wife] and her children and went off, so that proves he must have been here.

Several slaves were going back and forth from Nashville or just roaming the area. They came back to Wessyngton to check on their families and possessions. Once they were on the plantation, the Washingtons did not know what to do. Jane wrote George that "Old Axum came back home yesterday, not a very welcomed return. He looks worse for wear."[42] She also wrote that Dick Terry cut tobacco over the creek for a few days. During George's absences from Wessyngton in 1864, several of the former slaves returned and constantly harassed his mother. They made threats, refused to leave the property when ordered, refused to work or to hire themselves to anyone else. One of the returning slaves was John Harriet. Mary wrote:

> The children just rushed in breathless to report that John Harriet Washington is here. I went to see, and sure enough Blinkey is here, and sorry am I. He says he was hired as cook to a hotel. He left after the occupation with a regiment whose time was out, came to Nashville and remained there long enough to see all the absentees [runaway slaves].[43]

The war and chaos certainly impacted the lives of all the generations. At age sixty-eight, Mary was crumbling under the pressure. Jane wrote George in 1864, "Mama has been firing cartridges at the servants ever since you left."[44] Tragedy struck the Washingtons again when Jane had another stillborn son on October 31, 1864.[45]

Jane and George's daughter Lucy Washington Helm was a toddler during the war years and later described what life was like:

> Everything was gone. Only some work mules and two small mules which were excellent riding animals remained. We four girls rode them one behind the other. They were the only animals to hitch to the one carriage left of the many fine ones we had before the war. . . .
>
> Our coffee was made from dried beans and sweet potatoes. I have watched my father make ink from red and black oak balls. His tobacco—he could only make pipe tobacco, having always before the war and afterwards smoked the most marvelous Cuban cigars—was the heavy black tobacco raised on the

place, mixed with dried sumac leaves which we children loved to gather and put on the garret floor to dry and crush for him. I can see him now, as I, a little girl, stood by him in front of an open fire and watched him melt the lead to make bullets, melting it and pouring it into a mold. . . .

[Describing the house] [T]he curtains, as usual were drawn, and wide heavy bars were across the outside doors, and the wide iron, long bolts were on the windows . . . [M]y mother packed a large bolster-case with our clothes and would hide it under the hedge so if the house was burned we would have something to wear.[46]

Lucy related a story that had been told to her when she was older. One night two men knocked at the front door and said they were lost. The men conveyed to her parents that they were two of the band of Confederates under the command of John Hunt Morgan. This placed them all in great danger as "[t]here was a reward to the person giving information of anyone's harboring Morgan's men. Imprisonment and confiscation of all their properties were the penalties paid by those found guilty of such an act." George and Jane were rude to the men and said that they were deserters from the Union Army. "But as soon as the men had eaten and the servants could be sent to their quarters, they gave the men clean, dry clothes and sent them off before daybreak."[47]

Granville remained faithful to the Washington family throughout the war and had many conflicts with some of the other slaves because of that. Granville's position was certainly a very difficult one. He probably felt a sense of loyalty toward the Washington family because he was treated better than the other slaves, although both social and cultural realities would never allow him to be fully accepted as a true member of the Washington family. Other slaves on the plantation, even some of his relatives, no doubt mistrusted him due to his position. In 1864 Jane wrote: "Granville is afraid of being surrounded in his house, so he puts up in Marion's [a Wessyngton house servant] house."[48]

Even during the Civil War, some slave owners officially freed their slaves and gave them the means to start their lives as free men. My great-great-great-grandfather Henry White (born 1815) lived near Wessyngton and was freed by his owner, Mildred White, in 1864. He was given a wagon and a team of horses. His owner's will stated that if there was not enough money left for Henry to have the horse and wagon, he had the option of buying it himself, which indicated he could earn his own money. Henry was one of the first blacks in the county to purchase his own land.

Drewry Bell (1796–1865) emancipated twenty-nine of his slaves in January 1865 and made provisions for them. In his will Bell left his own nieces and nephews five dollars each, and all his real estate, livestock, household goods, one year's provisions, and money to his slaves.[49] Some of Bell's favored slaves received larger portions of the estate than others did. The Washingtons continued their practice: They did not "free" any of their slaves.

CHAPTER 12

No Longer Under
Washington Control

————◆————

T he Washington family, being the wealthiest in the county, was a prime target for outlaws and renegade soldiers in a time when law and order did not exist.[1] With the outbreak of war, poor whites took advantage of the state of lawlessness in the countryside. Men formed bands to prey on both whites and blacks; they were known as bushwhackers. According to Stephen Ash, these bandits "had no ultimate social or political purpose . . . but to pillage and scourge their fellow heartlanders from the basest of personal motives, notably greed and vengeance."[2] While the Washingtons had difficult times with their former slaves, they did not do major damage to their plantation. Rather it was the renegade white Union troops and roaming bands of white bandits who put their lives and Wessyngton in peril. In addition, the community was infested with guerrillas who often dressed in federal uniform as a disguise. These guerrillas, like the bandits, were men from the community and used brutal violence, but, as Jane wrote, unlike the bandits, they "though far from exemplifying any lofty idealism, at least symbolized the persistence of community, hierarchy, and ideology."[3]

In the early 1860s, such a band of outlaws led by a white man named Pollack roamed the area stealing horses and terrorizing whites and blacks. George wrote Major Lewis about his frightening experience with Pollack's band at the end of 1862:

> Some weeks since I was attacked at home by a party of six robbers; after being shot at three times. I shot and wounded one of the party; when they retreated but carried off two of my horses. Since then a portion of the gang have returned, burned my sawmill and lumber at the Dortch Place, together with one of my tobacco barns. I can occasionally hear of one or two of the band who formerly resided near here, prowling about my premises and am satisfied without the means of defense I would not be safe a day as I am informed they threatened to take my life.[4]

Pollack's band attacked Wessyngton again at the end of 1863; William reacted strongly in a letter from Toronto:

> I feel grateful that it turned out no worse. Pa's escape was truly miraculous for it is a wonder that he was not butchered in cold blood by those unfeeling demons. When I think of the manner they treated you, Pa and Grandma it makes the very blood boil in my veins, they do not deserve the name of <u>men</u>, for the appellation is far too noble for such bloodthirsty fiends in human shape. I can not see what encouragement there can be in attempting to raise anything, if the hard earned labors of a whole year is to be consumed in a few hours by desperadoes.[5]

George was involved in the prosecution of the Pollack case in Nashville.[6] Times were very tense indeed. Pollack and his gang swore to kill him and were still roaming around the area.[7] George advised Jane to have "Will and Granville keep their arms in good order."[8]

Granville reported to Jane (who passed the information to George) that Tom Gardner was harboring Pollack and his gang on his property. Granville got this information from one of the Gardner slaves when he drove Mary to Simpson Rosson's funeral. The Gardner slave told Granville that he wished someone would report Gardner to the federals. The slave hated Tom Gardner, Gossett, and Pollack because they whipped him so severely last winter.[9] The situation was so dangerous that a few of the former slaves stayed in the mansion during George's absences to provide protection to the family. Margaret slept in the room with Jane, and Monroe slept in the sitting room.[10] George admitted to Jane that they need to make plans:

> There is no use in longer deluding ourselves with the hope or belief that we can remain at home. So, you may as well begin to make your arrangements with a view to a change of residence, for a while, and it is important to dispose of all that can be sold off the place before leaving. The cattle must be sold before frost with the exception of about 4 oxen at both places & a few milch cows. . . . The wheat also will be for sale.[11]

Jane began to pack the linens, blankets, a selection of their best books, as well as the pictures, the parlor mirrors, and the only two good carpets.[12]

———•◦•———

The story of one fateful event and its aftermath were recorded in letters, newspaper articles, and legal depositions. Jane and Mary wrote William in Canada the emotional details of what transpired. At least two long articles were published. An article in the *Nashville Dispatch* was titled "An Unfortunate Shooting Affair."[13] A reporter in Springfield wrote an article and commentary that was published in the Dayton, Ohio, *Religious Telescope* with the title "A Disgraceful Affair in Robertson County."[14] In legal depositions taken on February 1, 1865, the participants described the events. Granville Washington and his wife, Irene, were among those involved and also gave depositions; they were identified as CM, Colored Male, and CF, Colored Female.[15]

During the first week of December 1864, several of the Washingtons' neighbors had been robbed by a band of four thieves dressed partly in federal uniform and partly in civilian clothing. The thieves made their first robbery on December 5 at the homes of the Traughbers, Red Burns, Squire Ayers, the Ledbetters, Jim Morrow, and several others. The next day the same band robbed a Mr. Stroud and Buck Darden and took a horse from Lon Polk. The thieves took money, jewelry, firearms, and other valuables. That evening, Dr. John R. Dunn, George's friend and family physician, alerted him that the band was in the neighborhood and to be on the lookout.[16]

On the morning of Wednesday, December 7, Dick Scott, a Wessyngton slave, reported that the group had been seen in the

Granville Washington (1831–1898), in Adams, Tennessee, 1892.

*Irene Lewis Washington (1842–1932) at
Wessyngton Plantation, ca. 1880s.*

Wessyngton Vanhook field. In the afternoon two of the robbers came to the Wessyngton mansion with the intention to steal
George's only remaining saddle horse, Old Ball. One man was
dressed in a black blanket, citizen's frockcoat, a civilian shirt,
civilian's light pair of boots, and army blue pants. The other man,
dressed mostly in civilian clothing, was sitting on a horse nearby.
While Irene, was out sweeping the walkway, she spotted the bandits. She and young Joseph ran to warn George.

George grabbed his shotgun and ran to the stable. He asked the
thief what he thought he was going to do with his horse and demanded
that he remove the bridle. The thief replied in a very insulting manner that he would not do so and started to reach for his seven-shooter.
Irene yelled, "Shoot quick, Mass George, he's getting his gun to shoot
you!" The man screamed, "I will shoot! I will shoot!" Just as the man
reached for his gun, George fired one shot from a distance of about
fifty yards. The bullet struck the man in the chest, and he staggered
backward a few steps into the stable and died.[17]

George and Granville then mounted horses to pursue the other culprit, who had jumped the orchard fence and was making rapidly for the Chestnut lot. Granville went through the peach orchard and fired at the thief but missed him. George rounded the pond and at the granary came in sight of four or five of Pollack's band on horseback who fired at him several times. He retreated to the house, had Granville called in, and prepared for a defense, expecting every moment to be attacked by the gang of outlaws.

In the meantime, the gang rode off in the direction of Cedar Hill. They were gone nearly an hour when they returned. While the robbers were still around the place, Jane wrote an urgent letter to Dr. Dunn asking him to get some friends to come to their assistance. Foster (Granville's son) delivered that letter to the doctor. She also sent a letter to Colonel Thomas J. Downey of the 15th Colored Regiment in Springfield requesting protection with a guard.

In less than an hour after Foster returned from Turnersville, Dr. Dunn came over with a company from the 7th Ohio Regiment. Colonel Garrard and the whole command of 160 men encamped at Wessyngton that night. They saw the thief's corpse and heard the circumstances. The colonel remarked that George was doing good border service, that he saw no evidence of the man having belonged to either army, and applauded his actions. He told George to "bury him in the most convenient place for I regard him as a robber." Colonel Downey sent down a squad, but finding Wessyngton amply guarded by Garrard's forces, returned to Springfield.[18]

It turned out that both robbers were from the 14th Regiment of the Illinois Cavalry. The man who died was Noah Fryar. They claimed that they were "pressing" the horse for government use. George, however, could not tell by their dress that the men were in the Union Army.

The next morning, not fifteen minutes after Colonel Garrard

left the house, twenty men of the 8th Michigan Calvary under the command of Lieutenant Crowley came thundering up to the mansion demanding to see George to interrogate him about one of their men who had been shot.

Wessyngton was under siege. Just days afterward, Jane described the terrifying events that then occurred:

> I took Lieut. Crowley to the room where your father was,
> he abused him for everything under the sun, but your
> father never answered him a word except that he was
> not conscious of having done wrong, but that before
> a proper tribunal he would answer any questions. His
> calmness only enraged them more. I saw they would
> murder him if they took him from the house and I and
> your grandmother in tears and on our knees besought
> that man to send him under guard to Springfield, he
> scoffed at our prayers and drove us from him with oaths.
> They finally took your father and started off with him
> but had not got to the top of Yellow Jenny's Hill before
> they were overtaken by a squad of the 14th Illinois [to
> which Fryar and his accomplice belonged] under Lieut.
> Evans and your father was brought back again. Crowley's
> command returned also and they began a scene which I
> shudder to recall. I stood by your father all the time feel-
> ing that his safety even for a moment depended upon
> me. The officers incited the men to greater fury than
> ever then possessed them, and after talking to them in
> a way to rouse their bad passions even higher left them
> without control to vent their fury at will. For two mor-
> tal hours threats, curses, jeers and taunts as to his fate
> were heaped upon him and I, pistols were snapped in his
> face, and shaken over his head, my prayers and tears were
> made a scoff and jest; a band of Indians could not have

taken more devilish delight in tormenting a prisoner. Your father stood confronting them calmly and fearlessly, steadily looking into their eyes, and they quailed before the steady gaze of an unarmed prisoner like cowards as they were. I felt the end was drawing near, and taking my arms from round him, I started to seek an officer, leaving the three little girls standing round his feet. I had not left him a second when I heard a shot and turning saw your father staggering from the shock, but in one instant he had recovered himself and was grappling the fellow's pistol with both hands. I rushed in between them and clasping my darling round the neck placed my body between him and the man, who cocking his pistol would have shot again through me, had not a comrade caught his hand with the remark "you have done enough." I shrieked murder with all my power, your father stood as calmly defiant as ever, the children screaming round our knees, and those demons gloating over our misery.[19]

Lucy, their daughter who was just four years old, wrote years later that she remembered, or was told, that one morning a crowd of soldiers came tearing into the grounds and house, swearing to find her father and Granville and kill them both. They had been told what a prize their capture would be. They broke into the cellar and found barrels of brandy, got drunk, and came through the house destroying everything in their paths. Later they tried to prove to Mary and Irene that they had found and killed George and Granville. After destroying all they could, one of them, to add to the terror, fired off his gun in the dining room where they all were. The hole made by the bullet was there until she was half grown, when it was papered over.[20]

Lieutenant Doyle of the 8th Michigan persuaded the men to allow him to take George to the house where he helped dress his wounds until Dr. Dunn arrived. In the meantime, George sent Granville to Springfield to get help from Colonel Downey. At the same time a man who had gone to Springfield to get a receipt for his horse overheard the threats of some of the officers and went to Colonel Downey and told him to go save Washington. Boyd Cheatham and Colonel Wiley Woodard also heard the same rumors and reported them to Colonel Downey.

Colonel Downey and one-third of the 15th Colored Regiment went to Wessyngton. They arrived just in time to save George from further harm by the unruly crowd. Seeing that the mob was determined to murder George, he locked him in a room in the house for his own protection. Soldiers of the 14th Illinois refused to respect Colonel Downey's authority; Lieutenant Crowley exclaimed twice, "I have nothing to do with Goddamned nigger officers!" and accused him of protecting Washington for hire.[21]

At the time Colonel Downey had only twelve men compared to fifty troops of the 14th Illinois. They could not prevent the unruly soldiers from doing further damage. The angry mob of soldiers ravaged the place. They pillaged the house, broke open trunks, and chopped the furniture to pieces. They cursed the elderly Mary and threatened if she did not give them $500 in gold, they would burn the house down over her damned old head. They took two gold watches from Jane, silverware, clothes, two revolvers and four shotguns, eight mules and three horses.

Several servants' quarters were robbed of gold, silverware, jewelry, and other valuables. They stole Granville's gold watch—the watch that George had purchased in New York with the twenty dollars Granville had given him.[22] In addition they took "Foster's and Lawson's [Granville's sons] boots and hats [and] every stitch of Granville's clothing."

Colonel Downey sent his adjutant to Springfield for reinforcements. While he was waiting, the men under Lieutenants Crowley's and Evans's command began to burn the plantation's outbuildings.

He had only enough men to guard the mansion; they had to let the other buildings burn. The 14th Calvary burned down the Woods Barn with the whole year's tobacco crop, then the shuck pens and corncribs, and the large barn where hay was kept. Some of the slave cabins then caught fire, but their occupants extinguished those fires. The Rocky Barn, which stored wagons, farming implements, threshing machines, and shingles, burned. The fencing caught fire and only the prompt exertions of a black Sergeant John Jackson saved the whole place from being consumed.

Some of the mob left "on the condition they were treated to as much brandy as they could drink." Lieutenant Evans and the rest of the marauders left after they had burned down the buildings. When Colonel Downey arrived in Springfield, he had all the men of the 14th Illinois Cavalry arrested, their arms taken from them, and their persons and saddles searched. He found in their possession one of the gold watches, two revolvers, four shotguns, a great deal of silverware, quantities of clothing, and a variety of other articles. He arrested Lieutenant Evans and had him placed under guard because he failed to restrain his men. Lieutenant Crowley was also arrested but later released when he received orders to report to Nashville.

Colonel Downey wrote a full report of the incident to his superior, Major Polk, and indicated that the soldiers' conduct was "outrageous and disgraceful to the Federal service." He further attested to George's character for honesty and integrity and as an excellent citizen, well known all over Tennessee. He confirmed that George had protection papers from General Rosencrans for all of his firearms that he often had occasion to use against guerrillas who had more than once attacked him. He had protection papers from General Sherman and nearly all the generals in the department for his property, but these protection papers were disregarded with scorn. The article published in the *Religious Telescope* condemned the officers of the soldiers who stole the horse as a disgrace to the service and called for their dismissal. The disgraceful conduct of the regiments which "must excite the hearty indignation of every true soldier" and to both lieutenants "must attach the blistering shame of the proceedings."[23]

Colonel Downey stated that George was perfectly justified in killing the soldier because he was not accompanied by a commanding officer while taking the horse from the stable at the time he was shot, had never been to the home to see Washington, and had not disclosed his business or authority. No authority could be shown empowering them to impress the horse. Washington's horse had previously been stolen by marauding robbers, and George supposed the two men to be robbers at the time he shot one of them.[24] According to an article in the *Nashville Dispatch* a week later, "Mr. Washington regretted having killed a soldier but felt that he did it in protecting his property from unlawful appropriation."[25]

Colonel Downey's attempt to save George and Wessyngton was viewed as courageous by the Washington family and at least one Northern newspaper, which commended "the bravery of the colored Sergeant [Jackson] and his men. It was an instructive spectacle: these cool, brave, disciplined Freedmen upholding law and order, and protecting the life and property of one of the lords of the soil, recently a large slaveholder. Is there no honor, no manhood in the negro? Can one not trust him? Ask Mr. Washington and his accomplished wife?"[26]

Colonel Downey's superiors and the black soldiers under his command did not share those same views. Young Joseph reported Downey's fate and the reaction of his soldiers:

> When I was in Springfield yesterday, as I was coming
> from the depot, going down in town, two Negro soldiers
> were coming along at the same time. One stepped up by
> the other's side and said, "Well, you know our old colo-
> nel is gone. He went off in full citizen's dress. General

Thomas has ordered him to take off his shoulder straps and his blue clothes and come to him in citizen's garb." One of them then said, "Yes, if he had not been so smart going down there to that Old Washington's house to guard him, he would not have had to leave here. He had better have let us have gone down there and killed him at once and been done with it. Now see what it has cost him. I heard him tell the Sergeant, this morning, goodbye and farewell for he did not know when he would see him again for he had to go and lay in prison for six months." The Negro then said "Now if he hadn't gone down to Washington's and had us out here talking about fighting them other Yankees. Now he's got to go to jail for it." This is the conversation that I overheard in walking from the depot. I was walking down the pike, and they overtook me. I heard them talking about Downey so I just walked fast enough to keep up with them listening attentively all the time without appearing to pay any attention to them.[27]

The historical irony was that the black Union soldiers and Sargeant Jackson were the ones who actually saved Washington's life and Wessyngton from complete destruction.

George estimated the total damages of the incidents to be in excess of $20,000. To prevent further loss of valuables, should a similar situation arise, he shipped many personal possessions such as silver, paintings, some by Gilbert Stuart, and other priceless heirlooms to a warehouse in Louisville, Kentucky, owned by his friend and business associate H. D. Newcomb.[28]

———•◦•———

It was no longer safe for George to stay in Robertson County. In December 1864, George traveled to New York City and attended to business interests, "to strike the market."[29] Jane joined him before January 1865. He considered moving his whole family to New York or Montreal, Canada. Jane wrote her mother-in-law about the living conditions in New York: "You cannot imagine how troublesome it is to find a furnished house we would or could live in. The parlors are well enough, but just go out of them, the carpets are worn out, the oil cloth in holes, the beds and bedroom furniture not as good as Marion or Irene [two house servants] has in their houses and hardly chairs enough in the whole house to seat our family at the table."[30] She called the Northerners "Good for Nothing Yankees."[31] Nevertheless, George and Jane stayed in New York and considered seriously a permanent move.

George's mother, Mary, refused to go to New York with them. She probably felt she should stay at Wessyngton to take care of everything. Mary managed the plantation and five children, ages four to fourteen. She kept George and Jane informed of all events at the plantation. As she wrote Jane, "I feel it is not safe for George to return, you ought to come and see after the children, he can let you come and he remain where he is until you could return to him."[32] Jane wrote Mary her concerns about their life in New York:

> You cannot imagine how I feel, the longer I stay among
> these people, the more I dislike them and their ways,
> and the more I love and long for, the old friends and the
> old home. I did not know how bitter the parting would
> be until I came here, my heart turns sick when I think
> that we soon will be self-banished exiles from home and
> friends. If I could convince myself that my Husband's life
> would be safe I would turn back this very day.[33]

Since George was in New York, the federal Colonel Collier of Pennsylvania and a regiment of Negro troops camped in the yard to "protect their house from soldiers and stragglers." Lucy Washington Helm believed that Major Lewis was instrumental in arranging for the protection.[34, 35, 36]

As the war was coming to an end, federal troops continued taking their property as well as that of the former slaves from the plantation. Joseph wrote:

> Yesterday we had a visit from the Springfield Yankees,
> they came to take all the mules and oxen that we had
> but the Captain got them out of the notion of taking
> the mules so at last they left after taking 2 yoke of oxen,
> one load of oats, 3 or 4 plows, and Step's [a former slave]
> wagon with 4 log chains. I believe that is the amount of
> what they stole. The commander was Lieutenant Wilcox, he said he had orders to do it from Major Armstrong
> although he did not have any written orders he said he
> had verbal orders.[37]

Mary added in her letter: "I am very certain the bucks [runaway slaves from Wessyngton] in Springfield sent them here. The officer could tell the names of the fields as well as if they had been living here. As the Captain said they knew more than he did. I believe they mean to take everything we have."[38]

This seemed to have been an ongoing pattern. In April the Union Army took for U.S. government purposes for twenty-five days: two yoke of oxen, three log chains, one lumber wagon, and three plows, as well as one load of wood.[39] The Washingtons knew that they would lose the few pieces of equipment that remained. Jane instructed Mary to have Granville collect all the tools, plows, hoes, shovels, picks, chains, road scrapers, and rock mason tools on the Home Place and the Dortch Place, and have Joseph record them in a book so George would know how much equipment was actually left in the event that farming was possible for the coming year.[40]

In addition, the returning former slaves would not be able to farm either: "if they [the Yankees] take everything off the place, he [Dick Terry, former slave] has to buy horses to plow with."[41]

Times continued to be chaotic for the former slaves. The Washington letters provide our only insight into how the former slaves reacted to their newfound freedom. For the first time in their lives, the former slaves felt that they could speak their minds to their owners without fear of being sold away from their families or suffering corporal punishment. A number of the returning slaves felt that they were entitled to some of the wealth they had created for the Washingtons and refused to work or leave the plantation. Monroe, who had helped guard Wessyngton from marauders at the onset of the war, was now one of the leaders of the former slaves. When the Washingtons wrote that so-and-so spoke to them "like they were Negroes" or were "imprudent," it showed that the blacks quickly knew that they could speak to all whites as equals.

Many former slaves roamed the countryside looking for relatives from whom they had been separated during slavery. In their letters, the Washingtons reported that a few slaves left the plantation and did not return. Abraham "left his family for better times." Henry Terry and his whole family left.[42] Godfrey, his wife, Lavinia, and her children left.[43]

Former Wessyngton slaves had a variety of personal experiences. While many of them were still in the Union Army, others returned from the contraband camps in Nashville and other places. Some returned to see if any of their possessions were left after the ravages of the war. Others merely came back to see their families and the only home they had ever known. Still others came back to consult with their families about what to do next: Would they stay on the plantation or venture into the unknown?

Mary's and Joseph's letters were filled with concern, anger, and even panic. They did not know how to handle the constant comings and goings of the former slaves. Jane's and George's letters tried to calm them and advised them as best they could how to handle the situation. As Jane wrote to Mary:

> We will get you out of that place as soon as possible. Don't say anything about where we are, or what we are doing, or what will be done when we come home. I know it will be hard for you to be silent when you see those Negroes, on the place, but I beg for your own sake as well as ours that you will not send them any messages by their wives or children or anyone else. If you happen to see them, don't speak to them, in a word, act as if you did not know they were on the place. . . . Don't make any threats within the hearing of any of the servants about what will be done when Mr. Washington gets home. Let them alone, if they do anything of their own accord in the way of work, let them do it, but if they don't choose to work, don't send them any word about it. Please let them alone until we come. Mr. Washington will probably come as far as Nashville with me, and try to get authority from the state government to do something with them. This letter must be strictly confidential, don't even let Joe read it.[44]

Jane had a difficult time persuading Mary that Wessyngton would never be like it was before the war:

> Ma, you talk about the prospect for a crop, why, we have nothing to do with crops now, we have no one to feed or clothe or care for. Why should you trouble about crops, there is plenty to eat here in New York and we can afford to feed and take care of you and the children yet though we have not enough for the Negroes, they are free now and they must take care of themselves.[45]

George Lewis and his wife, Jane, came back with Dick Terry.[46] "Mr. Hamp [Hampton Lewis] has been and stayed three weeks."[47] A family friend reported to the Washingtons: "Monroe and Jackson have been here for several days . . . , and George Smith Harriet had been here for a whole week and absolutely refused to leave. Monroe is the principal man among them."[48] According to Mary, "Monroe was at home walking about the place as though it belonged to him—saying that before long they were coming from Nashville to survey the land and divide it out among themselves."[49] Monroe's wife, Gilly, had been a nurse to the Washington children.

Joseph wrote his mother in February 1865 about more serious situations:

> Last night we had four visitors from Springfield, they were Allen, Simpson, Ike, and Archer. Colonel Alley and Mr. Gill passed them yesterday evening at Stoltz's still house and asked them where they were going. They said they were coming down home [back to Wessyngton]. Simps said he came to see his brother Irvin. Ike and Arch said they came to see the folks in general. Allen came to see his family, and Grandma sent him word to take them off with him. Granville went around last night after supper and found Allen holding the baby. Ike and Arch were standing out of doors at the lower houses. Granville told Arch if he caught him here anymore, he would shoot him. He then said he would not come back anymore.
>
> Day before yesterday, Mr. Clinton Simms [Clinton Washington] as he calls himself, was working in the ice house; he threw down his hoe and said he would not work another lick until he got some clothes for himself and his wife [Rachel]. Granville then sent for Grandma, and when she got there, Clinton asked her what he

sent for her for. She then told him to go to Springfield
or Nashville, whichever place he wanted to go to. He
said he was not going anywhere, but was going to stay
here. Grandma told him he should not stay here without working, but to go to his friends [Northerners and
Freedmen's Bureau officials] and get clothes and money
too, as much as he wanted. He said they were not only
his friends, but everyone else's, both white and black,
and both colors went to them when in danger. After
Grandma came away, he quarreled with Granville until
nearly night. He told Granville that he was going to
report him as having a government pistol. He also said if
Granville did not let him alone, he would stick him full
of holes with his knife. He made a great many threats
besides those. He ought to be driven off the place. He
talked to Grandma just like she was a Negro.[50]

Jane Washington responded to her mother-in-law:

I am sorry to hear such accounts of the Negroes, but do
not know what to advise you to do. . . . Mr. Washington
wants you to tell those Negroes at the Dortch Place, all
of them except Big John [White] and Hannah, [his wife],
to leave. Tell them Mr. Washington is not able either to
feed them or hire them and they must find someone else
to employ them. Tell John if he wants to stay and will take
care of the place and what is on it, Mr. Washington will
pay him, but he does not intend hiring any of the others. Tell those at home the same thing except, what few
Granville may think are needed on the place to keep
things going until we get home. Mr. Washington says
he is not willing to keep many there anyway. Let Louisa
Lewis, and Gilly stay until we come.[51]

Even earlier, in August 1864, Jane wrote that "none have left that lower place [Dortch Place] since Old Henry's [Terry] departure. Granville says they will not work, the grown ones are worse than the chaps, they are chopping tobacco for the last time."[52] That pattern continued through April 1865 as several slaves on the Home and Dortch places refused to work, leave Wessyngton, or work for other farmers.[53]

The house servants took an opportunity to express feelings they probably held to themselves for years under slavery as Joseph wrote to his mother:

> Clinton and Victoria spoke to Grandma just like she
> was a Negro. . . . Miss Vick is the most impudent one
> of all to Grandma that is on the place; she and Grandma
> are fighting and quarreling right now. She is giving
> Grandma all the impudence she can think of.[54] Captain
> Collier is still with us, but I do not know how long he
> will stay, he is already beginning to tire. The Negroes
> aggravate Grandma nearly to death. Captain Collier
> gave the Dortch Negroes their orders, but they do not
> want to leave.[55]

Mary conveyed some of her woes to Jane:

> I had a petition from Joe Cheatham to take his lovely
> family away. [Cheatham was a mulatto slave owned by
> Mary's brother Richard Cheatham; Joe's wife Marion
> was a Wessyngton house slave]. Shall I tell them to go?
> I think all about the house are ready. Vick is the most
> impudent bitch I ever saw. I came very near sending her
> off on Monday last. I am a good mind to send Lady Mar-
> ion off right away. No Negroes will ever leave until their
> houses are thrown down or burned down. I wish they

were all gone and we had a few Dutch or Irish to attend
the place.[56]

——•——

And then there was Dick Terry. Dick had run away from the Dortch
Place numerous times, had refused to take on the Washington surname, and had left for Nashville early in the war. There he met
Union officers and members of the Freedmen's Bureau. He made
several trips back to Wessyngton, made threats, refused to leave,
and once sent a message from Nashville that he was coming back
and would be running the "damned plantation."

Dick returned to the Dortch Place in December 1864. Mary
wrote:

> [Dick Terry] knows all things, said none of them Negroes
> were gone nor did not intend to go, if the men went off to
> work their families should stay where they were. Dick T.
> had gone to Nashville to get permission to remain there,
> they thought very hard they were to be turned off with
> nothing speaking of their crops of tobacco, they ought to
> have the money I was told. Some time ago he was talking
> saying George had acted badly in not paying them their
> money, he had made them worse than they would have
> been. He had his horse put up and moved a week ago,
> said to me yesterday the Negroes said and others too that
> George would be tried for killing that man, just came out
> plain about it, he wishes that himself. I have had enough
> of him, he is a great enemy as he is meaner than you have
> always said he was.[57]

In February Dick told Granville that he had given up his place in
Nashville: "he means to stay there [the Dortch Place] as long as he
lives that he has had orders to go there and he is going there and

stay."[58] After returning from a week's visit in Nashville, Dick Terry told Fletcher, a white farmer on the Dortch Place, that he "was no longer under Washington control and he expects twenty-five of the runaways to return and cultivate the land. He meant to be boss of the place and work the hands himself, keep plenty of everything to live on."[59]

Mary tried to order Dick off the Dortch Place, as she explained to Jane and George: "Dick Terry is cutting up. It was necessary to have someone here. He went on such a high rate yesterday that Captain [Collier] went to see him. He gave him his orders to leave. I feel safer by his being here. I am at a loss to know what to do until I see you."[60]

Again at the end of March:

> Captain Collier and Granville went down to the Dortch Place. . . . Dick Terry is still there and all the rest. They had orders, ten days to hunt homes and go to work for themselves, or find persons to hire them. They will not leave nor hire themselves to anyone. Sampson [Terry] and Sam Vanhook have pretended to hire but will not take their families away. He [Dick Terry] told them what to do. Some of them are pretty impudent. Several persons went to the Dortch Place last week to hire them. They would not hire to anyone.[61] [Two days later] Captain Collier have given the Dortch Negroes their orders but they do not want to leave. Mr. Hannam will hire Sam Vanhook and Mr. Epperson [the former overseer] will hire another.[62]

Days later Mary reported to Jane:

> I think Snipe [Dick Terry] wants those black skins to cut up and make a fuss about their tobacco as he calls

it. Not worth while to try to tell all I have heard. I know one great desire they have he [George] shall either be arrested or killed. A person told me they asked if he knew where George was, yes he had a house in New York and by God he was in hopes they [Pollack's gang] would run him from that as they had from this one here. You don't know how mean he is [and] he is not all, so he [George] has as well keep out of the way of all. I have no more faith of them devils in Nashville than I have of those out here. I think he has many enemies and but few friends. . . . All would like for us to be stripped of every thing and all things destroyed.[63]

Granville once again carried out the Washingtons' orders throughout these months. Granville reported the comings and goings of the former slaves and "complained" to Mary about some of those who had returned.[64] George and Jane trusted Granville with decisions regarding which slaves should remain on the plantation.[65] Granville's loyalty to the Washington family put him in a precarious position with the other slaves as well as whites.

According to George's daughter, Lucy Washington Helm, Granville's life was in jeopardy during this time because the remnants of the Union Army were determined to make an example to all by killing him. She believed that when the army thugs were threatening George's life at the end of 1864 that Granville was the target too.[66] Granville spent weeks in a cave deep in the woods later called Granville's Cave.[67] Granville saw Captain Collier's presence as protection for himself: "Granville has been somewhat alarmed, or was before the Captain came." He was also threatened by a few former slaves.[68]

Granville grew weary of dealing with both the runaways and the whites who resented his position of power and authority at Wessyngton. Joseph wrote his father that "He [Granville] was anxious to see his Master George," stating that he wished "he would come home and he never wanted to see him so much in his life."[69] Jane wrote Mary about Granville's future:

> Tell Granville that he can come here [New York] with us;
> he and Irene, or he can stay on the place and take care
> of what is left. Mr. Washington thinks it would be best
> for him to stay, but he can do just as he chooses. He has
> been so faithful and true that I cannot deny him anything
> he wishes. Tell him to think about it till I come and I will
> talk to him then.[70]

The war had also been difficult for Joseph and the other Washington children in the absence of their parents, with only their elderly grandmother, and constant turmoil on the plantation. Joseph was placed in charge when he was just a teenager. He had grown up playing with the black children before the war, then everything changed. Yet some relationships continued. As the war was ending, Joseph wrote his parents that he and Granville's son Foster had been plowing the garden and went to a bluff to find a cedar tree for his grandmother. Another day "me Foster and Grandvil [as young Joseph spelled it] plowed up the Irish potato ground and planted Grandma potatoes."[71] Joseph also reported that "Grandvil made me a pair of shoes but they hurt my feet so that I cannot wear them."[72]

———•+•———

Slaves in Tennessee were officially freed on February 25, 1865. In March 1865 the legislature and the voters ratified Tennessee's state constitution to abolish slavery; it was the only state to free slaves by popular vote. To celebrate that event, a group of blacks and United States Colored Troops staged a parade in Nashville.[73] "The procession was composed of both sexes and all ages, on foot and riding in carriages, hacks, and vehicles of all kinds[.] Two fine

Brass Bands were with them[.] Business and labor generally was suspended."[74] Even after the state's constitution was ratified, many slaves did not learn that they were free for several months. Some slave owners still refused to release their slaves until their crops had been harvested at the end of the summer.

On April 7, 1865, General U. S. Grant and General Robert E. Lee met at the Appomattox courthouse and agreed on the terms of surrender. The Civil War was over. George was philosophic about the future: "[A]s things cannot be exactly as we might have desired them, we must receive them as they are and make the most of them as we find them."[75]

The former slaves of Robertson County passed on to their descendants that by August 8, 1865, all the slaves in the county had received the news of their freedom. Former slaves refused to work for their owners beyond that date.

It was not until the ratification of the Thirteenth Amendment on December 8, 1865, that the institution of slavery was legally abolished throughout the United States. The slaves' prayers for freedom had finally been answered.

CHAPTER 13

August the 8th

———•◦•———

A fter the close of the Civil War, the Washingtons as well
as the freedmen were perplexed as to what to do next.
George A. Washington owned thousands of acres of land,
but it was worthless without someone to cultivate it. The freedmen,
many of whom had never left the boundaries of Wessyngton Plantation until the war, had to decide what to do in a state of uncertainty.
Freedmen all over the South faced similar decisions: Go back to
the familiar surroundings of the plantation or venture out into the
unknown? They had to contend with hostilities from whites: racism,
death threats, physical violence, and being cheated out of wages.

Once the Civil War battles were over, the reality of the Northern occupation made its impact in Tennessee. Since Tennessee had
been occupied by Northern troops since 1862, Northern officers
and soldiers were more entrenched in society; some married young
Tennesseans. Northern military and nonmilitary men came into the
area to buy up what assets were left. These carpetbaggers looked
for the best opportunities. Robertson County, with so much land
still in the hands of a small number of plantation owners, did not
hold as much appeal as Nashville and regions in the Deep South.
While each year brought new situations and new challenges, on
Wessyngton and in Robertson County, the period from mid-1865
to the early 1890s was a continuum of change.

Newspapers in Nashville and throughout the South were full of advertisements placed by former slaves looking for their relatives. Clara Brown, born in nearby Gallatin in 1803, was separated from her family in an auction in 1835. Her family was scattered throughout the South. In 1857 she purchased her own freedom and moved west where she started a laundry business and invested in real estate in Colorado. By the end of the war, she had accumulated more than $10,000. She eventually located thirty-four of her relatives, including one of her daughters, in 1882. There were many other success stories, but the majority of former slaves never found their relatives. Many black families set aside certain dates for gatherings to help locate family members. These gatherings later evolved into large and elaborate family reunions.

The White brothers, John, Tom, and Edmund, who had been slaves on the Washingtons' Dortch Place, were reunited with their brother David (Davy), who had been sold in New Orleans for constantly running away. My own great-great-grandfather Thomas Black Cobbs had been sold away from his mother, brothers, and sisters in 1854 when he was ten years old in the settlement of an estate. Thomas's family lived close by, and he was able to rejoin them after emancipation. The Blacks and Cobbs lived near the Wessyngton Plantation. Thomas worked as a day laborer on the plantation. The majority of Thomas's descendants live in Springfield and make up one of the largest families in Robertson County.

Another sign of freedom was that all African Americans began using surnames. Several of the Wessyngton freedmen already used surnames, but it was a time when they could change their surnames if they so chose. Lucy Washington Helm related in 1945: "To this day many of the descendants of our Negroes live on the place [Wessyngton]. They always were and still are proud of being 'Washington Negroes.'" However, not all the former slaves were

Thomas Black Cobbs (1844–1928) and
Minerva McClain Cobbs (1857–1928).

proud to be Washingtons and they chose to use other surnames based on their own connections to family members from whom they had been separated, more so than as an association to their former masters. They also took into consideration their sentiments toward their former owners. When they felt they were treated better by one owner versus another, they often selected the surname of the most favored master. Some freedmen adopted names of whites who had assisted them or treated them kindly. Others used surnames associated with wealthy or powerful families like the Washingtons, Lewises, or Cheathams. Many of the former Wessyngton slaves considered themselves in a higher social position than other slaves because of the Washington family's status.

Freedmen chose names of the historical figures: Washington, Jefferson, or Jackson. Others made up surnames such as Freeman that reflected their new status. Some got their names from

Descendants of Thomas Black Cobbs and George Ann Black Cobbs,
one of the largest African American families in Robertson County, at
Cobbs Family reunion, 1999. Organized by John F. Baker Jr.

their occupations. Bill, who was a blacksmith on Wessyngton, was
known as Billy "the smith" during slavery and became William
Smith after emancipation.

Most of the Lewis slaves given to George in 1844 when he married Margaret Adelaide Lewis retained the Lewis surname because
of their connection with the other slaves who had been owned by
Major William B. Lewis. One of the former Lewis slaves legally
changed his surname back to Lewis after having used the Washington surname. In an affidavit he stated that he was not changing his
surname from Washington for any fraudulent purposes, but Lewis
was the name of his family prior to coming to Wessyngton. Some
of the Lewises used the surname Fairfield, which was the name of
the Lewis plantation in Nashville.

Some descendants of the Scott family stated that they used the
Washington surname immediately after emancipation and, due to
bad behavior on one occasion, the Washington family insisted that
they revert back to their previous owner's surname, Scott. In the

Washingtons' opinion, their behavior was not becoming to such an honorable name as Washington. The family was listed with the Washington surname on a register from the Freedmen's Bureau in 1865, and Scott on all succeeding records. When slave Bill Henry Scott applied for his pension for military service in the Union Army, he was turned down because no record could be found to prove that he ever enlisted. When he reapplied, he stated that he had always been called by his father's surname, Scott, but when he enlisted in the army he was forced to use the Washington surname since that was the name of his owner. His records were found under the Washington surname and his pension was granted. Some of the Wessyngton freedmen interchanged their surnames with Washington and previous surnames during the years immediately following the war. It was not uncommon to see a former Wessyngton slave listed on one document as Washington and on another by a different surname.

In 1860 among the twenty-seven households of Wessyngton slaves on the Home Place, five surnames were used: Washington, Cheatham, Gardner, Lewis, and Smith. Twenty-three used the Washington surname; the other surnames had one each.

In 1870 Washington-headed households outnumbered all other African American surnames in Robertson County. This pattern continued for several decades. An account book from Wessyngton from the 1880s listed the names of many former Wessyngton slaves with the Washington surname, as well as several whites and blacks in the community. All the blacks were listed as "Colored" except the black Washingtons. A notation in the account book stated: "Note: all the Washingtons listed in this book are colored—former slaves of the Washingtons—hence the surname, 'Washington.' They are probably not marked as 'Col'd' because they had always been there and when someone saw the name in the register, he would know who it was."[1]

My great-great-grandfather Emanuel Washington, who had run away with federal troops to Nashville, returned to Wessyngton with his family. Several of his sisters and brothers also returned, though others did not. By that time his mother, Jenny, had been at Wessyngton longer than any of the other slaves. She had been there more than sixty years and was the matriarch of the largest family on the plantation. Jenny later moved with her daughter Clara Washington and her family to another farm near Wessyngton.

While many former slaves left the area never to return, a large number came back to Wessyngton. This included at least twenty extended families, a very unusual pattern in the postwar South. At the end of 1865, Jane wrote her husband informing him of the number of former slaves who were returning to Wessyngton:

> Axum has moved his family back, and Man [Emanuel
> Washington] will be in on Sunday night to regular work.
> I employed Melissa at seventy-five dollars per annum; I
> see no prospect of Amy coming and told Edmund you
> would feed a boy in her place. I've hired Foster as driver.
> Old Brit wanted to know yesterday what was to become
> of him, his "folks were all gwine away." I told him he
> could take lodgings with Silvy and remain until you came
> home. No removals have taken place except Axum's fam-
> ily; I don't know what Hannah is going to do.[2]

Many freedmen who returned to Wessyngton found themselves doing the same things they had done for decades, living on the same planta-tion they were born on, and living in the same cabins that their par-ents and grandparents had built a generation earlier. On Christmas Day 1865, George drew up contracts with some of his former slaves specifying the terms under which they would work in 1866. These included contracts for domestic work and as well as farm labor. The terms and conditions varied somewhat depending on the needs of the freedmen. From that time onward, many of the former slaves from Wessyngton worked there as domestic servants or did general work around the mansion. Pay generally ranged from $0.25 to $0.50 per day during the mid-1860s through the early 1880s.

Many of the house servants at Wessyngton had felt that they were the aristocracy among the slave community and saw it as a step down in society to work for anyone of a lower social status than the Washington family. Granville Washington was hired for $160 per year and was responsible for his own doctor's bills and clothing. George provided his food. Granville contracted the labor of his wife, Irene, and son Foster for $50 each per year, and his younger son, Lawson, for $30.

Emanuel Washington's contract stated that he was to cook for the Washington family for a salary of $125 per year. He was to be charged for all lost time, and he was to have every other Sunday off to spend at his wife's house. George was to feed him, and he resided in the mansion. He was responsible for clothing himself and paying his family's doctor's bills. The contract stated that George had no obligation to support Emanuel's family; Emanuel was responsible for supporting them. An 1880 account book revealed that Emanuel Washington paid $5 for a dress for his daughter Cornelia, $3.50 for a pair of boots for his ten-year-old son Amos, and $1 for a hat. He also purchased material, which was probably made into clothing by his wife, who was the head laundress. Emanuel and his wife, Henny, appeared to have prospered.

George hired Hannah Washington as a domestic for $60 per year. Joe Washington was hired for $100 per year and was responsible for all his expenses. Louisa Lewis worked as a domestic for food, shelter, and clothing for herself and five children. George hired Amy Washington (Joe's wife), Sylvia Washington, and Martilla Washington each for $72 per year and fed them; they were responsible for all other expenses.

Emanuel Washington was succeeded as cook by John Phillips, Beulah Green, and Minerva Washington Lewis. Housekeepers were Gilly Lewis (before and after emancipation), Matilda Washington, Lucy Washington, and Carrie Williams Washington. The maids were "Cousin Louisa" Lewis (before and after emancipation), Winnie Washington Long Biggers, and Mattie B. Terry Washington. The nursemaids included Margaret Lewis Washington and Annie Terry, and the coachmen were Granville Washington, his son, Foster Washington, and John Green. Foster Washington also served as overseer at the farm briefly during Reconstruction. Chambermaids included Cornelia Washington and Mandy Washington. Joe Washington, Jackson Gardner Washington, and Joe Scott were gardeners. Joe Washington also served as hostler, caring for the horses. Gabriel Washington and Woodard Washington picked up the mail in Cedar Hill.[3] Allen Washington was the head dairyman. Milkers were Silvy Washington, Hannah Washington, Prudy Washington, Lucy Johnson, and Betty Gardner. Mary Lewis worked as a dining room maid.

According to Mattie Terry, before the time of washing machines, doing the laundry meant they had "to carry water from the creek in the bottom up the hill to the Big House."[4] Clothes were boiled in huge wash kettles and rinsed. They were wrung out by hand, hung out to dry, then ironed in the loom house. Henny Washington was the head laundress for forty years or more. She received $6 per month. She normally worked three days per week. Others who worked in the laundry room were Rachel Washington Terry, Caroline Dunn, Belle Ayers, and Sarah Jane Scott Harris. Lady Terry Williams (1878–1981) worked from 1912 to 1953. She and Sarah Jane started working as young women under Henny's supervision.

Some of the servants resided in the quarters above the kitchen, the loom house, and in the basement of the main house. The coachman lived in a small frame house in front of the mansion. The farm

Wessyngton Plantation servant doing
laundry, ca. 1880s.

manager and his family resided in a small frame house near the mansion.[5] Aunt Henny and Uncle Man lived in a log cabin near a stream at the bottom of the hill. According to Mattie Terry, Aunt Henny's house was always very neat and they often held prayer meetings in her house.[6] Gabe Washington lived next door. Gabe's son Joe recollected that there were two cabins in the yard side by side (Emanuel's and Gabe's). The other cabins were scattered about.[7] According to George's daughter Mary in 1867, "Granvill [sic] is a free man. He is set up for himself and he is going to live in the Easly house where the cotton is, but they did not move there they moved to Creek Betty's house."[8]

George and Jane returned to Wessyngton from New York City in April 1865. The plantation bore only a faint resemblance to what it had been at its peak only a few years earlier. Most of the buildings were burned, the livestock was gone, fields were overgrown, most of the slaves had left, and the few who remained refused to work. In addition, almost all their treasured possessions stored in Louisville had been destroyed by fire; only the box in a vault that contained their silver was saved.[9, 10]

The Washingtons must have wondered if it was even worth it to return to Wessyngton, and how to start to get the plantation in operation again. Jane felt that "[t]he good old times will never be again, the glory has departed and the fading light of those times shines but upon ruined homes and blasted hopes."[11]

George and Jane had a rental home near New York City. The North offered advantages of investment security, freedom from the chaos of war and its aftermath, safety and security for their family, and vastly better educational options for their children. However, this was always balanced against the loss of their family ties, social position, networks, and their lifelong home; the inflated expenses to live in the North in urban congestion; the unfamiliar people, cultures, and attitudes; and the prospect that their children would grow up in what appeared to be a foreign land. George commented in a letter to Jane about his quandary:

> So far as I am concerned personally, would prefer remaining at home on the old place. But in view of advantages in education for the children think it may be better for them that we should remove to Nashville, [where they owned a house[12]] and keep the old place up as a resort in Summer, by which their health will be benefited and they will not altogether forget the place of their birth.[13]

Perhaps the strain of the war brought the onset of heart problems for George; he called them "heart-aches."[14]

However, by September 1866 they clearly had decided to stay home and resolved their major concern—the education of their children. Nearly all the private schools in the South were destroyed or closed after the war. The Washingtons had no alternative but to send their children to school in the North. William continued for a time at the University College in Toronto. Joseph attended Georgetown College Preparatory School in Washington. Joseph then graduated from Georgetown College in 1873. George and Jane constantly admonished him to perform well at college: "Oh Joe, try and make yourself a man I can be *proud* of, as well as *love*." His mother stressed the need for good manners, a well-trained mind, and warned him not to "fall [into] bad habits which often cause people never to come to any good, but simply eat and sleep through their life."[15] Since Jane's alma mater, the Nashville Female Academy, suffered greatly during and after the war, Martha and Mary were sent in 1872 to the fancy Mrs. Reed's School for young ladies in New York City. Mary must have missed her life at Wessyngton; she sent letters to her siblings from "Reeds Prison."

The decision to remain at Wessyngton was significant, not only for the family, but also for the freedmen and for Robertson County. The Washingtons had been a pillar of economic and societal stability before the war and would remain so for more than another hundred years. They revitalized a broken economy and provided leadership in a time of uncertainty when the community and its security forces appeared paralyzed. In the post–Civil War era, many plantation owners lost their land due to insufficient production caused by labor scarcities and a high tax burden. The aftermath of the war created a land-rich, cash-poor former upper class. The Washingtons, however, fought to avoid that outcome.

The effects of the war had exhausted the aged Mary Washington. She felt that "[a]ll would like to see us stripped of everything."[16] She died on November 28, 1865. Her will, written November 16, 1860, had been placed in a bureau that was sent to Louisville during the war. When no will was found after her death, it was assumed that she had no will, and that George would inherit her entire estate. Six months after Mary's death, her will was discovered in their possessions stored in Louisville. Mary left her grandson, William Lewis Washington, all the real estate left to her by her husband (including the Thompson tracts of land), land she inherited from her father (the Flewellyn land), and land she inherited from the estate of her sister Francis Cheatham. She left William $50,000. Mary explained in her will that she made the bequest to her grandson because she had made a promise to his mother on her deathbed and because of the love and regard she had for her. Furthermore, her other grandchildren would have the whole of their mother's fortune independent of their father's estate. She left the remainder of her estate to her son. Her will instructed George to purchase $5,000 diamond necklaces for her two granddaughters Martha and Mary. Mary's will provided "there should be new capping put on the wall around the graveyard and such repairs as are necessary, an iron gate put to it and paid out of my estate."[17]

George drew up an agreement with William to give him other property instead of that specified in Mary's will: George gave William eight hundred acres in Dyer County valued at $13,000; seventy-four acres in Davidson County, at the mouth of Brown's Creek, valued at $12,000; and $50,000 in bonds of the State of Tennessee.[18] William had sat out the last part of the war in safety in Canada. We do not know if the decision not to return to Tennessee was made by William, his parents, or the communal decision of their social group. George and Jane were very concerned about William. George confided in Jane: "Will is loafing around seemingly without object, I much fear he will fritter away his life in that way if he has, or continued to have the means to defray his expenses. I most fear he will do nothing useful."[19] Jane warned Joseph not to adopt the "useless driveling existence which your Brother has chosen."[20] William's grandfather, Major William B. Lewis, died at the end of 1866 of a severe cold with virulent fever;

William was his only heir.[21] With his substantial inheritances, William was able to live in Europe, Washington, Philadelphia, and as far west as California. According to his letters, he visited spas, had various mistresses, and enjoyed the good life of the idle rich. He seldom returned to Wessyngton.

After the war two more children were added to the Washington family. Jane Augusta was born in 1867, and George Augustine Jr. was born in 1868. Unlike their older siblings, Jane and George grew up in a time of growth and prosperity within the family with no personal memory of wartime. Mary, eleven years old in 1866, reveled in the return to normalcy. With Joseph away at school, she kept him up to date with news of the family, the plantation, and the changing lives of the freedmen.

———•◦•———

The United States government established the Freedmen's Bureau in 1865 to assist the former slaves in their transition to free citizens and to give them more stability. Although the bureau was part of the War Department, it primarily engaged in economic and social work. Bureau officials supervised labor contracts between black employees and white employers, helped black soldiers and sailors collect bounty claims, pensions, and back pay, and performed numerous other functions. D. D. Holman was appointed superintendent of the Freedmen's Bureau in Robertson County on October 10, 1865. Washingtons outnumbered all other freedmen in the county when the Freedmen's Bureau created an 1865 register of former slaves who entered into sharecropping contracts.

Wessyngton and other plantations and farms throughout the South introduced the sharecropping system. Nearly one hundred of George's former slaves signed sharecropping agreements with local farmers. The Freedmen's Bureau drew up contracts in an effort to prevent the landowners from taking advantage of the freedmen.

Most blacks were illiterate and signed their agreements with an "X." Some of the landowners were no more educated and signed with an "X" also. There was a $1 dollar fee for drafting a contract.

By June 1866, D. D. Holman's register contained 2,281 contracts between freedmen and landowners in Robertson County. These contracts covered the work of about 3,400 people because a cropper's agreement in many cases obligated the labor of the entire family. Twenty-three of these contracts were with minor children who worked as apprentices. Some farmworkers chose to work for wages rather than a share of the crop. These laborers received rations, quarters in which to live, and from $100 to $180 per year. Nearly one-third of the contracts were for a share of the crop; the others included domestic work and day labor. The average day laborer received $12 per month. Altough sharecropping was another form of economic exploitation, unlike slavery, the new system was more class- than race-based. Black and white sharecroppers worked on property owned by blacks and whites well into the mid-twentieth century. Also, small children as young as seven were often "hired out" to work for white families. In census records from the 1870s and 1880s there were a number of small children listed alone living in white households.

In 1867 George had Wessyngton surveyed and assigned tracts of land to black and white families. Tracts generally consisted of forty to eighty acres of land planted in tobacco, corn, oats, rye, and wheat. As it was before the war, tobacco was the cash crop. In the Wessyngton contracts, George furnished the land, tools, draft animals, barns, and other provisions, and received two-thirds of the crop. The sharecropper provided the labor and received one-third of the crop. George provided the tenant with a house and firewood from the estate. The contract stipulated that the tenant had to work for George at a rate of $0.67 a day, whenever needed, unless he was working on his own crop. He could not work for anyone else without George's permission and had to tend George's stables seven days a week, and water and feed the stock. The share-croppers' obligations included the repair of fences, cleaning out fencerows on the farm, and giving George three days' work free each year for every adult male in the sharecropper's family in order to put up hay for the animals in the winter. George also reserved the right to terminate the contract at any time if the tenant was guilty of bad conduct or getting drunk.

The first men to enter into these contracts were Allen Wash-ington, Jackson Gardner Washington, Jacob Washington, Dick Terry and family, Sam Vanhook and his stepson Leroy Lewis, John Lewis, and Granville Washington, all of whom had been slaves at Wessyngton. Dick Terry had been adamant about his demands for land when he returned to the plantation during the months when George was still in New York. However, upon George's return he was willing to enter into the sharecropping arrangement with him. Other black sharecroppers included Jim Darden, George Fort, and Cain Gaines.

An early agreement with former slave John Lewis and his fam-ily stated that George would provide a team of draft animals and tools and in return, they would cultivate as much land as they could for one-third of the profits. The contract stipulated that he was responsible for his mother, Caroline Lewis, and his sis-ter Lucy.[22] A similar agreement was made with Jackson Gardner Washington to operate George's Dortch Mill to grind grain for one-third of the profits. George generally stated in the labor con-tracts that the freedmen were responsible for their medical bills and those of their families. In only a few agreements, if the ten-ant provided his own team of draft animals and tools, he received two-thirds of the crop instead of one third. Granville Washington was one of those who received two-thirds of his crop. These con-tracts had fewer restrictions than the later sharecropping agree-ments George used in 1867.

Although George thought some of the former slaves would not be satisfied with the tracts they were given to cultivate, his wife assured him they were well pleased with them: "You thought the Negroes would hardly be satisfied with the land they are to cultivate but so far as I know they are perfectly delighted, for they know that those lots always produced fine crops."[23] By 1870 eleven former slave families were working on the Home Place, consisting of fifty-two individuals. This did not include the Terrys, some of the Lewises, Vanhooks, Whites, and other former slaves who resided on the Dortch Place and other properties.

Even with a number of his former slaves cultivating his land, George still needed additional labor and hired white sharecroppers whom he housed in former slave cabins. Even the former overseer Ed Epperson became a sharecropper. Many day laborers worked at Wessyngton. Wages ranged from $0.25 to $0.75 per day depending upon the work. Most workers had an income of $180 per year. In comparison, most other workers in that era in the South earned $60 per year.[24]

White sharecroppers on Wessyngton Plantation, ca. 1890s.

Black and white sharecroppers on Wessyngton
Plantation, ca. 1900s.

Sharecropping became a mainstay at Wessyngton for generations as it remained a major tobacco enterprise for many years
after the Civil War. Wessyngton under Washington ownership
raised tobacco for more years after the war (1866 to 1983), than
before the war (1796 to 1865). However, between 1860 and 1870,
Tennessee's black population decreased by 20 percent, and there
was an exodus of 13 percent of Robertson County's black population. This labor shortage directly affected the county's tobacco
industry, which declined 10 percent during that period.[25]

By 1869 nearly the entire farm was rented out to black and
white sharecroppers. Jane wrote Joseph:

> Dick Terry and company live in the cabins and work
> part of the Old Dortch place on shares, and two of Jim
> Andrews' sons live in the house and cultivate the balance,
> the Sory field is divided out among the Sherrods, Hollo-
> ways, Procters, Dardens, Roaches, and Granville. Old Cain

a Negro who used to belong to Gaines and Old Jacob
[Washington, America's husband], Billy at the Old Reed
place, and John [Lewis] and Allen [Washington] cultivate
the Cheatham and Fyke fields. I believe that is about the
sum and substance of your Pa's rent roll. It sounds like a
good deal to read about, but when the rents are collected
they do not more than pay taxes.[26]

George was not too impressed with some of his new tenants (sharecroppers) and encountered difficulties with both groups. He wrote
to Joseph that "[a]lthough I have tenants on all the places that
have houses, I cannot say that many of them are desirable; indeed
they are generally a thriftless indolent set. I believe the white men
are worse than the Negroes in a general way."[27] Alfred Washington (Emanuel's brother) returned to Wessyngton to sharecrop after
he had worked for three years for another farmer. Jane wrote,
"Old Alfred was here today wanting land, tools, and team, having
worked three years for the Dardens and no money to show for it,
he wishes to try here again."[28]

Some aspects of life on the plantation continued as it had for
decades. Slaughtering hogs required considerable labor and was
a major event. Mary wrote: "They killed hogs in the later part of
last week. We had a holiday on the last day and I helped cutting
the lard and ground sausage meat and was useful in every way. I
wish you were here for you would enjoy the sausages so much."
And another time: "The hogs have been killed. They were in splendid order."[29]

Britain Washington, eighty years old in 1880, was the only
slave who had been brought from Virginia still on the plantation. The seventy-two-year-old Axum Washington was proba-

Hogs slaughtered at Wessyngton Plantation, ca. 1890s.

bly the oldest former slave who was born on the plantation still residing there in 1880. Twenty-eight former slaves remained on the Dortch Place, including the families of Dick Terry, Sam Vanhook, Leroy Lewis, Amos Washington (brought to Wessyngton in 1836), Claiborne Washington, Harrison Washington, and Jefferson Washington.

The pattern of daily life was similar to during prewar times.

Women processing pork at Wessyngton Plantation, ca. 1890s.

During slavery, the slaves had worked Monday through Friday and a half day on Saturday. They usually ate at noon, often taking meals in the fields when they worked far from their quarters. They were not required to work Sundays. This same work pattern was followed by both black and white sharecroppers.

Wages were very low at that time, but most managed to support their families. During that period the following items could be purchased at Wessyngton: ham, 14 cents per pound; 1 gallon of coal oil for 35 cents; 1 pair of shoes for $1.75; pork cracklings for 5 cents; 1 bushel meal, 60 cents; 1 pork shoulder, 12 cents per pound; 16 gallons salt, $1.20; 1 pair brogans, $1.50; 1 pound butter, 15 cents; mutton, 6 cents per pound; 1 gallon vinegar, 40 cents; lard, 16 cents; 1 gallon molasses, 65 cents; 50 pounds flour, $1.50; 1 bushel potatoes, 75 cents; and bacon, 10 cents per pound.[30]

Freedmen, former slave owners, and local citizens were slowly adapting to their new status, but still tensions existed. Jane's reactions were quite strong at the end of the war:

> I saw yesterday an exemplification of "whither we are drifting." Mr. Willis Patterson and Mr. George Bartlett both of ebony came to see your Pa on business. I went into the room to sit down but on entering changed my mind as I saw the colored brothers sitting before the fire as large as life. I thought it was time to get away from the chance of such familiarity, you don't know how I was shocked for the moment, but why should I be, they are our equals before the law and have as much right to a chair as you or I, but I don't feel yet like looking on patiently when they take a seat in my house. If I have to be on equality with those socially below me, I at least want them the same color.[31]

Through the Washingtons' letters we can learn about how the former slaves were beginning to exert their new freedoms and taking control of their lives. Some of the house servants left the Washingtons to do their own work as Jane wrote in 1866:

> I had occasion to reprove Irene [Granville's wife], for the time she was cleaning the sitting room and suppose I insulted her very much as Granville asked me the next day if I could do without her to let him pay her board, that she was every much dissatisfied with him for hiring her and caused him to see a heap of trouble. I told him if I could get Amy [Washington] or Melissa [Washington] either she might go out of the house never to return. Monday I sent out the wash and told her to go and help Margaret. She did so that day but the next morning she announced to the Negroes that she was done with the house, and I have not seen her since. She keeps to her cabin as close as if she was confined. I am doing very well without her, but if it was not for Granville I would drive her off the place.[32]
>
> Since Christmas, our troubles have commenced. Would you believe that the day after Christmas, Louisa, yes, Cousin Louisa told me she was going to leave the next day. And she did too, bag and baggage leaving Bob with his grandmother, giving Beck to Hannah Johnson, and taking Ad, Alice and Lizzie with her to Springfield, where I understand she has rented a room and intends living for the present. I can't imagine what fool notion she got in her head unless she thought her two precious daughters had too much to do. Well the day before Louisa left I paid Margaret up her wages and dismissed her for she had become so worthless and impudent. I would not keep her, and you see I was flat not a servant in the

house for Amy had gone to visit Betsy and I did not know
if she was coming back or not. So for the last two days
the children and I have been doing all the house cleaning and dining room work with the assistance of Martilla.
Of all the servants we had last year only Man, Step, Silvy
and Tilla have agreed to hire, what I shall do for a wash
woman and a seamstress I don't know.[33]

Mary described their new way of life without servants: "Cousin
Louisa is moved and we have to do our own work and we get up at
six o'clock and clean up the house. We eat in the sitting room and
I wait on the table and I have fine old times waiting on the table.
Cousin Louisa is gone to Springfield and Olive is back and Ant
Amy is here yet and Ant Lindy [Malinda] and Ant Prudy too."[34]

Three years later, Jane still did not know how to deal with the
freedmen:

Amy left me week before last, Joe [Washington, her hus-
band] was not willing she should stay. Henny [Washing-
ton] does the washing for the present after a fashion, and
I have Margaret for nurse and Tilla for housework, but
they are more idle and worthless than they were before.
I cannot say that anything is done unless I have seen
to it myself. We have no man or boy at all except Step
[Stepney Washington], he is the only chance for hostler,
gardener, and man of all work. I can hire Axum [Wash-
ington] by the day, and the weather is so fine that I think I
shall try to get him to plant some young fruit trees.[35]

At the end of 1866 Jane reported that Granville Washington took
his family away at Christmas "either to the Frey or Carr place to
work for himself. I am sorry he is going, but I am glad to lose Irene
and those boys, but he would not go except on her account, she

keeps him miserable all the time."[36] Jane described her household to Joseph:

> I have pieces of Negroes enough to run a small farm and they all don't amount to one good one. Step, Gilbert, and Jim, and Old Brit, Man. Jim feeds about twenty-five head of cattle and takes care of his horses, he does pretty well, Man cooks and thereby saves me some trouble, but the other three are not much. We hired Gilbert because there was so much fencing to be done, but the weather has been so cold that he and Step do not more than get firewood. Henny does my washing for six dollars per month, Mandy comes up in the morning and cleans the bedrooms, and one day gives a general cleaning, this for her meat and meal. I have Josie for two dollars per month, Gabe for clothes and thirty-five per annum, Hannah and Prudy for what they cost. Lucy Johnson I feed to milk, and Betty Gardner I pay twenty-five per annum to do the same. So you see how the work of three good servants is divided out among a dozen.[37]

The relationship between the Washingtons and their servants was not always difficult. In fall 1866 Jane wrote Joseph, "Gilly came last night to see the children and you can't imagine how delighted Lucy was. Gilly looks very well and inquired for you."[38] Joseph often sent gifts to his family and some of the servants from Washington while attending college and always had his mother remember him to all the servants. His mother wrote him when Granville received his gifts: "Granville grinned when he saw his watch, cravats, and pipe. He said he would not need the pipe to remind him of Mass Joe, 'I clare, I never did miss anybody so much, I ain't had no fun since Mass Joe been gone, I ain't got nobody to play with o'nights.'"[39] Joseph also sent handkerchiefs to Granville's wife, Irene, and their son "little Grants capered and laughed at his five cents."[40] Mary even passed on to Joseph that "Tilla says bring her something nice when you come home and she says Howdy."[41]

Joseph wrote his mother from Washington asking that Emanuel Washington bake him a birthday cake and some cornbread and send it to him in the mail. His mother replied:

> I have just packed a box to send you, and it will be
> shipped tomorrow by express. In it are your grey jacket
> and pants, two white shirts, three pairs of new yarn socks,
> some chestnuts, some cornbread and a cake. I hope it will
> reach you on the 10th for a birthday present. Uncle Man
> thought it very funny that "Mass Joe" should send home
> for cornbread. I expect everything will be stale and dry
> when you get it but it started fresh.[42]

Another time Irene sent Joseph a large cake.[43] Jane wrote Joseph in 1872: "Monroe brought Gilly down to spend the day with the children, so you see we are quite intimate with our colored friends."[44]

Uncle Man's Cornbread Recipe

Make 3 pints of sour milk into a stiff batter with corn meal, add 3 eggs well beaten, 2 oz of shortening, 1 gill [1/4 pint] best molasses, a little salt, and saleratus [baking soda], grease a pan well, and bake quick.[45]

Wessyngton had been entirely self-sufficient before the war, and many slaves had learned a number of skills in addition to doing agricultural labor. They were blacksmiths, stonemasons, and carpenters. They manufactured bricks, built buildings, worked in sawmills, operated gristmills, made whisky, slaughtered animals, and processed meat. The women had served as cooks and laundresses, spun cloth, made clothes, churned butter, and did other domestic work. They used many of these skills to support themselves as freedmen and freedwomen.

For generations the slaves had viewed the North as their Promised Land or the land of freedom. Once they were freed, the North was the first place the former slaves thought about going to start a new life. Thousands of freedmen went north in the decades after the war and others ventured west to Texas, Oklahoma, Kansas, Missouri, and California.

Although several former Wessyngton slaves were discharged from the U.S. Army in 1866 in places far away from Robertson County, they did not remain there. Otho and Frank Washington were discharged in Chattanooga.[46, 47] Miles Washington was discharged in Huntsville, Alabama.[48] Thus far we have found no evidence that any former Wessyngton slave migrated south of Tennessee during this time.

Many slaves who left Wessyngton during the war never returned to the plantation. Some of them settled in Cheatham, Dickson, Montgomery, and Sumner counties. Other freedmen lived throughout the area in Cedar Hill, Turnersville, Coopertown, and Springfield. Grundy Washington (Emanuel Washington's son) was a minister and later moved to Clarksville. Jacob Washington (a former Union soldier) relocated to Wilson County. Frank remained in Springfield and lived in the Kirktown settlement. Several of the Lewis slaves and others who once worked on the Dortch farm migrated to Cheatham County and later to Nashville. Dick Lewis

Washington, Sylvester Lewis Washington, Samuel Lewis Washington, and Washington Lewis Washington and their families lived in Cheatham County. Others went to Dickson and Montgomery counties, where some of their descendants remain.

Ford Washington was living in Clarksville and listed as a white barber. By 1880 he settled in Lincoln County, where the family was listed as mulatto. After his death the family migrated to Cleveland, Ohio. Others settled in Kentucky in Todd, Logan, and Christian counties. Martin Washington, Warren Washington, Mahala Washington, her son Mason Washington, and several others migrated to Christian County. Several former Cheatham slaves also moved to Christian County.

Some freedmen settled in Nashville in the contraband camps that became the black neighborhoods of Edgefield and Edgehill. In 1866 Clinton Washington, his wife, Rachel, and his brother Ford resided there. In 1865 they had asserted their new rights during visits to the plantation, and the next year they made a claim against the Washingtons through the Freedmen's Bureau:

> Dear Sir: We are colored men residents of Edgefield, and formerly the slaves of Geo A. Washington. In the year 1863 we made a crop of tobacco, two hundred pounds each and sold it to our master, who has never paid us for it. The wife of Clinton Washington worked for him all of the year 1864 up to the last of March 1865, and he never paid her or even clothed her. Her name is Rachael Washington and lives in Edgefield.

This claim, made through D. D. Holman of the Freedmen's Bureau, was sent on to General Clinton B. Fisk, assistant commissioner of the bureau, who endorsed the claim, writing, "the Courts of Tennessee hold a master to a contract made with his claim."[49] We do not know if the Washingtons paid off these claims; they might have paid the sum due for the personal tobacco cultivation but probably did not pay Rachael as they still considered her a slave at the time.

Nashville city directories from the late 1870s through the early 1900s listed many Wessyngton families who had relocated and established new lives for themselves. Cornelia Washington (Emanuel Washington's daughter) gave notice to the Washingtons in 1880 that she would soon be leaving the plantation to get married and then move north. Her plans did not work out, and she moved to Nashville where she died in 1882. She was brought back to Wessyngton for burial in the slave cemetery.

Most of the Wessyngton families in Nashville ran into each other frequently since they lived in close proximity to one another. Some of them attended the same churches and worked for the same employers. They would have shared information about friends and relatives back at Wessyngton.

In addition, as an effort to permit the freedmen a chance to leave the South, the Nicodemus Town Company was incorporated in 1877 by six blacks and two whites from Kansas. It was the oldest of twenty such towns in the west established by blacks. In 1878 large printed sheets (broadsides) were posted by the Edgefield Real Estate and Homestead Association in Nashville urging black citizens to join the western migration. This movement was led by former slaves Benjamin Singleton of Davidson County, along with Reverend Columbus M. Johnson of Sumner County and Abram Smith of Nashville. Singleton and the association raised funds and transported thousands of blacks to Kansas.[50] Two freedmen from Wessyngton, Henry and Susan Washington (Emanuel Washington's sister), joined the western migration and settled their families in Topeka, Kansas. So many of Singleton's migrants settled in the northern suburbs of Topeka that it became known as "Tennessee Town."

The freedmen held various occupations. They were ministers, porters, railroad workers, store owners, bakers, tailors, nurses, cooks, brick masons, barbers, teachers, Fisk University students, plasterers, carpenters, painters, elevator operators, shoemakers, chauffeurs, bartenders, seamstresses, hostlers, grocers, restaurant owners, butchers, blacksmiths, jockeys, laundresses, steamboat men, hucksters, candy makers, and day laborers. The doors of opportunity opened, and they walked through them.

CHAPTER 14

In Their Own Words

O ver the years, I made many visits to Wessyngton Plantation, but my research continued in spurts. My obligations as a student in high school and in college, and then working full time meant that my research would slow down but never quite stop. Any free moment was devoted to going to our local library, only five minutes away, and jotting down the slightest bit of data or any remote lead and saving it until I had the opportunity for further exploration. Census data, various old records, and even dead ends would often lead me back to some of the elders for answers, which they could usually give me. At times it seemed that I worked on it nonstop. Luckily, I don't need much sleep!

When I finally got my driver's license, my parents were relieved. They no longer had to take me on my roots-tracing adventures. At that point, my mother would let me borrow her car or my father would let me use his truck. I am one of three children; but my brother and sister were fifteen and fourteen years older than me, so I grew up very close to their children who were nearer to my age. On the weekends I had my father's truck I would take my nieces, nephews, and some of their friends for rides in the country, just as my grandfather did when I was little. We'd have a great time. I took them swimming to a nearby creek and even got a small raft for them. Sometimes we would cook out or just ride. They rarely paid any attention to where we were going. They were too busy laughing and joking, talking or just having a good time being a kid, I suppose. I often stopped and asked if they knew how to get back home, and they never did. One day I decided to take them to Wessyngton so they would know the history of our family and know where we came from. Before we left home I told them to pay close attention which way we were going because I was taking them to a place where our ancestors came from and they needed to know how to get there when I was gone so they could show their children. This time they seemed to pay close attention to every detail of our trip. We finally reached Wessyngton and drove up to the mansion. I showed them the grounds, the slave cabins where our ancestors once lived, and the slave cemetery. They were in awe, knowing that our history went back to this place so many years ago. As we were leaving, I told them they would have to bring their children here and not let them forget the history of our family. Years later, I took their children to Wessyngton too and told them about our family's history. I hope I will be around to take the next generation. Several of my great-nephews go there often with me and joined me in one television interview.

———•———

As time passed and the word spread, more people found out about my work. A number of people who had ties to Wessyngton approached me. They shared the stories their ancestors had passed to them in their own words. Some even had portraits and photographs of their parents or grandparents who had been enslaved there. It was astonishing to see actual likenesses of some of the people I had learned about during my research. Often the image seemed to match how I imagined their personalities were. The pictures and portraits were priceless and were in many cases the sole copy. I tried to persuade the owners of these precious photos to let me copy them and spread them throughout the families in case something were to ever happen to the originals. Most everyone agreed. I remember my great-aunt Maggie Washington, then in her nineties, showing me a group family photo that had been taken when she was three or four years old. I asked her if I could take it and have a copy made of it. She always complied with anything I asked but insisted on going to the photo shop with me. She showed the clerk her picture as a child and told him to be very careful with it. She was delighted when she got an enlarged copy. She was supportive of my research and very proud of it. At one family reunion at her home, she insisted that a collection be taken up for me for the family trees and information on our family I had provided. I didn't want her to do it, but she insisted. She stated boldly, "Listen, now I have made up my mind and that's what I'm going to do."

John Polk (1861–1909) and Mary Lewis Polk (1863–1946) and family, ca. 1908. Front row: Mary Lewis Polk, Henry Polk (baby), John Polk, Maggie Polk [Washington], Rachel Polk [Dowlen]. Back row: George Polk, Walter Polk, Arthur Polk, and William Polk.

She was a true matriarch, and whatever she said to do, the whole family did with no questions asked.

There were thousands of documents in the Washington Family Papers, but they still could not answer all my questions. I wanted to find out about the personal lives of some of the slaves, so I asked their closest descendants. No matter how busy I was, I always made time to spend time with anyone who had a story to tell me.

My great-aunt Maggie Polk Washington was a constant source of information and inspiration until her death on August 27, 2003, at age ninety-nine, and was the last of the original group of people whom I have interviewed since the beginning of my research. Aunt Mag possessed an extraordinary memory, knew how nearly everyone in the area was related to each other, and could recall events from her childhood to old age with remarkable accuracy. Aunt Mag was well known throughout the area for being a person who would speak her mind and tell you exactly how it was, no matter who you were or thought you were. She was also well known for her cooking. Each time I visited, she offered me a piece of cake, pie, homemade preserves, or ketchup (homemade sweet relish). I always looked forward to our Washington family reunions held at her home. Her greens and cornbread was a favorite of mine too. When I told her once that her cornbread was good as cake, she laughed and remarked, "That's funny you should say that because your grandfather Joe Cobbs told your grandmother the same thing when they first married. You know, when it comes right down to it, you can't hardly beat me cooking some things."

I replied, "Most things."

She smiled and chuckled in agreement. During the Christmas holidays she always set aside some apple cake and jam cake for me. We were very close, and I really miss visiting with her and listening to her stories.

Over the years, I interviewed her numerous times about the history of Wessyngton and various families. She often told me stories that she had been told as a child by former slaves or their children. Her mother was born at Wessyngton during the Civil War.

Not only was Aunt Mag a tremendous help to me with genealogy and history, she also assisted others who sought my help. As a genealogist and historian, many people from all over the country who have Robertson County roots often contact me about their ancestors. I would then go to my aunt's house, less than five minutes away, and ask her how different people were related. Ninety percent of the time she could tell me right off the top of her head. On the few occasions she could not remember right away, she would say, "Let me think about it and I will call you." Many times before I reached home, she would call and say she remembered what I had asked her. One good thing about her was that she provided information not found in mere census records and often had personal stories to tell or described their personalities. I was amazed many times because some of the same personalities she described in the earlier generation I could see in their descendants. Some things never change.

Maggie Polk Washington, 1904–2003

I'm Maggie Polk Washington, the daughter of John and Mary Lewis Polk. My mama was born at Washington. Grandpap John Lewis, his mother, Caroline, and his sisters were given to the Washingtons from the Lewises in Nashville. My mama's mother was named Minerva Washington; she was born at Washington too. Minerva's mother, Sally, and grandmother, Esther, were inherited by Joseph Washington in 1819 from his brother's estate.

Grandpap had a brother Jim who was sold on the block by his owners, not the Washingtons, and was never seen or heard from again. I was told that he was very muscular and brought lots of money when he was sold. The old people used to tell us all kinds of tales about slavery when we were little.

The Washingtons owned many slaves, and they went by different names such as Lewis, Gardner, Scott, Terry, and Washington, but they all came from down there at that Washington farm. The way slaves were bought and sold, it was hard to keep up with just how everyone was kin, but I was told the Washingtons didn't sell their slaves. When the slaves were first freed, some of them stayed on the plantation and some of them bought farms of their own. My mama's daddy, John Lewis, owned a farm that once had been part of Washington and so did Joe Scott and Wiley, Sellie, and Richard Terry. When I was a child lots of blacks owned their own land, more so than they do now. Areas around Mt. Herman, Cedar Hill, Turnersville, and Fisers was like a black town. The Pitts owned lots of land.

One time when I was young, I was working for a white lady. The lady told me, "My father had lost everything he had when the Civil War broke out because he had just bought some colored people and never got a chance to work them." I told her, "He had no business buying people in the first place and that was good enough for him that he lost everything." The lady replied, "Maggie, that's just the way things were back then." I told her, "It would never happen again because this new generation sure wouldn't stand for it."

My family sharecropped on a farm in Coopertown, Tennessee. When the man who owned the farm died, his widow let my father run the farm for the most part. After Daddy died in 1909, the widow felt since she had young sons, and my mother had sons of the same age, they would not get along well enough to operate the farm together.

My mother had no choice but to move her family to her father's farm in Turnersville. I attended Scott's School and Sandy Springs School while living in the Turnersville area. My grandfather's farm had a small family cemetery where my grandparents, my father, and brothers William and Arthur, and other family members were buried. His farm was just about one hundred acres. After my grandfather's death, the farm went to my uncle Ed Lewis.

I married Bob Washington in 1921 and we raised a family of thirteen children. [Bob was my grandmother's older brother.] We sharecropped on several farms throughout Robertson and Summer counties. We worked hard but had a good life raising our children. My mother taught me to cook when I was a little girl. Her mother was a cook at Washington at one time too. My mother taught me how to make quilts. I love to make quilts and give them as gifts.

Aunt Mag gave quilts to nearly everyone in our Washington family—for birthdays, wedding gifts, and Christmas, or just to be giving them. She gave quilts to many friends. At her funeral, one minister asked to see a show of hands of those people who had been given one of her quilts, and the majority of the congregation raised their hand. She was always active in church and many social activities in Springfield. She was somewhat of a celebrity, being one of the county's oldest citizens who was still so active. Aunt Mag often remarked, "You know, I'm just about the oldest thing in Springfield now that's still on the go." She was always very proud of her family. Aunt Mag had acquired hundreds of friends, extended family, and acquaintances after living nearly a century.

At the conclusion of her ninetieth-birthday celebration, she told us, "I'll see all of y'all in ten years," and laughed. In her later years, I always reminded her that she could not leave us until she at least made it to one hundred as she promised. She replied, "I guess I will just have to stay here because you are determined to make me stay here one hundred years." During my last visit with her, five months before her death at ninety-nine, she declared, "Well, you know, I may not make it to a hundred, but I sure put a good dent in it!" I dearly miss her.

When I first started the research on Wessyngton, I attended the Greater South Baptist Church in Springfield, only a few blocks from my house. Then the church was composed of three main families: the Gardners, Yateses, and Dowlens. The Gardners' and the Yateses' ancestry through the Lewis family came from Wessyngton. Reverend Sam Gardner was the patriarch of a very large family, most of whom attended the church, and Mrs. Goldena Lewis Yates's family was there as well. The original church started in the home of Mrs. Yates's parents, Will Lewis and Eliza Scott Lewis. While waiting for afternoon services I would often talk with Mrs. Yates, Reverend Gardner, and Miss Matt Terry about their ancestors at Wessyngton. The three of them were related through the Lewis family line. Each one would take a turn telling me about their ancestry while the others would sit quietly and listen or nod their heads in agreement as they recalled a similar story.

Reverend Sam Gardner, 1901–1999

I'm Reverend Sam Gardner, I was born in Robertson County, Tennessee, in 1901. My father and mother was Will Gardner and Etta Pennington Gardner. My grandmother on my mother's side was Mariah Lewis, her mother's name was Caroline.

My granddaddy Daniel Gardner, according to what was passed down in my family, was bought by the Washingtons when he was a young child along with his parents and two younger brothers. They always told us that the Gardners would not let the Washingtons buy them unless they could keep the Gardner name. That's why we are Gardners today, but we are really supposed to be Washingtons. The slaves usually took the last name of whoever owned 'em back in slavery times, but our family didn't because they had been with the Gardners who brought them out here from Virginia. It was a whole lot

Daniel Gardner (1829–1911),
portrait.

of slaves down there at Washington. Your people came from down there too.

When I was a child, I lived next door to my granddaddy Daniel and used to go to his house every morning and drink coffee with 'im. Grandpa Dan'l had zigzagged whip marks all over his back from whippings he got back in slavery times when he was on the Washington farm. Boy, times were rough back then, thank the Lord all that can't happen no mo'. Grandpa Dan'l and Grandma Melissy had eighteen chillun. Grandpa Dan'l's brother George Gardner owned a farm of about ninety acres in the Fiser community near Kinneys that he willed to Papa. The land stayed in our family for a while and Papa lost it during the Depression like lots of folks did.

There's a church on some property out at Fisers that some white people gave to our family to have church. As long as there's a Gardner living, we still have access to it. The church membership kept getting smaller until they stopped havin' regular services there, but at one time all the Gardners would get together and go once a year.

My wife, Odell Scott Gardner, and I had twelve chillun in all, including three sets of twins. So you see, I have a big family and I'm kin to nearly everybody in town. Me and Goldena and Matt Terry are all kinfolks.

We've been having a Gardner family reunion every year since 1935 and never missed having one yet. You never seen so many people. We've got a big family and you can tell they're all Gardners. We have the reunion on the third Sunday in August.

After Reverend Gardner told me the story about his ancestors that had been handed down for generations, I searched through the Washington Family Papers and found an 1839 slave bill of sale that listed five slaves; Aaron, his wife, Betty, and their three sons: Dan-

Daniel Gardner and family. Front row, second from left: Amy Gardner; center: Daniel Gardner; and Bessie Gardner next to Daniel.

iel, George, and Jackson. They were purchased from the estate of Henry Gardner for $2,270. Gardner's will stipulated that the slaves were to be sold at a private sale and they were not to be sold "down river"—meaning to the Deep South. I was very excited to tell Reverend Gardner what I had found, and he was thrilled. He knew the names of his uncles George and Jackson but did not know the names of his great-grandparents. "If it wasn't for you, I never would have known their names in this life," he exclaimed. Sadly, the story of his grandfather getting whipped was also confirmed in the documents. Apparently, Daniel and his brother George were very defiant and ran away several times and were whipped when they were captured. I found this information after Reverend Gardner died.

Lewis family. Front row: John T. Lewis, Eliza Scott Lewis (1875–1952), Will Lewis (1870–1960), Goldena Lewis Yates.
Back row: James Lewis, Jesse Lewis, Sarah Lewis, Ezadean "Bezo" Lewis, Fannie Lewis Fort, Joe Lewis, Alice Lewis Buchanan.

Goldena Lewis Yates, 1905–1991

My name is Goldena Lewis Yates. I'm the daughter of Will Lewis and Eliza Scott Lewis. My father's parents, John Lewis and Minerva Washington Lewis, were Washington slaves. My grandfather bought a large farm that was once part of the Washington estate.

My mother's parents were Joseph Scott and Fannie Biggers Scott. My grandfather on mother's side was a slave down at Washington too. He told me that he used to help the mistress, Mary Cheatham Washington, in the flower gardens at Washington when he was just a young boy. He said that he was well treated as a slave and was very young when he was freed. He said Washington was the largest plantation there was, and they had over two hundred slaves.

After my granddaddy Joe Scott was set free, he sharecropped on the plantation until he bought his own farm that was once

Joseph Scott (1843–1932), and
Fannie Biggers Scott
(1843–1928).

part of the farm he was a slave on. He was a preacher too. A part of his land is near a family and community graveyard called Scott's Chapel Cemetery. Several of the former Washington slaves are buried there. The earliest marked grave there is about 1880.

When I was small, our family moved to the community near Fairview Baptist Church, about twenty-five miles away, to share-crop, and we didn't get to see Grandpap and Grandma but once or twice a year as the trip back to Turnersville took nearly all day long in a horse and buggy. So when we went back to visit, we stayed several days.

As a youth I was in church for nearly every service, especially singings, and rarely missed a Sunday. Our church at that time visited other churches for joint worship services. On one occasion we visited the Antioch Baptist Church in Turnersville. The church was founded in 1869 by former Wessyngton slaves and others in the community. Its first pastor, Edmund White Washington, was a Wessyngton slave. At the time there were several members of the church who descended from Washington slaves. One of them was Deacon Henry Polk.

Henry Polk, 1907–1990

I remember lots of people when I was a child that had been slaves; in fact, most of the older people when I was coming up had been enslaved. My mama was born just before slavery times were over. Those people back then had a hard time. They had to work from Can't to Can't. It would be so dark when they went to the fields you couldn't see and so dark when they finished you couldn't see. Wasn't no calling out sick either. I guess they would have killed me. Some of them were treated pretty good and others were very mean to them. Thank the Good Lord it's all over now. Some of those slaves did pretty well after they got free to have come up under all they went through. Several besides my grandfather John Lewis owned their own farms. Ol' man Joe Scott, Wiley Terry, and several others who had been slaves down there at Washington owned their own places. They tell me they had so many slaves down at Washington that it looked like a black town. After slavery a whole lot of them stayed there and sharecropped, and white families did too.

I've been a deacon here at Antioch for years. The old folks used to tell me that some of the slaves from Washington and others built it shortly after they were set free. Most of the Lewises attended the church and went to the Antioch School. Some of them are buried in the church cemetery. You know the church burned several times. I remember when Uncle Ed Lewis died in the winter of 1951 and during his burial, a white man came up and interrupted the burial and asked some of the men to push his car out of a ditch. Uncle Ed's son, that they called Gander Lewis, gave the man a good cussing for disturbing the service. Later that night the church burned to the ground. We couldn't ever prove it, but I know that man did it.

He concluded, "I think you're doing a mighty fine job looking up all this history. Our people need to know what all those people went through back then for us to get to where we are now, especially the young folks."

Mr. Polk told me if he could help me in any way with the research to be sure to come visit him. At the time he and his wife lived on the next street behind my home. Mr. Polk's wife, Lula Williams Polk, also had ancestral ties to Wessyngton from the Terry, Williams, and Washington families.

Whenever I spent time with members of the senior generation, I felt that I was on the receiving end since I was learning so much. Aunt Mag looked at me and my life differently and constantly encouraged me to pursue my research. She often told me, "I don't care what anybody says, the Lord meant for you to do all this. Look at all the Washingtons and others that have come along long before you and gone and never thought about this. This story had to be told before the end of time about what our people went through and He sent you to do it."

CHAPTER 15

The Church in the Hollow

———•·•———

George A. Washington rebounded in the postwar years. Due to time spent in New York during the Civil War by himself and with Major William B. Lewis, and afterwards in New York with Jane, George mastered the skills necessary to successfully invest in stocks, bonds, and treasury notes.[1] George served as a Democratic representative in the Tennessee House of Representatives for Robertson County in 1873 and became even wealthier than before the war. Years later the *Nashville Banner* wrote that when "Tennessee bonds were at their lowest, and could find few takers [during the Panic of 1873], Col. Washington purchased $950,000 of the bonds and his confidence in the credit of his native State helped to tide her credit over a dark period of her financial history."[2] In 1891 he held more than $1 million in stocks and bonds, including large blocks of shares of the Nashville, Chattanooga & St. Louis Railroad; the Louisville & Nashville Railroad as well as other railroads; and various banking institutions.[3] He conducted business with banks in Nashville and credit houses in New Orleans and Philadelphia. In New York he dealt with the United States Trust Company of New York (a subsidiary of U.S. Trust), the Bank of New York, and the Bank of Manhattan (a predecessor of JPMorgan Chase). By 1892 George's land holdings were only about 7,188 acres; he had gifted George A. Washington Jr. 1,192 acres in 1888, and as time passed, he sold more land, including parcels to some of the freedmen.

George took an active part in the Edgefield & Kentucky Railroad and served as president in the early 1870s. He served as a director and vice president of the Louisville & Nashville Railroad Company (L&N Railroad) after it merged with Edgefield & Kentucky. He was one of the original stockholders in the Nashville, Chattanooga & St. Louis Railroad in 1881 and later a director of the company.[4] Even as influential as George was, the local railroad never did go through Wessyngton.[5] George looked for new opportunities to invest in Tennessee's future and the new industrialization taking over America. In 1852, the Tennessee Coal, Iron & Railroad Company was founded in Nashville and after the war became a leading manufacturer of steel. George served as one of its directors in the 1880s. The company expanded so much that it was chosen as one of the ten stocks that made up the first Dow Industrial Average index in 1896.[6]

The lives of the Washingtons were those of the very wealthy. The house was maintained by a large staff of servants. George's daughter Lucy Washington Helm described her life and her relationships with the servants whom she had known all her life:

The housekeeper, whom I can remember, wore in the early mornings the cleanest and stiffest of cotton dresses. After her morning duties were attended to, she dressed as an English housekeeper in a full black silk dress with the white embroidered collar and wore gold hoop earrings. She was a rather large woman, very light in color and had straight raven black hair. A bunch of keys was always at her belt. I remember her well. We had two nurses: one for the baby and one for the older children. My father's valet, Granville, my grandmother's coachman, a dining room man, my mother's maid, Louisa, whom I insisted on calling "Cousin Louisa," because the Negroes called her that, chamber maids, a dining-room maid, yard men, and gardeners were our other servants.[7]

. . . We, living as we did on the big place, were reared like English children. We had teachers from the East and Europe, a northern woman for English, etc., and a European for languages and music. There was a dear old lady who had known better days living in a village a few miles from us. She made our clothes and kept house and was our comfort when our mother was away. . . . I was always in difficulties with the governesses from the North. They were strict and New England and did not know the South or a Southern child's love of Negroes. So what we didn't eat at one meal we had to eat at the next. No Negro or Southern child could understand that. So, if we were sent to bed without supper, some one of our colored friends would slip up to our bedroom window on the upper porch and knock gently on the window and in a quiet voice call to us. Whenever I could slip off in the evening after supper, I managed to get down to "Uncle" Joe and "Aunt" Amy's room to sit with them by a big fire, and have "Uncle" Joe tell me stories. Sooner or later I was yanked upstairs. The two old servants had a basement room under the dining room. We had a lovely free childhood anyway, in spite of New England rules and ideas. While we were young we went for long walks through the woods, over creeks with swinging bridges—our joy but the terror of governesses who only knew the city.[8]

George and Jane's children married people from similar social and economic backgrounds.[9] Their spouses were from the area around Wessyngton, Nashville, and other Southern states. Martha Jackson married Judge George Newton Tillman of nearby Bedford County, and Mary married James Stokes Frazer, who was the law partner of Jacob McGavock Dickinson, the president of the Tennessee Bar Association (1889–1893), later the counsel for the Alaska Boundary Tribunal (1903), and Secretary of War under President Taft (1909 to 1911). James's sister, Sallie Murfree Frazer, married J. Hart Hillman, the founder of the Hillman dynasty. Bessie Adelaide married Atlanta judge Henry Bethune Tompkins. Lucy Amelia's husband was John Larue Helm II, the son of the governor of Kentucky (1850–1854 and 1867). John Helm Sr. had been president of the Louisville & Nashville Railroad from 1854 to 1860 and was credited with bringing the railroad into operation between Nashville and Louisville. Jane Augusta married Felix Grundy Ewing from the prominent Ewing family of Nashville, related by marriage to the Grundy and McGavock families. George A. Washington Jr., a widower, was married to Marina "Queenie" Woods of Nashville, whose grandmother was a Cheatham.

Joseph graduated from Vanderbilt University in Nashville in 1874. He served in the Tennessee legislature from 1877 to 1879 and then as a member of the U.S. Congress from 1887 to 1897 as the Democratic representative from Robertson County district. In 1879 Joseph married Mary Bolling Kemp of Gloucester County, Virginia. Joseph's ancestors were personal friends of her family in the 1840s.[10] They had four children: George Augustine II (1879), Anne Bolling (1882), Joseph Edwin, Jr. (1883), and Elizabeth Wyndham (1888).

Although the former slaves obtained their freedom, they still faced hostility from local white citizens. The rising political power of the blacks and the Republicans caused a violent reaction from Democratic whites who believed that the Radical Republicans were taking racial equality too far, too fast. White vigilante groups called Regulators burned freedmen's schoolhouses, churches, homes, destroyed crops, maimed draft animals, and lynched black leaders. Poor whites who resented blacks and blamed their difficult eco-

nomic circumstances on the former slaves comprised these groups.
Due to wealthy slave owners purchasing the best and most fertile
lands, poor whites were left with land of the poorest quality, if any
at all. Poor whites lived in conditions far worse than many former slaves, especially servants of the wealthy. After emancipation,
many whites sought to take out their frustrations on the blacks,
since they could not do so when the blacks were enslaved. Jane
Washington wrote about some of the violence toward blacks:

> We have never found out who burned the old house at
> the Frey place, but suppose some of the neighbors burnt
> it to keep that old Negro from going there. There have
> been several houses burnt in this county that were to be
> occupied by Negroes, and a great many notices stuck
> up at cross roads and public places warning those who
> employed Negroes that they would be burnt out if they
> worked for a part of the crop. The most of the citizens are
> opposed to these "Regulators," as they call themselves,
> and I do not think they will do much more mischief.[11]

Jane was wrong in her assumption that the "Regulators" would not
do any more mischief. Several freedmen in Robertson and Sumner
counties were assaulted, threatened, raped, and murdered in the
years immediately following the war. In 1866 the freedman Henry
Willis of Robertson County reported to the Freedmen's Bureau
that a group of three armed whites attacked his family, sexually
assaulted his twelve-year-old sister Mandy, and burned the home
of his parents after robbing them. Willis also stated that the group
had gone throughout the county and killed several black men who
were Union soldiers.

A few months later, Eliza Jane Ellison, a freedwoman of Cross
Plains (twenty miles from Wessyngton) was killed by Dr. L. B. Walton. Ellison worked for the Walton family and demanded money
from Walton's wife for doing extra washing not included in her

freedmen's labor contract. Mrs. Walton refused to pay and stated that she should do what she was asked. An argument ensued between Mrs. Walton and Eliza Jane. Dr. Walton then came on the scene, cursed Eliza Jane, and ordered her off the premises. Eliza refused, stating that she had a contract to work for twelve months and would leave at the expiration of the contract. Walton then drew his pistol and shot Eliza through the abdomen, and she died the following day. He was cleared of all charges.[12]

In 1867 the "Regulators" put up posters in Robertson and Summer counties citing warnings to blacks and whites who violated the following rules and regulations:

1st • No man shall squat Negroes on his place unless they are all under his employ male and female.

2nd • Negro women shall be employed by white persons.

3rd • All children shall be hired out for something.

4th • Negroes found in cabins to themselves shall suffer the penalty.

5th • Negroes shall not be allowed to hire Negroes.

6th • Idle men, women or children, shall suffer the penalty.

7th • All white men found with Negroes in secret places shall be dealt with and those that hire Negroes must pay promptly and act with good faith to the Negroes. I will make the Negro do his part, and the white man must too.

8th • For the first offence is one hundred lashes, the second is looking up a sapling [hanging].

9th • This I do for the benefit of all young or old, high and tall, black and white, anyone that may not like these rules can try their luck, and see whether or not I will be found doing my duty.

10th • Negroes found stealing from anyone or taking from their employers to other Negroes, death is the first penalty.

11th • Running about late of nights shall be strictly dealt with.

12th • White man and Negro, I am everywhere, I have friends in every place, do your duty and I will have but little to do.[13]

Similar incidents were perpetrated against blacks throughout Tennessee and the South with little protection or recourse. Lucy recalled the county being in a state of turmoil and lawlessness following the war:

Well, finally the war ended and the reconstruction and carpetbag rule were in. Things got completely out of hand in our county. Bushwhackers, as they were called, made up of bands of murderers and thieves, terrorized the people. Finally they got so bold that a man named Whitehead, who was their leader, lay behind a log and shot a leading citizen riding home from the county seat one evening. He was on horseback with his little boy behind him. They shot him, and the little boy was sprinkled with his father's blood. The community and law seemed paralyzed. My father, as always, came to the front. He went to New York and at his own expense hired Pinkerton's men, brought them out, and tracked and brought to justice these creatures. As soon as he took the work in hand, they sent him word if he didn't stop his prosecution, they would shoot him on sight. During that time we were never allowed to answer anyone who came and asked us to tell where our father was, for fear it was one of Whitehead's gang. When the leaders were arrested and taken to the county seat for trial, my father had to be there every day of the trial. He would leave Wessyngton before dark, and usually return after ten at night. The road was a lonely one, and he had the knowledge that men were lying in ambush to wait for him; yet he never gave any evidence of fear.[14]

Order was eventually restored in Robertson County by 1870.

In addition to adapting to a new economic system, the freedmen were living under new social institutions and structures. The Freedmen's Bureau aided them in solemnizing their marriages, which had taken place during slavery. Tennessee enacted a law in 1866 that stated all persons of color who were living together as husband and wife in the state while in slavery were declared to be man and wife, and their children legitimately entitled to inherit property acquired by their parents, to as full an extent as the children of white citizens.[15]

According to the 1866 law, anyone with multiple spouses had to choose which would be his or her partner. Due to the dissolution of slave marriages by sale of a partner and slaves remarrying, a number of the freedmen found themselves with multiple families and spouses. It was not uncommon for a slave to have been sold and married several times. When the slaves were freed, many of them located spouses from whom they had been separated for years. They faced major problems relating to their marriages as former spouses reappeared in their lives.

Several Southern states such as Alabama, Mississippi, Florida, Georgia, and Virginia passed a series of laws regarding former slaves and the status of their marriages. In August 1865 Mansfield French drew up for the Freedmen's Bureau rules meant to deal with ex-slaves who had more than one living spouse, but civil marriage laws quickly superseded them. Georgia ex-slaves with two or more reputed spouses had to select one immediately or face prosecution for adultery and fornication. The South Carolina law allowed ex-slaves three months to make a similar choice.[16]

Anxious to have their marriages legalized, freedmen flocked to the Freedmen's Bureau in scores. Several former Wessyngton slaves indicated to census takers in 1900 that they had been married in excess of forty years. Often there were so many freedmen seeking marriage that bureau officials performed mass wedding ceremonies. The bureau licensed black ministers to perform marriages.

When a freedmen couple was married, they were issued a certificate, and their marriage was recorded in registers that were later sent to the bureau's headquarters. The registers included the names and ages of the couples, their complexion, and those of their parents, the number of years both spouses lived with another person, the cause of separation (such as a sale), and the number of children they had together and from previous marriages.

Granville Washington and Irene Lewis were two of the first freedmen in the county to marry in 1865. Granville's first wife, Malinda, whom he had married during slavery, married Jackson Gardner Washington.

Clara Washington (1832–1925), a former Wessyngton slave, applied for military benefits of her husband, Reuben Cheatham Washington in 1908. She stated in the application that she and Reuben were married in the 1840s by a black minister, Reverend Horace Carr. Clara and Reuben were married again by the Freedmen's Bureau agent D. D. Holman at Wessyngton in 1866. Holman probably married several couples, as it was unlikely that he made a trip to Wessyngton from Springfield to marry only one couple. Holman married 451 couples and recorded them in a register. He also recorded the couple's ages, the names and ages of all their children, and the date of the marriage certificate. The freedmen paid $1.25 for the certificate. In addition, many freedmen in Robertson County were married by local officials. In some areas in Tennessee the Freedmen's Bureau performed marriages because white officials refused to do so.

———•◦•———

Despite the threat of physical abuse and loss of life, the freedmen in the area pushed forward to take advantage of all the rights freedom had promised. Their goal was to achieve full citizenship. In

Tennessee, African Americans were given the right to vote in local elections in 1867. Black Tennesseans voted in their first presidential election during the November 1868 election and cast almost all their votes for General U. S. Grant. The Fifteenth Amendment to the U.S. Constitution, passed on February 3, 1870, gave them the right to vote in national elections.

Most white citizens felt that the freedmen were given too many liberties too soon. Jane wrote Joseph that every man on the place who was over twenty-one was registered to vote, but they did not do so in the November 1866 election. In her view, "The election passed off quietly, all going one way, but strange to say, not a Negro on this place went to vote; they were all too busy. I suppose the mule and the forty acres not being forthcoming last summer, they rather 'smelt a mice' and concluded that a day's work at home would be more profitable."[17] Jane expressed her own fears and concerns:

> Our enlightened and refined legislature have just passed
> a law giving every Negro fellow over twenty-one the right
> to vote and as the franchise law passed last year excludes
> two thirds of the white men from the polls, we are at the
> mercy of the Radicals and Negroes; combined a pleasant
> prospect for a man, who once was free![18]

The freedmen were indeed frustrated with the political system and the many unfulfilled promises made to them, including the rumored forty acres and a mule. Nevertheless, they voted in all the succeeding elections. Blacks in Robertson County made up the largest majority of the Republican Party. Few whites belonged to the "Grand Old Party," and those who did had fought for the North or sympathized with the North during the Civil War.

Freedmen experienced repercussions for exercising their new rights in those early elections but still they participated. William Hilliard and W. N. Jamison of Springfield were fired by their employers for voting.[19] Scores of freedmen were fired from their jobs in Nashville for voting the Radical ticket in an election held in August 1867. Still, as a result of their new political power, black Tennesseans gained several public offices and enjoyed a relationship with the Republican Party for more than three generations after emancipation. Through the 1880s, blacks in Nashville and other towns held city and county positions including being magistrates and justices of the peace.[20] Henry "Cat" Thomas was the leader of the black Republicans in Robertson County. He was born a slave and joined the Union Army in 1861 and came to Springfield with the USCT regiment commanded by Colonel Thomas Downey. Henry Thomas was known for saying that "he came to Springfield 'with freedom in one hand and a spelling book in the other.'" Thomas remained in Springfield, where he championed "the education of the freedmen and black political action."[21] Political meetings were important events; in 1870, according to young Mary Washington, "There was a large Negro Meeting at Turnersville and I believe every one went that was able."[22]

Another indispensable matter for the freedmen was education. They faced many obstacles throughout the South in trying to educate themselves and their children. This only made many of them even more determined to get an education. The Freedmen's Bureau assisted in organizing schools in Robertson County. No whites objected to the establishment of schools for the black children near Wessyngton. However, when a school was opened in Springfield in 1865, "Fellows of the baser sort" broke up the benches, knocked down the door, and gave the instructor "such broad hints" of visiting him with their wrath, he left town.[23] Bureau agent D. D. Holman reported in June 1866: "One school of thirty scholars was taught two months by a very faithful and Praiseworthy lady from Ohio—she was however unable to obtain support and the school is discontinued. There has been no interference with the school and public sentiment is reported as in favor of educating the Colored people."[24]

The Highland School opened shortly after the close of the Civil War in Robertson County. Missionaries came from the border of Kentucky into this area of Tennessee to teach the freedmen. During the summer months school sessions were held in an open field.

White members of rural communities sometimes donated land on which black schools were built. Daniel Fiser deeded land to the board of education of the Eighth District in 1869 to be used as a "school house for Colored children." This institution was known as Fiser's School. The Fiser family had been among the first in the county to emancipate their slaves.

The first black school in Turnersville (Antioch School) was in session by January 1869. Mary described the event to Joseph while he was in Georgetown attending college:

> The Negro school in Turnersville is in full blast. Gran-
> ville has brought Lawson back from Springfield [where
> he boarded and had to pay fifty cents per month for his
> schooling] and he, with Minerva's [Lewis] two children,
> Sampson and Harriet went last week and this week Allen's
> [Washington] two, Gabe and Loney [Maloni], are to go.
> Man [Emanuel Washington] expects to send his children
> [General, Grundy, Winnie, Cornelia] before long.[25]

In 1869 Jane reported that Preacher Edmund (Edmund White Washington), Melissa's husband, "has entered as a scholar and Tilla and Margaret are talking about going also. I believe Grantz [Granville's son by Irene Lewis] is to go in warm weather. They pay one dollar per month."[26]

Although they were adults when the Turnersville School started, Tilla and Margaret still felt the importance of getting an education.

Pastor Edmund White Washington moved from student to teacher and was assisted by Matilda (Washington) and his wife, Melissa. Miss Lula Young, one of the Fisk Jubilee Singers from Nashville, was the first trained teacher at the school. Professor Taylor Fisk, who was also from Fisk University, succeeded Miss Young. The fee to attend the school increased over time to $1.50 per month. The school term was only two months each year, since most students, especially the boys, had to work in the fields. Paying $1 per month for their children to attend the school was a great sacrifice, considering most freedmen earned only 50¢ per day for their labor. But they realized the value of education and gladly paid it.

In 1872 Jane expressed concern that the whites were planning to make a strong fight against a proposed school tax:

> I fear a pretty heavy one [tax] will be assessed for the Radicals [the newly empowered Republicans] are all bent on that point, and they want to raise it by taxing lands more than anything else. The Negroes will be the greatest beneficiaries, particularly in the country for where they are scattered as they are here, they will be obliged to have mixed schools, and as a consequence, the whites will stay at home, for you know a Negro will go to school whenever he has a chance and modesty will not restrain them from pushing forward.[27]

The first free school session (Antioch School in Turnersville) was held in 1873 to 1874 and was taught by Miss Tennie Grant of Nashville. The teacher paid no board and was housed with different families who volunteered for the honor.

The freedmen's new status also affected the religious life of the community. After emancipation most whites no longer wanted black members in their congregations and therefore helped them establish their own churches. Many churches and their members deeded land to the freedmen to build their own churches. Many of these deeds stipulated the ownership of the land would revert back to the original owner if the land were used for any purpose other than worship.

The church was the focal point of nearly all activity for blacks because it was the only institution where they were totally free from white surveillance. The church was much more than a mere building for worship. It was a place for self-improvement where members learned to speak before the public and participate in biblical debates, and where children learned to recite poems. It served as a meeting place for the black community to organize and discuss political and social issues. The church served as a shelter for any members who could have lost their homes due to fire or any other unfortunate incident, and it was a place of refuge where members could help comfort each other through difficult times.

Jane described the blacks' religious devotion:

> This is [her daughter] Mary's thirteenth birthday and
> to celebrate it even more than usual, she and Hannah

*Baptism in Sulphur Fork Creek, near Wessyngton
Plantation, ca. 1890s.*

cooked the dinner. Perhaps you would like to know why, well, I will tell you, there was a grand Negro preaching and baptizing in Turnersville today, and every Negro on the place, I believe except Old Hannah and Prudy, went, and among the rest, Man [Emanuel, the cook]. So Mary got dinner and did pretty well, with roast mutton, sweet and Irish potatoes, rice and corn and a pound cake and boiled custard for dessert, the latter Miss Susie made. Mrs. Baxter and Lucy rode over to Turnersville, this morning, and Mrs. Baxter says there were at least forty Negroes soused under the water, and "Washingtons," of course, largely outnumbered the others; John, Allen, and Mavern from here, and as your grandmother would say the whole "Kit and Tuckin" from the Dortch Place even, to the Vanhooks and Old Fat Lucy [Lucy Lewis Van-hook] went in like ducks.[28]

Jane then reported that they built a church also used as a school:

The negroes have erected a church at Turnersville and now they are having a school taught over there by a negro, Tom Carr by name, who used to belong to James Darden's sister. I believe everything that can walk is going from here, at least Billy Wynne says so, and he ought to know for they say he has been trying to persuade the negroes to go themselves and to send their children. Peggy [Gilly Lewis Washington's sister] tells the [Washington] children that she is not going to such a school as that, for her mama is getting her clothes ready to send her to a boarding school in Nashville.[29]

In 1869 some of the former Wessyngton slaves and other blacks in the community named the church Antioch, which was one of the first black Baptist churches in Robertson County. Antioch Baptist Church opened on the second Sunday in June 1869, with the assistance of Cindy Clinard and Mary Connell along with their pastor.[30] The first church site was about seven miles south of Cedar Hill in the community of Turnersville. The land was donated by Oliver Darden, a freedman, and was referred to as "the church in the hollow." Whites from nearby farms donated the logs used to build the church. Blacks and whites in the community cut and hauled the logs to the mill. Religious fervor was so high that Reverend Althus Carr, Reverend Edmund White Washington, and Reverend Willis Patterson baptized 135 people during 1869.

Mary described the church dedication in October 1869:

> We went to see the new church dedicated. We went in Granville's wagon and had a splendid time. It was basket meeting but as we did not know it and had promised Mother to be home to dinner we would not stay. The church was full and the aisles were filled with chairs, and many were there that could not get in at all. The church is not been quite paid for. It lacks three hundred dollars so they were asking for money and you never saw men get out so fast in all your life, but it did no good. Dr. Dunn went out after them and collected some money.[31]

The social part of church life was certainly important as well. Mary wrote her brother that "Tilla has bought a sack and a pair of earrings which she got the last time Miss Susie went to Nashville. Miss Susie gave her a dress. Sunday being church day she went to church and wore all her finery. Irene says she looked better than any one at church."[32]

Tragically, the church burned to the ground on April 1, 1870, but this did not deter nor discourage the members. Dr. John R. Dunn donated land approximately one hundred yards north of the original church on the side of a hill. Again whites in the community furnished logs, and Mary Connell's husband had all of them hauled to the mill and sawed. In 1871 the church members organized a picnic to help defray the completion costs. Various people donated nineteen hogs, and each barbeque meal was sold at 25¢ per pound. With the freewill offering the next day, the church members raised over $500. They completed the new church in 1872. Mary Connell donated a solid cherry communion table, and Jane Washington gave two sparkling cut-glass bottles to complete the set. It served as a place of worship until 1894.

During those years the church building was used as the schoolhouse as well. Woodard Washington, whose father was a Wessyngton slave and later a sharecropper, recalled that the school had only one room that was just about fourteen feet square or a little better: "The teacher had to teach all the children and didn't have any help at all. And all of my going to school, we had to walk about five miles a day, going and coming. I was fortunate enough to be promoted to the fifth grade. I didn't have a chance to go regularly, because when I was large enough to work, I had to help with the crops and mostly in the wintertime, I had to cut barn wood for the next year."[33]

Many freedmen established Masonic lodges in Cedar Hill, Port Royal, in Robertson County, and in Nashville. These lodges were secret fraternal orders that undertook social and philanthropic work. They also organized several benevolent societies that continued some of the work started by the Freedmen's Bureau to help those in need. The Benevolent Lodge #210 of Port Royal was founded in 1872 and still serves the community. The King David Lodge #187 of Cedar Hill was founded shortly after emancipation. It established a King David cemetery for its members and their families. The earliest marked grave there dates from 1876.

After the war the freedmen had more choices in choosing a

final resting place. Many continued to be buried in the former slaves' cemetery on Wessyngton. However, after 1869 others were buried in the church graveyard at Antioch Baptist Church. Prior to 1880, Joseph Scott bought a farm in Turnersville that once had been a part of the Wessyngton estate. A portion of his land was used as a family and community graveyard called Scott's Chapel Cemetery. Several of the former Wessyngton slaves were buried there, the earliest marked grave dating from 1880. Other blacks were buried in Mt. Herman Cemetery in Cedar Hill, and several other black landowners had small family cemeteries.

The first years after emancipation were times of celebration. We do not know who actually started the Eighth of August celebration in Robertson County to commemorate Tennessee's Emancipation Day on that day in 1865. Black Union soldiers from the area or the Freedmen's Bureau could have initiated the tradition. Each year the day was a joyous event. People came from miles around. Some rode in trains from Nashville; locals came in horse-drawn carriages, buggies, and wagons; others walked for miles. Some dressed in finery, others in plain clothes. Food of every description was on hand. The locals embraced friends and relatives who had moved away and introduced their children to them. Over the years hundreds of people from all over the country have returned for the celebration. Around the turn of the twentieth century, the King David Lodge took charge of the celebration. Joe Washington told me that even after his family left the area, they would come back to Cedar Hill each year for the event. People would come from everywhere to get old-fashioned whole-hog barbeque. Joe boasted that Lawson "Pimp" Gardner could "prepare the best pulled pork barbeque you'd ever eaten."[34] Lawson got the secret recipe for the barbeque from his father-in-law, Irvin Washington, who was born at Wessyngton. Larger celebrations are still held in Port Royal and nearby Allensville, Kentucky.

The African Americans kept faith in God that He would take care of them in any situation as He had done during the dark days of slavery. In spite of all odds, they achieved many accomplishments. They made sacrifices and educated their children to better their lives and pave the way for the next generation.

CHAPTER 16

Digging for the Truth

————— ·•·• —————

Most of the information we have on slavery comes from plantation records, diaries, and other documents created by slave owners. Archaeology helps give voice to the slaves from the materials they used and left behind. In 1989 Caribel Washington, president of the Bloomington-Normal Black History Project, approached Dr. Charles Orser and David Babson, director and archaeologist of the Midwestern Archaeological Research Center, about the potential investigations of the slave cabin area at Wessyngton Plantation to get an interpretation of slave life there. Similar digs have been conducted at the Hermitage, Mt. Vernon, and Monticello. The group first went to the Tennessee State Library and Archives to do research in the Washington Family Papers to gather as much information as they could on the number of slaves on the plantation, the number of slave dwellings, and their families. An archivist informed them about my research and suggested that they contact me.

When Caribel Washington called me and told me about their interest in the plantation, I was very excited and agreed to meet them at Wessyngton. I shared many photographs with the group and told them stories I had collected from descendants of the slave families. After investigating the slave cabin site at Wessyngton and from information I had given them, it was decided that the site on the plantation would be good for archaeological exploration. The actual digging at

Wessyngton did not start until 1991. The thought of actually walking in my ancestors' footsteps and holding objects they used in their everyday lives one hundred years earlier was surreal to me. The dig yielded fragments of pottery and dishes used by the slaves as well as coins. I took a few days' vacation from work and participated in some of the digging at the slave cabin site with David Babson and Jerry Moore in the early nineties, and later with Melanie Cabak and Mark Groover. I felt that I was digging for the truth.

After the second dig, a report was compiled to present to the state of Tennessee to have the slave cabin area nominated to the National Register of Historical Places. I submitted a chapter for the report about the black history of Wessyngton for which I earned a national history award from the National Association for State and Local History.

While helping with the dig, David Babson told me that a descendant of the plantation owners had written him when she found out about the dig and had sent him a photograph of some of the former slaves. He thought one of the men in the photograph was my great-great-grandfather because he remembered the skullcap

Sarah Jane Scott Harris (1852–1925), Emanuel Washington (1824–1907), and Henny Washington (1839–1913).

he always wore. I immediately thought it must have been the same one that was in my seventh-grade history book, as that picture is spread throughout the Washington family.

To my amazement it was a photograph of my great-great-grandparents and another Wessyngton slave. I had never seen this photograph of them. David told me that the photo was sent by Mary Washington Holley, who lived in Lake Placid, New York. I looked up her number and called her. I told her that Emanuel and Henny Washington were my great-great-grandparents, and I was interested to know if she had other pictures of my ancestors. Mary replied that she was delighted to hear from me. She said she had that picture of my ancestors for more than fifty years, and her father, Joseph Edwin, had spoken so highly of them. Mary always wondered what became of the family, if they moved away or simply died out. I told her that our family alone was at least five hundred strong, if not more.

Mary grew up on Wessyngton. She remembered that her father knew all the former slaves on the plantation and knew exactly how they were related to one another. As a child, her father had shown her where the slave cemetery was located. The graves were unmarked other than a few scattered stones. She always was saddened that their family cemetery had elaborate markers and the slaves didn't; she felt that their family should have done something about it. Mary told me it was not too late to change that, and she offered to pay to have a monument erected in the slave cemetery if I would document the names of people who were buried there. Two of Mary's cousins, Thomas Blagden and Preston Frazer, also made contributions for the marker. The granite monument inscribed with thirty-nine names was erected in the slave cemetery in 1995 in honor of the slaves and their descendants.

The director of the dig, Caribel Washington, told me that her late husband, Arthur A. Washington, was a direct descendant of Wessyngton slaves. His father was General Richard Washington

Memorial monument at Wessyngton Plantation slave cemetery.

and his grandfather was General Washington. I looked through my genealogical notes and found that her father-in-law was actually a first cousin of my grandmother Sallie Washington. She told me that her husband's family left the plantation in the early 1900s and went to work in the coal mines in Earlington, Kentucky. The family returned to Wessyngton during the Depression when the coal mines closed down and left again after the mines reopened. Caribel said the Washington family was very large. When her mother-in-law, Amanda Washington, died in 1971 there were more than one hundred males in the family carrying the Washington surname. Caribel told me that her husband's uncle Joseph Washington was still living and was in his late nineties and was of excellent memory.

In June 1997, eight years after my initial meeting with Caribel

Washington, I finally had the honor of interviewing Joseph Washington in Mansfield, Ohio, on his one hundred second birthday. I met him through his great-niece, Argene Washington, who contacted me when she decided to do research on her family. At the time Joseph lived with his nephew, Reverend Henry Washington. In preparation for the trip to Mansfield, I brought many photographs and documents I had collected.

As soon as he saw me, he exclaimed, "I don't know who you are, but the Washington blood runs deep in your veins!"

I told Cousin Joe about my research and showed him the book of the photographs I had. The first picture I showed was of the "Famous Four," which is what I call the photo that led me on the initial search. Joseph pointed to the picture of Allen Washington. "That's my granddaddy." He then identified Emanuel, Henny, and Granville. Allen and Granville had died before he was old enough to remember them. He turned each page of the photo album carefully and could identify nearly everyone and had a story to tell about each of them.

Joseph Washington, 1895–2002

The last time I was in Tennessee, the cabin I was born in was still standing. It was about twenty feet by twenty feet with a brick-end chimney. There was a loft upstairs where we children slept. My parents, Gabriel and Margaret Washington, sisters and brothers, Amanda, Annie, Mattie Belle, Charlie, Henry, Allen, Woodard, and Grandma Jenny, who they called Jincy, all lived there. Grandma Jincy was a small-framed woman and had good aim with a shoe if any of us children got out of line. She lived with us until she died. My mother died when I was very young, and my father remarried in 1902. One day he pulled up to our cabin in a one-horse wagon with my new stepmother, Ora Killens Strain, and her children, Lucille, Floyd, and George Strain.

Joseph Washington (1895–2002), on his
one hundred second birthday.

When he came to a photo of Fannie and Wesley Williams, he said "There's Aunt Fannie and Uncle Wes Williams." Fannie and Wes Williams were not related to Joseph, but children of that time called most adults aunt and uncle as a title of respect. Joseph added, "They were Indian people, and their son, old man Kinchem Williams, was my father's best friend. They used to live across the field from us. That house is still standing too."

I asked him many questions about my ancestors and his memories of them, and I shared things I had found with him. He mentioned several things that happened when he was young and was surprised that I knew so much about what had taken place decades before I was born. He stopped talking at one point, laughed, and then asked, "Now how old did you say you were?" His nephew Reverend Washington remarked that it was like listening to the conversation of two hundred-year-old men.

Do you remember my great-great-grandparents Emanuel and Henny Washington?

Of course, I remember them. We lived within handshaking distance on the Washington farm. Our cabins were close enough to each other where I could stand on my father's porch and reach out and shake hands with someone on the porch of Uncle Man's cabin. They were wonderful people, and I have many fond memories of them during my childhood. Uncle Man could really sing well and led most of the songs during our prayer services. You know a lot of those old folks could sing back then. His favorite song was "I Just Come from the Fountain, His Name Is So Sweet." I can see him now singing and slapping his knees with those big old hands of his'n. [Joseph then sang it for me.] When I left Tennessee for the North, I was in several singing groups and I often sung some of the songs they used to sing back on the old Washington plantation. Uncle Man was tall and so was Aunt Henny. Their son Grundy, and his son, Emanuel (who was called Manny), looked like giants above other people. Manny Washington later moved to Evansville, Indiana.

If you become as good a man as Uncle Man when you grow up, you will have really done something because he was certainly a great old man. [I was thirty-five at the time, which may have seemed like a baby to a man who had lived more than a century.]

Did you ever eat Uncle Man's cooking?

Lord, yes, every chance I got. He would bring things he had cooked from the Big House and give it to us children when he came home. Uncle Man went blind due to cooking when he was older. His relatives would feed him on a very large plate. Me and the other children would wait anxiously for any desserts he did not eat.

I remember some of the older folks mentioning Axum Washington and another slave named Britain. Lots of the old people back then had some Indian in them too. Aunt Henny Washington, my grandmother Jincy, and some of the other older slaves were partially mixed with Indian blood.

I have fond memories of my life on the farm, although the work was hard. The Washington family was very nice to all the workers on the place. My father told me that George A. Washington treated them well when they were enslaved. I'm named after George's son, old man Joe Washington. Father said George Washington was very nice, but remembered one incident when a storm hit the farm and did a lot of damage. George was then very ill and looked up at the sky and cursed God, which my father thought was awful.

During Christmas everyone on the plantation, black and white, would gather at the Big House and everyone on the place would get presents.

Washington was so big that they rarely had to leave the plantation to get anything. It was very big and had large peach and apple orchards and all types of other fruit trees. There were huge numbers of hogs, cattle, sheep, horses, mules, and everything else. Sheep were much bigger when I was young than they are now, and we often rode on their backs. As a young boy I was always small for my age and some of the larger boys tied me to a sheep and I was taken a good piece [distance] before I could get off.

The Washingtons had some of the finest horses to be found anywhere, so comfortable that riding one was just like sitting in a fine rocking chair. I took Shetland ponies to Nashville for the Washingtons. My brother Woodard used to pick up the mail for them in Cedar Hill. Sometimes I would join him. One time I was nearly thrown to the ground when the horse I was riding across the old covered bridge was spooked and went wild. I was thrown forward, but being small I managed to hold on to the horse's neck.

My first schoolteacher, Ida Grimes, used to ride me home in their buggy when her father, Dan Grimes, came to pick her up on the weekends. She would stay in the homes of some of the students during the week. I was the teacher's pet. The school was in Turnersville about five miles away, and we walked there and back. The name of the school was Scott's Chapel. The schoolhouse was named after an old man by the name of Joe Scott that owned that land up through there, which had a little cemetery right out there on the schoolyard, you might say. I later attended school on the Washington Plantation built for the children of the black sharecroppers.

Some of the families on the farm who I remember are: my father, Gabe Washington, Emanuel Washington, General Washington, John Phillips, John Adams, Earl McCroy, Bose Adams, Robert Williams, Kinchem Williams, Gilbert Hulsey, James Frazier, Tillman Williams, John Green, Mattie Terry, Emma Carter, Tom Brewington, Otho Terry, and George Terry.

There were many children on the place, as most people in those days had large families. When I was young there were many sharecroppers on the plantation. White and black—they all got along very well. And all the children played together with no problems at all.

There was an old Indian graveyard on Washington, and when we were children we used to play there and many times we found arrowheads and other stuff. Many of the sharecroppers also found old things like that when plowing the fields.

In 1909 a ten-year-old boy named Charlie Terry was in the woods with his father when he was chopping wood. While his father was cutting wood, Charlie was swinging on a grapevine on a dead tree, and the tree fell and killed him.

I remember another tragedy in 1919. Kinchem Williams's brother Robert and his family lived at Washington. Robert and a white man had taken a load of tobacco to Clarksville, and it had rained very hard and several people tried to get them to stay overnight and wait for the water to go down, but they decided to take their chances. When they tried to cross a creek, Robert and his team were swept away by the current and he drowned.

When I was a young man, my friend Joe Killens and I used to play in a band, and we were the best musicians around. I played the guitar and harmonica. We'd go to different places and we'd have 'em kicking up dust. My father didn't want me playing that kind of music in a group, though.

[When Joseph told me about him playing in a band, his niece Argene said she had never heard anything about it. When we went out she bought him a harmonica.] I'm a little rusty because I haven't played in so long but I used to really play. [He then played a tune or two for us, which was quite impressive at one hundred two years old.]

One Sunday afternoon my friend Curtis Frazier, who also lived on the plantation within hollering distance of my house, and I decided to leave for no cause at all no more than just got tired of being on the farm. So we set out walking. I never will forget it. We ended up going to Earlington, Kentucky, where my older brother Henry lived. Henry had left the area several years before this to work in the coal mines. Henry took us sightseeing at the mine, it was called Heckley mines. It was on a Sunday and of course they weren't working on Sundays back then. Curtis did not like it at all after we went down in the mine, so he headed right back to the farm. I stayed.

In later years several members of my family moved to Kentucky and from there to other Northern areas. Mining work was very dangerous and the conditions were quite bad. I would be so tired when I got in from work, I would have to lay down and rest before I could eat. Some parts of the mines were as low as four feet high. Ephraim Biggers Jr., Uncle Man's grandson, got killed in one of the mines. His father, Uncle Eph, could have gotten money on account of the death, but you couldn't get older people to go that far from home back then. His mother, Winnie, was dead by then.

Even after our family left the area, we would come back to

Cedar Hill each year for the Eighth of August Celebration. Each year hundreds of people from all over the country would return for the celebration. Some of us came back to the Antioch Baptist Church homecoming, which is still held the fourth Sunday in May.

Joseph Washington died in 2002 in Memphis, Tennessee, at one hundred six years old. He was taken back to Madisonville, Kentucky, for burial.

Sadly, just a few months before his death a storm destroyed the cabin in which he was born.

The connections I made from the experience of the archaeological dig confirmed what my great-aunt Maggie Washington always said, "The Lord meant for you to do all this research because it seems that you are always at the right place at the right time to make a new discovery."

CHAPTER 17

Generations in Transition

———•◦•———

A s Wessyngton entered the last decade of the nineteenth century, life for the Washington family was about to change. The new generation and the division of Wessyngton would bring a new way of life. For the freedmen, although they faced many obstacles, they were about to embark on new paths.

Health was precarious for all. Jane and George's third daughter, Bessie Adelaide Tompkins, died in 1887 after a miscarriage.[1] Mary Washington Frazer, their second daughter, in April 1892 lost

George A. Washington (1815–1892), portrait. *Jane Smith Washington (1830–1894), portrait.*

her husband, James Stokes Frazer, to a sudden "hemorrhage" after several years of poor health, perhaps from typhoid fever; he left seven children thirteen years of age and younger.

George's health had been "feeble" for a number of years as he "suffered from gradual paralysis" from the late 1880s.[2] Each summer the extended Washington family gathered at Wessyngton. The family thought that the summer of 1891 might be their last with the family's patriarch so they hired a professional photographer to take photographs of family groups posed on the front porch and steps of the mansion. Children and grandchildren were photographed on the steps and on the lawn. Former slaves who were then house servants appeared in various photographs.

On the same occasion, a posed photograph of Emanuel Washington, Henny Washington, Allen Washington, and Granville Washington was taken. Their poses showed both dignity and high stature. This was the photo used in my textbook and the newspaper article.

Washingtons at Wessyngton Plantation, ca. 1891.

Joseph Edwin Washington and family.
Front row: Anne Washington, Joseph E. Washington,
Elizabeth Washington, Mary Kemp Washington.
Back row: George A. Washington, Joseph E. Washington.

On December 4, 1892, George Augustine Washington died at the age of seventy-seven. Newspaper accounts of his funeral services held at Wessyngton mention the involvement of his former slaves. "The coffin was borne from the residence to the grave by the family servants whose ancestors had been in the family for generations. At the grave, the exercises were concluded by a song from twenty or more of the family servants. Their melodious voices and deep earnestness touched all hearts."[3] This was the end of an era.

At his death, George possessed assets in excess of $1 million, excluding the value attributed to Wessyngton Plantation.[4] According to his 1888 will and codicil, his widow was to receive the Wessyngton Home Place surrounded by approximately 1,400 acres as a life estate. At her removal by remarriage or death, it

Hostler at Wessyngton Plantation, 1920s

would revert to Joseph Edwin, the eldest son. The remainder of his real estate was divided into seven equal parts, and according to family lore, the seven surviving children drew lots to decide the division of the rest of the Wessyngton acreage. Joseph Edwin Washington received an additional 799 acres. William Lewis Washington received various tracts totaling 1,509 acres. Martha Washington Tillman drew the Dortch and Adams tracts of 904 acres; Mary Washington Frazer received the Frey, Ayers, and Ellis tracts of 1,443 acres; Lucy Washington Helm drew the Carr and Barber places of 875 acres; Jane Washington Ewing received the Norfleet Dortch tracts of 865 acres; and George A. Washington Jr. received the Vanhook tracts of 934 acres. In addition to the land, each of his children, and the children of his deceased daughter, Bessie Washington Tompkins, received $231,514.[5] George remembered Granville Washington, his life-long valet, and perhaps his unacknowledged son, in his will: "I give and bequeath to Granville Washington, colored, $500 for his fidelity to me."

The passing of the generation was complete when George's widow, Jane Smith Washington, died in 1894 at the age of sixty-

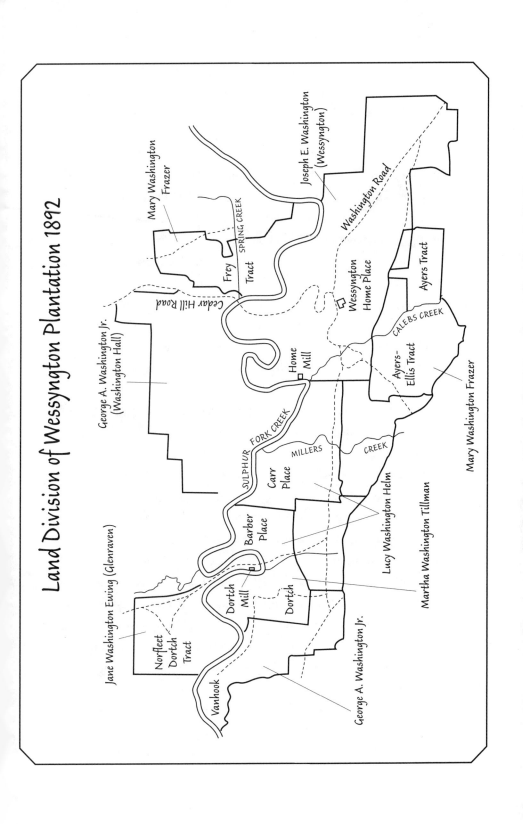

Land Division of Wessyngton Plantation 1892

Mary Washington Frazer

Joseph E. Washington (Wessyngton)

SPRING CREEK

Frey Tract

Washington Road

Wessyngton Home Place

Ayers Tract

George A. Washington Jr. (Washington Hall)

Cedar Hill Road

Home Mill

CALEBS CREEK

Ayers-Ellis Tract

SULPHUR FORK CREEK

MILLERS CREEK

Carr Place

Mary Washington Frazer

Jane Washington Ewing (Glenraven)

Barber Place

Lucy Washington Helm

Martha Washington Tillman

Dortch Mill

Norfleet Dortch Tract

Dortch

George A. Washington Jr.

Vanhook

four. She passed away at her daughter Mary Washington Frazer's home in Nashville after a short illness.

A special train and a procession about a quarter mile in length from the station preceded her funeral services in the mansion and in the family cemetery. The *Daily American* reported "a moving incident at the grave just before the benediction was the singing of 'Hark, from the Tombe,' by the old family servants and their children."[6]

Several newspapers wrote obituaries that described her character. The *Nashville Banner* noted she had "a charm of manner for entertaining and gentleness in her treatment of her friends that won for her a host of friends who loved and honored her. Her home, Wessyngton, has long been noted for hospitality. The sorrow of the poor in the neighborhood at the knowledge of her death speaks volumes for the charity and benevolent kindness of the mistress of the estate."[7] The *Nashville American* wrote that the basis for her character "was the intense loyalty to duty . . . [She met all her duties well] whether as wife, mother, mistress, friend, and helper of a numerous tenantry or neighbor."[8] According to another newspaper, "none save her own children will feel a deeper grief at her going than the poor, both white and black, who were so long blessed by her kind acts and kinder words of cheer and sympathy."[9]

To honor their parents, George and Jane's children commissioned several stained-glass windows for Christ Church in Nashville. The magnificent large rose window in Jane's honor still beautifies the front entrance of the Episcopal Church. On a subsequent visit to England in 1910, Joseph Edwin Washington and his sister Jane Washington Ewing endowed two stained-glass windows on the sides of the altar in the Church of St. Nicholas, Islip, in honor of their Washington ancestors who came from that area of England.[10]

Joseph Edwin managed Wessyngton and was influential in Nashville and Tennessee. He was responsible for an exhibit of African American contributions to the State of Tennessee's Colored Citizen's Exhibit at the State's Centennial in Nashville in 1896. He

Mrs. J. W. Thomas and Mary Kemp Washington in Tennessee Centennial Parade in 1897, driven by former Wessyngton slave.

also provided an exhibit showing the production of Wessyngton tobacco, including a small log barn for curing.

————•••————

The older generation of both former slaves and their descendants was passing away. I needed a lot of luck and detective work to learn the story of Granville's later years and his death.

One day while at work in 1992, I was discussing with a coworker, Corrine Horner Vaughn, how several people in my family had lived to very advanced ages. Corrine said she remembered two of her neighbors, Oscar Washington and his sister Fannie Washington, who both lived to be in their late eighties. It then occurred to me that they—like most Washingtons—might be related to me. I looked through my records and found that was indeed the case. Oscar was born in Robertson County, and Fannie in Dickson County after their parents, Foster and Mary Frey

Washington, relocated there sometime between 1900 and 1910.

Corrine told me that Oscar Washington's children, W. D., Oscar Jr., Mary Ann, and Dianna, still lived in the area. Fannie never married and resided in their family home, which adjoined Corrine's mother's farm. Dianna also worked with Corrine's mother in the county school system.

We arranged a meeting. We were to meet at Shoney's Restaurant in Dickson. In my excitement we just set the time, and I failed to get a description of them, the kind of car they would be in, or anything. However, as soon as I saw W. D. Washington, I could see his resemblance to Granville. I asked, "Are you Washingtons?" and they answered, "Yes."

I had brought several photographs of their ancestors, documents, pictures of Wessyngton, and other things I had collected. They knew the family had originally come from Robertson County, but that was all. They had never heard of Wessyngton Plantation or the Washington family that owned it. They also had a portrait of Granville Washington and always thought he was white and jokingly stated that they were related to President George Washington. Little did they know that they were actually related to the president! They later came to our Washington family reunion, and I took them to tour Wessyngton Plantation.

Another discovery for Granville's family came in 1996 when I found the 1951 obituary of his daughter Joyce Washington Nixon that listed the following survivors: daughter, Miss Irene Nixon; nieces Mrs. C. A. Davis of Knoxville, Mrs. Mary Graves, Mrs. Hattie Ready of Nashville, and Mrs. A. B. [Ann] Cooper of Atlanta, Georgia; nephews James Dozier and Will Graves of Nashville and A. B. Cooper of Atlanta; dear friends Frank Berry Sr. and Allen Berry, and other friends and relatives. In view of the forty-five-year span, I felt it was probably a long shot, but I still was going to give it a try to locate these people.

Fortunately, I didn't give up and reached Mrs. Ann Nixon Cooper, who was then ninety-four years old and living in Atlanta. After the death of her parents, she was raised by her aunt-in-law Joyce Washington Nixon in Nashville. During many fascinating conversations, Mrs. Cooper told me about Granville's life after he left Wessyngton and about his family.

> In the 1890s Granville moved to Nashville, where he bought a house on Division and Fairmount streets. Granville, Irene, and their daughter Bessie lived in one side of the house; his daughter Joyce and her family lived on the other side. Both sides of the home were furnished with expensive antiques, some of which came from Wessyngton. The house had an organ that Bessie played, a victrola, ornate furniture, figurines, and many nice furnishings that most people, white or black, did not have. They even owned a telephone, the only one in the neighborhood.[11]
>
> Granville was very close to Reverend Preston Taylor, whom Joyce dated at one time and everyone thought would marry. Reverend Taylor was one of Nashville's most influential black business and religious leaders. In 1888 he established Greenwood, Nashville's second oldest cemetery for blacks. In the same year, he founded the Taylor Funeral Company on North Cherry Street (now Fourth Avenue). Taylor also helped organize several other Nashville black businesses, including the One Cent [Citizens] Savings and Trust Company Bank. Reverend Taylor remained close friends to the Washington family and pastored some of its members.

Granville took his own life on August 22, 1898, six years after George's death. The story of his death was shrouded in mystery until Mary Ann found an unidentified newspaper in her grandfather Foster's family bible, which had Granville's obituary pasted inside the front cover. The obituary reinforced the perceived connection to the Washington family:

Granville Washington was born in Robertson County on January 17, 1834 [1831], a slave of George A. Washington, and was with him constantly, his body servant until after the war, and long after freedom was given him. Until the time of Mr. Washington's death, a warm affection existed between him and his master, each one ready at all times to stand by the other. He married his first wife in 1845 [1852], and she was the mother of three children, Foster, of Robertson County: Lawson, of Nashville, and Fannie of St. Louis. He married his second wife in 1864 [1865], and she has three children, Grant [Grantz], Joyce and Bessie. They all live in Nashville.

After coming to live in Nashville, he became devoted to Elder [Preston] Taylor and through the influence of him, joined the Gay-Street Christian Church. On August 22, 1898, he died at 9 o'clock in the morning in his 67th year, by a pistol shot fired by his own hand, while alone, and probably not in his right mind. Last Friday he sat talking to his dear wife of the many kindnesses shown to him by white people and of how good she had always been to him. "Oh, how I wish I could see all my white children [the Washington children]! Why don't they come to see me?" After hearing that Mrs. Tillman [Martha Washington Tillman] and Mrs. Ewing [Jane Washington Ewing], [both daughters of George A. Washington] had come and gone and he hadn't seen them, he sat down and wept like a child, and said: "How kind Mr. Tillman has been to me. Every time he meets me, he takes my feeble hand in his and talks to me of how I am getting along and is always ready to help me. O, wife, how I love him," and then he spoke of all the Washingtons, how kind they had all been to him and how much they had done for him. And he kept saying, "O, I wish I could see them all once more."[12]

Another obituary in the *Nashville Banner* gave more details as to what might have led to Granville's suicide:

AUGUST 22, 1898

COLORED MAN'S SUICIDE

GRANVILLE WASHINGTON SENDS A BULLET THROUGH
HIS HEAD, SUPPOSED TO HAVE FIRED THE FATAL SHOT
WHILE SUFFERING FROM TEMPORARY INSANITY

Granville Washington, a well-known colored man who lives on Fairmount Street, committed suicide about 9 o'clock this morning by shooting himself through the head with a revolver. Death ensued almost instantly.

Washington was well known throughout the city, he for years having been employed in the bath rooms of Charles Breyers, on Church Street. He was polite and courteous to all and made many friends among the patrons of the shop. As a slave, he belonged to the father of ex-Congressman Joe Washington. Yesterday he returned from a visit to his old home in Robertson County, where he was ever welcomed by the Washington family, and stated that he felt better than he had for years.[13]

Mrs. Cooper had been told about Granville's suicide—that he lost his mind and that was when he killed himself. She thought it was odd because you never heard of black people committing suicide in those days.

Granville Washington was buried in the Mt. Ararat Cemetery in Nashville. His will stated that his property in Nashville was held in trust for him by Joseph E. Washington. Granville must have given his sons money as indicated in his will: "I leave nothing to my three sons: Foster Washington, Lawson Washington and Granville (Grantz) Washington in this will because I have from time to time already given to each of them, Foster, Lawson and Granville, property, money and various articles of value in the nature of advancements which collated and equalized would aggregate an amount greater than the value of the property herein devised."[14]

Mrs. Cooper told me about Granville's family:

> His widow, Irene, was a very fair-skinned mulatto who looked white. She was a very large woman weighing more than three hundred pounds. She had very long hair that I loved to comb. Irene belonged to a white congregation on Church Street, believed to be Christ Church. Some white people, probably the Washingtons, would visit Irene sometimes and take her to church. The Washington family also gave her money. Irene always had money to give to her grandchildren when they wanted to go to the store. She was a large-busted woman, and would ceremoniously take out the money she tucked in her bosom to give to the children. Irene cooked the most delicious turnip greens.

before 1898   *after 1898*

Joyce Washington Nixon (1864–1951).

Using her special recipe, the greens would be a bluish green.[15]

Granville's children followed very different paths after his death. Joyce was devastated by his suicide; she wore black for the rest of her life. She was a striking woman and had been voted as the most beautiful woman in Nashville when she attended Roger Williams College. Aristocratic, proper, and polished, Joyce knew the governor, senators, powerful political figures, and other important whites. Joyce worked for W. W. Berry, president of the First National Bank. She was in charge of all the domestics at the Elmwood estate owned by the Berrys. Joyce could get whatever she wanted from any exclusive store in Nashville at a time when most blacks were not allowed any credit or even allowed to enter some of the stores.[16]

Granville Washington's oldest son, Foster, moved his family to Dickson County and purchased more than two hundred acres of land around 1910. Foster, along with William Mallory, Dick Long, James Dickerson, and E. W. Washington (also from Robertson County),

Foster Washington (1852–1919) at Wessyngton Plantation.

Grantz Washington (b. 1862).

were the first settlers and founding fathers of a small black community called Hortense. The town had been organized by J. B. Mullins of Nashville in 1911 for some of Dickson County's black citizens.[17] In contrast, Grantz Washington was driven out of town for dating white women and moved to Texas.[18] Grantz had one daughter, Georgia Washington, who married a dentist, Dr. Charles A. Davis of Knoxville. Mrs. Cooper said they had a son, Washington Davis, who moved to California. Lawson Washington was a handsome brown-skinned man who everyone called Dr. Lawson because he performed illegal abortions. Lawson was a shrewd businessman, and it was said that no one ever got the best of him in a business deal. In the 1880s he had as many as eight families sharecropping for him on his own farm and other farms he had rented. He died in Nashville in 1921.[19] Bessie remained in the house with her mother. Bessie's son, James A. Dozier Jr., passed into white society, married a white woman, and lived in the exclusive Belle Meade section of Nashville.[20] When his aunt Joyce died in 1951, family members contacted James, but he did not attend any of her memorial events for fear of being detected for passing. He was, however, named in her obituary.

In 2008, Mrs. Cooper became part of American history. After CNN television news chronicled her voting early in the presidential election, Senator Barack Obama telephoned her. At the conclusion of his historic acceptance speech on Tuesday, November 4, the first African American president-elect of the United States drew on her life as representative for all African Americans, and indeed all Americans. He acknowledged that the stories of the election will be told to future generations, and that he was thinking of Ann Nixon Cooper, who at one hundred and six years old cast her ballot in Atlanta. And then he reflected on what "she's seen throughout her century in America— the heartache and the hope; the struggle and the progress; the times we were told that we can't, and the people who pressed on with that American creed: Yes we can." And the last lines of President-elect Obama's inspiring speech brought her into the future as well, when he wondered about our children and his own: If they live as long as

Ann Nixon Cooper on her
hundredth birthday, 2002.

Ann Nixon Cooper, "What change will they see? What progress will we have made?"

By 1900 only Emanuel and Henny Washington, their son General, and his family, and Jenny (Jincy) Washington, her son Gabe Washington, and his family remained on the Home Place. General Washington had been put off Wessyngton in 1882 after a disagreement with the foreman Perkins. He returned by the 1890s. Some of the Terrys, Lewises, Scotts, Gardners, and other Washington families resided on the Dortch Place.

The Washingtons were very close to Emanuel, known affectionately as Uncle Man. His descendants related that he was

Emanuel Washington (1824–1907),
Henny Washington (1839–1913), and Winnie
Washington Long Biggers (b. 1860).

always treated like a member of the Washington family. When he died in 1907 at eighty-three years of age, George Augustine 2d, then practicing law in New York, conveyed his sympathies by way of his mother: "Uncle Man's death was very sad. He was certainly a wonderful old man whose place can never be filled. Please tell Aunt Henny how sorry I am and how I sympathize with her."[21]

Everyone loved Aunt Henny. She was very sweet and loved to talk. The Washington family was very fond of her too. She died in 1913 at seventy-four years of age. Her funeral was held in the front yard at Wessyngton and hundreds of people—black and white—attended. According to Mattie Terry, Reverend Stoner of Antioch Baptist Church really did preach that funeral. As the procession made its way to the old slave cemetery, the mourners sang hymns; it was a Wessyngton tradition.[22]

In 1902 William Lewis Washington died in Philadelphia after being in failing health for several years. After the Civil War, Wil-

William Lewis Washington
(1844–1902).

liam inherited considerable property and assets from his grandfather Major William B. Lewis and his grandmother Mary Cheatham Washington. He traveled and lived in many places in Canada and Europe, only occasionally visiting in Tennessee. He married three times but left no children. William was laid to rest in the Washington family cemetery. His obituary read, "After life's fitful fever, he sleeps well." Another obituary stated that his father, George, was "one of the wealthiest citizens of Robertson County, and the family is one of the most prominent in the State."[23] The substantial property William had inherited from his grandparents and his father was divided among his siblings.[24]

Once the land was divided after George's and William's deaths, George and Jane's children made different choices as to the future. Since Lucy Washington Helm was married to John Helm, son of the former governor of Kentucky, and lived in Kentucky, she sold the land she had inherited to Gus Elliott, Irvin Elliott, and their half-brother Irad Murphey. Gus later bought out his brothers, and

Washington Hall.

Ballroom inside Washington Hall.

the land remains in the hands of his son and daughter, Gus Elliott Jr. and Maxine Elliott.

By a December 12, 1888, codicil to George's will, George Augustine Jr.'s inheritance of personal property (including stocks and bonds) was held in trust for him until his thirtieth birthday in 1898. He had been given 1,065 acres in 1888 and later received an additional $25,000 to make his inheritance equal to that of his brother Joseph. George and his wife, Marina "Queenie" Woods, built the magnificent Washington Hall on his land starting in 1896. Their mansion was a three-story white brick house with forty-four rooms. It has been said that the sweeping staircase in the movie *Gone with the Wind* was fashioned after the one at Washington Hall. There was a ballroom on the third floor of the mansion that could accommodate two hundred guests. Most of the furnishings were imported from France and Italy. Washington Hall contained priceless antiques: a lamp used by President Washington at his Mt. Vernon home, a secretary built in 1620, an antique bed used by

Glenraven mansion.

General Lafayette during his stay in New Orleans, a linen handkerchief that was a gift from King Edward VII of England, a chair
belonging to President James K. Polk, paintings by Gilbert Stu-
art including one of President Washington, and a Regency-style
piano made in 1820. In addition, Washington Hall was decorated
with fine old laces, old English silver, European china and glass-
ware, Italian tapestries, ornate French mantelpieces, and a collection of American mahogany furniture of several periods handed
down through the family.[25] Washington Hall was one of the show-
places of the South and known for lavish hospitality. George and
"Queenie" entertained some of the crowned heads of Europe,
including King George of Greece and his sons Prince Constantine
I and Prince George. Their farm was the only place in the South
where full-blooded hackney horses were bred and sold.

The same December 12, 1888, codicil to George's will stipulated that Jane Washington Ewing's personal property inheritance
from her father was to be held in trust until her thirtieth birthday
in 1897. Jane purchased an additional 550 acres from her sister

Martha Washington Tillman. She and her husband, Felix Grundy Ewing, then began construction of the Glenraven mansion on her land. The mansion was completed in 1904. It had three stories and a full basement. Most materials used to construct the mansion came from the estate. The six twenty-eight-foot stone columns at its front entrance were quarried locally. The mansion had twenty-four rooms and ten baths, and the entire third floor was used as a ballroom. The Ewings entertained some of the state's most affluent and distinguished guests. Guests would often come from Nashville by train to Cedar Hill and then be driven to Glenraven in fine horse-drawn carriages.

Washington Hall and Glenraven in many ways continued life as it was on Wessyngton. Several former Wessyngton slaves and their descendants sharecropped at Glenraven and Washington Hall. A number of other black and white families sharecropped on both estates. Glenraven was entirely self-sufficient with its own mill, store, post office, church, school, barns, stables, two-story tenant houses, and an electrical generating plant.

Washingtons at Glenraven pavilion house, ca. 1890s.

Mary Washington Frazer built a house on the land she inherited called Frazer Hill. However, after the death of her husband in 1892, she and her seven children continued to live in Nashville in the house she and her husband had built there. Mary married again and eventually sold the land in Robertson County.

Since the pattern of a Northern preparatory and university education had been started in the earlier generation with Joseph Edwin, his daughters attended schools in the North. Elizabeth went to the National Cathedral School for Girls in Washington where undoubtedly she met her future husband, a Hotchkiss from Connecticut, and left the South. Anne married a Blagden and moved to New York.

Joseph Edwin and his family lived at Wessyngton. Around the turn of the century, he made architectural changes to the mansion. A service wing was added to the southeast side and a framed addition to the south side of the house. That addition served as a temporary accommodation for wedding guests at the marriage of Anne Washington to Augustus Silliman Blagden.

After the land division among George's children, Wessyngton was only about 1,000 acres. Sharecroppers worked most of the land. As some of the original Wessyngton families died out or relo-

Wessyngton mansion, 1920s.

Five-generation photo taken on farm of Richard Terry, 1925. The child in the photo, Maxine Williams Washington, now has fifth-generation descendants making a total of nine generations she has seen.
Front row: Jane Bigbee Killins (1852–1946), Maxine Williams [Washington] (b. 1922), Huldah Jones Bigbee (1831–1923). Back row: Bettie Killins Terry (1886–1975), Annie Mae Terry Williams (1904–1995).

cated, there were new black and white families to take their places. Black families included Drake, Williams, Connell, Darden, Phillips, Terry, Green, Tribue, Ellis, Washington, Frazier, and Dowlen. The white families on the estate included Adams, Whitman, Webb, Hulsey, Hornberger, Knight, Marshall, Hunter, Gossett, Gourley, McCroy, Inman, Harris, Farmer, Rummell, and Cooksey.

Education remained a priority. In 1894 a one-room school building was erected facing the Antioch Baptist Church, with a deep well between them. Prior to 1894, the church also served as school. At one time, as many as ninety children were enrolled under one teacher in the little school.

Joseph Edwin established the Washington School on the farm. In 1908 the Washington family formally asked the Robertson County Board of Education for a teacher. The Washington School was made up of the black children of the employees on the farm including the sharecroppers' children. Joseph Washington (1895–2002) attended classes on the Washington Plantation in that school built for the children of the sharecroppers.[26] The Coleman School was opened nearby for the black children in the area in 1910 so the Washington School probably closed. The Coleman School was a one-room school with about thirty-five students.

A clear demonstration of the African Americans' belief in the importance of education was the event remembered by Herschel Williams (1898–1993). He and his wife, and Annie Mae Terry Williams, were sharecroppers at Wessyngton for a number of years:

It was very important to me that my children get an education because I didn't have a chance to go to school that much. One day in 1941, as all the black children on the place were on their way to school, the farm manager Hornberger told them that they couldn't go to school because they would have to help take down tobacco, but he didn't stop the children of the white sharecroppers. My children then started back home. I

*Jenny Washington (1866–1950) and
Geneva Gleason.*

met them and asked where they thought they were going, and they told me what Hornberger had said. I immediately sent my children back on their way to school and told Hornberger that he didn't have any black children and that my children weren't hired to work on the farm! I sternly told the manager that he wasn't to ever tell my children they were not to go to school again. The farm manager then put me and my family off the farm. My children were always proud that I stood up for them and spoke up in a time when few black men felt they could. I didn't take nothing off people back then and I don't now.

Cousin Herschel lived a few blocks away from me on Thirteenth and often visited our home. He was in excellent physical condition well into his nineties and could be seen walking all over town. He would often tell me, "I'm over ninety years old and I can walk from here to town and back, sit down a few minutes, and go right back."[27] He was the great-grandfather of the rapper and movie star Clifford Smith, aka Method Man.

———•·•———

Joseph Edwin died on August 28, 1915, after a two-week struggle with typhoid fever, still a deadly menace in rural Tennessee. A special train was run from Nashville to Cedar Hill, stopping at Springfield to pick up friends to attend his funeral.[28] Newspaper accounts and magazine articles described the Episcopalian funeral with Masonic rites that was attended by hundreds of dignitaries, friends, and local mourners. According to *The Nashville Banner,* "one section was reserved for the Colored plantation hands and Colored people of Robertson County, who came in great numbers." *The Springfield Herald* wrote, "The house servants who had been faithful to Mr. Washington for many years followed the family."[29] *The Nashville Woman's Magazine* described that "the family, the connections, the friends, the neighbors, the associates, the tenantry, the servants, some of the old slaves of the family or their children— each one's face bore the imprint of regret and sorrow."[30] Many articles, editorials, and obituaries reviewed his illustrious career: his five terms in the United States Congress; his close personal and professional relationship to the Democratic president Grover Cleveland (president from 1885 to 1889 and 1893 to 1897), to John G. Carlisle and Chief Justice White; his deep interest in education indicated by his terms as trustee of Vanderbilt University; and his terms as director of the N.C. & St. Louis and Nashville & Decatur railroads. He achieved the high rank of 32nd Degree Mason.[31, 32]

———•·•———

Wessyngton was inherited by Joseph Edwin Washington's widow, Mary Bolling Kemp Washington. Their son Joseph E. Washington Jr. was placed in charge. Joseph had attended several Northern preparatory schools, including St. Paul's and Phillips Academy (known today as Andover), and graduated from Yale University. His brother, George Augustine 2d, graduated from Yale University and Harvard Law School, and by the early 1930s, he left his New York law practice to run the plantation. George commissioned a "Farm Management Corporation Report" that concluded that its approximately one thousand acres of cultivatable land needed to be managed by a paid manager to improve its earnings.[33] When Joseph Edwin's widow died in 1946, her funeral was described in detail in the *Nashville Tennessean:*

> Never, perhaps, in this Southern section of the country, will there be an occasion such as took place in Robertson County, Tennessee, a few days ago, harking back to the old South now fast disappearing. . . .
>
> After simple services in the rambling old home, nearly 200 years old, to the strains of "Abide with Me," there came from the white porch an impressive and solemn procession, which had in its rarity the character of a pageant. First came the clergy in white vestments, the lily-covered casket, the family, friends, and neighbors, followed by a long line of family servants and tenants, many bent with age, youths and young children, each carrying a floral design, sent from far and near. The procession moved slowly through the old garden, bright with spring flowers, between lilacs and flowering fruit trees, to the stone-walled burial grounds.[34]

Her estate passed to her sons, George Augustine 2d and Joseph Edwin Washington Jr., and her two daughters, Anne Bolling Blagden and Elizabeth Wyndham Hotchkiss.

Many customs and rituals continued at Wessyngton. Descendants of the black and white sharecroppers recalled everyone getting along very well. An 1893 description of a wedding of African Americans on Wessyngton illustrated the evolving relationship between the Washington family and its servants. The bride was the forty-year-old Anne Bernaw, who came to Wessyngton from Virginia possibly upon the marriage of Mary Bolling Kemp to Joseph Edwin, and worked in the mansion. The groom was the widower Austin "Aus" Terry, who was a sharecropper on Wessyngton and born a slave there. The Washingtons were intricately involved in the preparations. Jane wrote to one of her grandsons about the summer wedding:

> I must tell you about Mammy's [Anne Bernaw] wedding. She wore the muslin dress your mother [Mary Bolling Kemp Washington] gave her, a white ribbon round her waist, a white veil over her hat, Aunt Mary Frazer pinned it on, a pair of white gloves and a cream colored fan which

Austin Terry (1844–1916) and
Anne Bernaw Terry (1853–1918).

Aunt Mary gave her and her watch and the handkerchief your mother gave her stuck in her belt. Austin [Terry] had on light pants, black coat and vest and a red necktie. Mary Lip was very nicely dressed and had a big bunch of pink roses pinned on her breast. Amos [Emanuel Washington's son] took Mary in his buggy and Aus took Anne. When they walked into the [Antioch Baptist] Church Mary went with the groom and Anne with Amos. While the ceremony was going on Aunt Sarah [Sarah Washington Cheatham] began to shout "Glory, Glory, I'm so happy Aus has got a good wife, Glory." Anne said it made her ashamed. Mammy asked me to let her go out of the front door that it was bad luck to go out of the back door. So I said yes and Austin came in at the front door and took his Bride. All the children threw old shoes after them for good luck.

I gave Anne all the things for her wedding supper. Molly [Terry Washington, Austin's sister] cooked it except the cakes which Mary Lip made. She had biscuits and chicken enough for all, two large iced cakes, two glass bowls of peaches and two of pineapple jelly and preserves and a big freezer of ice cream and the groom furnished some blackberry wine. The table was set in the loom house where Henny [Washington] irons. I gave them a white table cloth, the plates, dishes, glasses, knives and forks, indeed everything she used. I tell you she had a "splurgis" wedding. She and Aus drove home in the moonlight and the next day she came for her things. And that's the end of Mammy.[35]

Reverend Woodard Washington remembered that "[f]rom the time I was big enough to remember, everyone went up to the Big House on Christmas morning and everyone, sharecroppers and hired hands, got presents." Joe Washington (son of Gabe Washington and named after Wessyngton's owner, Joseph E. Washington) remembered that during Christmas everyone on the plantation would gather at the Big House, and everyone on the place would receive gifts.[36] Lucy Washington Wilcox had the same recollection. Even in the 1930s, Christmas was still a special day shared by the Washingtons, the white sharecroppers, and the slave descendants. A Washington family member's journal described "Wednesday, December 25, 1935, Christmas Day":

Had Christmas tree on kitchen porch with five in washroom. John Terry acting as Santa Claus with masks and red leggings and woolen coat of Mr. Farmer's. Had presents for all people on place sent by Anne Blagden, each present wrapped in red paper with name on Christmas tag. About 85 presents from Anne and Gus [Blagden]. Betty Hotchkiss also sent box containing presents for household servants and Farmer and myself. Mother [Mary Bolling Kemp Washington] also sent presents for household. Had tree and presents distributed at 10 a.m. Weather cold about 23 or 24 degrees with snow storm in moving about 3/4 inches of snow. Christmas night thermometer down to 10 degrees above zero.[37]

In another notation in the journal on December 26, 1935, one of the Washingtons described the result of too much Christmas spirit in the African American community:

Will Neville arrested by Joe Hardin on complaint of Herschel Williams' wife [Annie Mae Terry Williams]. It appears that Will Neville and Wesley Mallory attended a concert Christmas night at the Washington Hall Lodge room on Turnersville Road and had too much Christmas when they went there. Herschel Williams' wife who was running the concert said they broke up the concert, so she had them arrested today. I went on appearance bond for Neville to appear 10 am, Saturday, 28th before Ed Lokey at Cedar Hill. Herschel Williams' wife said that any institution that was opened with prayer was entitled to the protection of the law and that is why she had Will Neville and Wesley Mallory arrested.[38]

A cannon on Wessyngton's great lawn was fired every Christmas morning. The tradition ended when the cannon was donated for scrap iron during the second World War.

In the 1890s the Washington family commissioned portraits of several of their former slaves. [Maria] Howard Weeden, the most famous artist of the time who specialized in portraits of African Americans, painted these portraits. Most likely, the family sent the artist photographs of some of the former slaves from which she drew their likenesses for the paintings. The portraits measured

*Henny Jackson Smith, portrait
by [Maria] Howard Weeden.*

Wessyngton servant, portrait by [Maria] Howard Weeden.

approximately 5 inches by 7 inches and were done in soft pastel shades. The portrait of Henny Jackson Smith was based on an 1849 photograph. In the photograph she had a large basket by her side sitting near the Wessyngton mansion, but the portrait was only head to shoulder. Two portraits were also painted of Emanuel Washington. Another portrait of a slave showed the columns of a plantation house in the background. The portraits hung in prominent places in the Wessyngton mansion, along the grand staircase in Washington Hall, and now in the homes of Washington descendants. Also a full portrait of Granville Washington hung in the mansion.

The achievements of the Wessyngton freedmen were more impressive in view of the institutionalization of Jim Crow, the system of laws and customs that perpetuated racial segregation and discrimination, after the end of Reconstruction in 1877. Jim Crow was also the name of a character white performers in blackface used to mock black people. By the beginning of the twentieth century, blacks were constantly reminded of their second-class citizenship.

For the former Wessyngton slaves the first decades of the twentieth century were years of change. According to their descendants, the stereotype of the poor blacks was not correct: not all blacks were poor. Some of them bought farms, built houses, and purchased automobiles. African Americans commissioned portraits of themselves and their relatives to hang in their homes. These oil paintings usually were painted by itinerant artists. Many of them also had their pictures taken by professional photographers.

Sellie Terry was the first African American in Robertson County known to own an automobile—a Model T Ford—which he bought in 1918. His brother Richard purchased a car at the same time but sold it after he had an accident.[39]

Some African Americans amassed enough money to purchase their own farms. According to Maggie Polk Washington, so many blacks owned land in the areas around Mt. Herman, Cedar Hill, Turnersville, and Fisers, it was like a black town.[40] John Lewis had purchased his own farm of 100 acres in 1886. There was also a

Sellie Terry and Callie Williams Terry and family with Model-T Ford, 1918. A. C. Terry, Ewing Terry, Sellie Terry, Ethel Terry, Annie Bell Terry, Legusta Terry, Callie Terry, Bertha Terry, Gertrude Terry.

Sellie Terry (1875–1946) and
Callie Williams Terry (1880–1964).

small family cemetery located on the farm, where his wife, Minerva Washington Lewis, and other family members were buried.
The last burial there was in 1909. Goldena Lewis Yates recalled
that her paternal grandparents, John Lewis and Minerva Washington, were Washington slaves and their land had once been a part
of the plantation.

Wiley Terry and his sons Sellie and Richard purchased several
hundred acres of land that had once been part of the Wessyngton
Plantation. Some of the property is still owned by their family today.
A deed dated January 1, 1905, shows that Wiley, Richard, and Sellie
Terry purchased 429 acres of land from George T. Parrish and William McMurry for $7,000 to be paid in seven installments from 1906
to 1912.[41] Sellie Terry and his wife, Callie Williams Terry, donated
some of their land near their home to establish the Sandy Springs
School (also called Scott's Chapel School) for African Americans.

The Terry family also had a cemetery on their land. Rachel
Washington Terry was buried there in 1918. An expensive tombstone placed on her grave was later moved to Scott's Cemetery

when Wiley Terry was buried there in 1931. Lady Terry recalled that her father Wiley Terry bought his own farm.

Joe Scott bought 18 acres, part of which was later used as a family and community cemetery and was near Scott's Chapel School.[42]

George Gardner, who was a Wessyngton slave, owned 71 acres by 1879 and purchased an additional 98 acres in 1885. Henderson Chapman Bell, a blacksmith who married a former Wessyngton slave, Olive Cheatham (1833–1928), owned 106 acres.

Granville Washington's two sons, Foster and Lawson, purchased 101 acres near the Glenraven estate together in 1880. There is a small cemetery on this land where their grandmother, Marina Washington, was buried in 1884. There are approximately thirty graves in the cemetery.

Many of the former Wessyngton slaves and their children who could not purchase their own property in the latter part of the nineteenth century managed to do so during the early twentieth. Jordan and Nelson Washington both owned town lots in Cedar Hill;

Nelson Washington (1865–1943).   *Irvin Washington (b. 1870).*

Sampson Terry owned a 100-acre farm; Everett Washington, 150 acres; his son, General Washington, owned 81 acres; William Scott owned 114; Doss Washington, 95; Love Lewis, 165; Joe Lewis, 74; and Granville Washington's grandson, also named Granville, owned 57 acres. Henry Darden owned 505 acres. Most of this property was in the 6th, 7th, 8th, and 14th Districts of Robertson County that were near the Wessyngton properties. Irvin Washington purchased property in Cedar Hill. Irvin and his brother Nelson Washington and their families were prominent members of the St. James Baptist Church in Cedar Hill. Irvin and Nelson were instrumental in continuing the August Eighth celebration in Cedar Hill, which was held on their land. In later years the Masons and Eastern Stars (the organization then open to Masons' female relatives) sponsored the celebration and sold fish and pulled-pork barbeque. Irvin's barbeque was the culinary specialty of the event.

A few African Americans became large property owners. Alford Pitt (1830–1900), a carpenter, purchased land from the 1880s through 1900 until he had amassed 550 acres. He was the largest black landowner in the area closest to Wessyngton, and

Arry Fort Pitt (1836–1918). *Nicie Pitt Ross (1885–1910).*

Robertson County's largest black landowner with black and white sharecroppers on his land. His wife, Arry Fort Pitt, who bore him eleven children, filed for divorce in 1900 citing him for mental cruelty, death threats, and adultery with three black women and one white woman (the wife of one of his sharecroppers). Alford believed that since he and Arry married prior to emancipation that their marriage was not valid, and therefore she was not entitled to any of his property. Arry was represented in court by Joel Battle Fort, whose family had owned her family during slavery. The court denied Alford's defense citing the 1866 law which legalized former slave marriages and ordered him to give Arry one thousand dollars in cash, one hundred acres of land, a buggy, and livestock. The case put a strain on the Pitt family as half the children sided with their mother and the others their father. Alford died shortly after the court decision from a severe cold caused by traveling to court in bad weather. Some of the Pitt land remains in the family, and a street that runs through the property is named in the family's honor.

Some freedmen left Robertson County and purchased property in other areas. Others, like Granville, moved to Nashville and purchased homes in the city. Ford Washington moved to Montgomery County, went into the barbering business, and then relocated to Lincoln County, where he purchased property. After Ford's death, some of the family moved to Cleveland, Ohio, and others migrated to Chicago.

New business and educational opportunities opened for African Americans. Joseph Green and Marion Simms Washington Green moved to Nashville, where some of their descendants became very successful and influential citizens, serving as teachers, or operating groceries, laundromats, dry cleaners, hotels, and rental businesses. By 1904 Inman Green had started Green's Grocery. He later expanded

Green Family, 1942.

the business; he built a $200 investment in 1913 into a grocery store that was grossing $25,000 annually by 1920.[43] Ford Green became principal of the Ford Green School, which later became Pearl Cohn High School. Ellen Green married into the Pitt family.

Some of the former slaves of Mary Cheatham Washington's brother, Richard Cheatham, became very prominent citizens. Fanny Cheatham's children became educators, entrepreneurs, and landowners. Anderson Cheatham was in the first graduating class at Fisk University in Nashville. Harriet Cheatham married Humphrey Bowling and, after his death, Sam Bransford whose family were tour guides at Mammoth Cave, Kentucky. Sam operated a barbershop on the town square in Springfield for an all-white clientele. After he suffered a stroke, the family business was run by his son-in-law, Ike Henderson. Harriet and Sam's daughters, Susan Bransford Kitchen and Lena Bransford, were among the first black teachers in Robertson County. They taught at a school founded in 1884. It was one-room building on Cheatham Street (named for

Colonel Richard Cheatham) in Springfield. It became a high school in 1913. Students throughout Robertson County had to go to that school to go beyond the ninth grade. Many walked several miles to school to complete their educations. The school was later named in honor of Lena Bransford. Most of the Bowling-Bransford family migrated to Nashville and then to other states.

During the early 1900s, many blacks left the farms and moved to the city of Springfield, where many of them worked in the tobacco factories. Others worked as day laborers and domestics. The city at the time was segregated, and many of the blacks operated their own businesses. There were various black-operated businesses throughout Springfield, but the greatest concentration of them was located on Thirteenth and Cheatham streets. In this section there were several black-owned restaurants, saloons, hotels, grocery stores, dry cleaners, shoe shops, barbershops, undertakers, nightclubs, dance halls, poolrooms, and beauty shops. There

Bowling-Bransford family reunion, 1928.

were two churches and a doctor's office in the area as well. Practically everything needed from the cradle to the grave could be found in that one spot all within walking distance. After former slave Joseph Scott's death, his property in the rural area was sold, and his daughters, Jenny Scott Washington and Eliza Scott Lewis, purchased property in the city of Springfield. Some of the property remains in their descendants' possession. Will Gardner purchased property in Springfield after selling the property he inherited from his uncle George Gardner.

———•••———

Even with so many people moving away, still certain aspects continued as before. Woodard Washington, the son of a Wessyngton slave (Gabriel Washington) and then a sharecropper, stayed on the plantation in the same house in which he was born until 1914. He

Amos Washington (1870–1955) (right), daguerreotype.

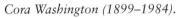

Cora Washington (1899–1984).   *Bob Washington (1897–1977),*
World War I soldier

then joined the army in the 9th Calvary. He recalled, "[w]hen I got out of the service, I was called to the ministry. I embraced Christianity when I was eleven years old. Religion was important to the people on the farm."[44] Woodard commented on how times had changed: "But I will say this, although times were hard, we weren't able to have things like we do now, I believe we were happier than we are now. People were more neighborly and cared for each other. If my father or someone else would get sick and could not care for their crops, the other neighbors around them would come and carry the crops to the barn. If my mother got sick and wouldn't be able to take care of the children in the family, the neighbor women would come around and carry things on until she got able. We were just happy together in one thing, and after we became Christians, we gave a lot of time to the Lord, more so than we do now. And the Lord blessed us."[45]

Under the leadership of Reverend J. D. Ramey, Antioch Bap-

*Servant with Pauline Tillotson Washington
(b. 1919), in front of gazebo at
Wessyngton Plantation.*

tist Church in the "Hollow" was torn down and a new building
was erected on a scenic plot of ground donated by the Benevolent Order of Turnersville. Descendants remembered that one
could hear singing, the rustling of wagon wheels, and the proud
stepping of horses' hooves bringing people from far and near
to the house of the Lord. The Antioch Baptist Church served
as a spiritual beacon for many blacks. Mattie Terry recalled the
high-spirited church meetings and revivals at Antioch when she
was a young woman: "We really had a time back in those days,
we would walk for miles to go to church during revivals and it
would sometimes be pitch-black when church turned out, but we
didn't get tired. People would be singing and shouting all along
the way and going back home. There would be crowds of us
walking. And we would meet others who would join us. When I
got baptized, it was so cold they had to break ice on the creek to

baptize me, but when I came out I was hot because I was filled with the Holy Ghost."[46]

Antioch Baptist Church lost many members when some African American families joined the Great Migration to the North in the 1920s. Some of the Wessyngton descendants also attended the Mount Herman Baptist Church and the Saint James Baptist Church in Cedar Hill.

Burials continued at Wessyngton in the slave cemetery until July 1928. Henry Drake, a sharecropper on the estate, died while in the fields and was buried in the cemetery. His family had no connections to Wessyngton. Guss Washington Jr. made his coffin and Henry was taken to the cemetery in a mule-drawn wagon. Maxine Williams Washington recalled that her mother took her and her sister, Mae June, by the hand to the cemetery where prayers and songs were conducted. Then the body was lowered in the grave; there was no other funeral service.

Guss Washington Sr. (b. 1858).

In the 1920s, the children at Wessyngton, white and black, had close ties. Maxine Williams Washington said she and the white manager Mr. Harry Webb's daughter, Ethel, were as close as sisters. The manager's children would even spend the night with them in their house. Maxine said they all had a great time while Mr. Webb was manager. He died at Wessyngton after falling from a barn. After Webb's death, a Mr. Farmer and a Mr. Hornberger were managers. Maxine recalled that she and Mary Washington Holley and her sister were very close. The Washington children used to come to their house all the time and even ate supper with them.[47]

Black Tennesseans migrated to Northern industrial cities such as Indianapolis, Chicago, Cleveland, Louisville, and Detroit, both in the 1890s and in the 1900s. The largest portion of the Robertson County migrants relocated to Indianapolis, Evansville, and Chicago. During the 1920s and 1930s, several families from the area migrated to Earlington, Kentucky, to work in the coalmining industry. General Washington and his family were among the first to move to Earlington. During the Great Depression when the mines closed, Reverend Woodard Washington and his large family returned to Wessyngton. After the end of the Depression, the mines reopened and the family moved back to Kentucky. From there the family spread throughout Ohio, Kentucky, Illinois, and Indiana. Other Wessyngton descendants joined this large Northbound wave—the Great Migration—relocating to Maryland, Pennsylvania, Virginia, Connecticut, New York, and Michigan. Some moved west to Texas, Kansas, Nevada, and California. Bill Henry Scott Washington, who was born at Wessyngton and served in the Union Army, moved to Lawton, Oklahoma, where he purchased a home. He received a pension for his Civil War service.

Mattie Terry recalled telling Aunt Henny and Sarah Jane Scott Harris, who still worked in the laundry at Wessyngton for fifty cents per day, that they should get more money and how well people got paid in the North for the same work. She stated that Mrs. Washington (Mary Bolling Kemp Washington) overheard her, didn't like it, but didn't say anything.[48] Many Southern blacks were lured to the North when friends and relatives from the North came home to visit and told them how well they lived and how much they were paid.

My great-uncle Baxter Washington (1903–1988) told me that he did not like farm work, and it was one of the main reasons he moved up North to Chicago.

I raised one crop of tobacco after I got grown and that was the first and the last one. I wanted to get a horse and buggy to impress the young ladies and dress up. I always dressed well and looked good in my clothes. After I raised the crop, my father took most of the money to help out, so I left and went to Chicago in the

Baxter Washington (1903–1988).   *Sallie Washington (1909–1995).*

1920s and have been there ever since. I married your grandfather Joe Cobb's sister, Mattie. She used to write to me every day. She worked for a white woman who asked, "Why in the world do you write him everyday?" When she met me in person and saw how good-looking I was, she told Mattie she saw why she wrote every day. [He then laughed.] I worked until I had saved enough money to send for Mattie and she then came to Chicago and later died from childbirth. I sent her body back to Springfield and left our son with my in-laws and was going to come back and get him when he got older. He died as a baby.

Emanuel Washington's sister, Sue Washington, had moved to Topeka in the 1870s. She returned to the plantation in the early 1900s. Sue often talked about how good everyone lived in Kansas, and that it was a land of plenty. Hearing this as a young boy Joe Washington often wondered, if things were so good, why she ever came back. [49] Many who left the South never returned.

Racial tension, poverty, advancement in farm mechanization, and limited opportunities prompted thousands of blacks to leave the South in the Great Migration from 1916 through 1930. More than 1.5 million African Americans left the South in search of "the Promised Land." The migration of African Americans continued in great numbers throughout the 1930s and 1940s.

———•◦•———

Time began to catch up with the Washingtons. Unlike their grandparents and parents, who rarely entertained and did not live lavishly, local tradition has it that Jane Washington Ewing and George A. Washington Jr. were in fierce competition to have the grandest home in the area, and each tried to entertain on a more elaborate scale than the other. We can only speculate that since they were born after the Civil War and did not suffer through the chaos, they might have had a different set of values than did their older siblings. During the Depression, Glenraven, owned by Jane, was heavily mortgaged and ownership was assumed by the Metropolitan Insurance Company. In 1941 Robert D. Moore bought the Glenraven estate; it is owned today by his descendants. Glenraven was placed on the National Register of Historic Places in 1973.

In the 1930s and early 1940s, George Augustine Jr.'s son, Robert Woods Washington, and Washington Hall started to have financial difficulties, making a sale inevitable. In 1948 Washington Hall was sold to Howard Werthan of Nashville. A warehouse auction of the Washington Hall furnishings took three days with 736 lots sold. Many of the furnishings left the area, as many of the purchasers came from the North.

For years Washington Hall was abandoned and fell prey to vandalism. It was reduced to a faint memory of its former glory and was used to store hay before its destruction by fire in 1965. Today the Washington Hall property is privately owned.

George A. Washington 2d (1879–1964),
portrait by Max Westfield.

The Washington family name still carried considerable influence in Robertson County in the 1950s, as a local folklore story showed:

> George A. Washington 2d would call the Cedar Hill train depot to have the train stopped whenever he needed it to go to Nashville. A Mr. Lawrence began working there; he was from the North and did not know of the Washingtons. George called and said, "I'm George Washington and I need you to stop the train." Mr. Lawrence replied, "I'm Abe Lincoln, and we don't stop the train for anyone." And he banged down the phone. Lawrence admitted that he later found out the hard way who George Washington was, and the train was stopped when requested.

Gabriel Washington (1857–1932).

In 1932 Gabriel Washington (1857–1932) died. He was the last of the former Washington slaves who had remained at Wessyngton to pass away. Mary Washington Holley recalled his funeral: "All the white Washingtons attended the funeral held at the Antioch Baptist Church in Turnersville, and a special place was reserved for them with the family."[50] George A. Washington 2d spoke for the Washington family. He told the assembly that he had known the elderly Gabriel all his life, from the time he was a young boy, and talked about the relationship that existed between both Washington families. Gabriel was buried in Scott's Chapel Cemetery, a few miles from Wessyngton Plantation.

CHAPTER 18

Back Through the Centuries with DNA

———◦◦◦———

For more than twenty years, I conducted my research along traditional lines. I then heard about DNA testing in relation to President Thomas Jefferson and the controversy with the descendants of his slave Sally Hemings in 2001. When I learned that DNA could also be used to trace African lineages before the time of slavery, I realized that the technology could expand my research. Of course, I wanted to test my DNA first. I completed the easy DNA swab test. When I received the results, my connection with my African roots, specifically with the Ibo in Nigeria and the Mende and Temne in Sierra Leone, seemed so real. I felt I had jumped back centuries.

I organized a Wessyngton DNA project for the Wessyngton families whose present-day descendants I could trace. Many of these families have remained in the area since emancipation so they were easy to locate. Locating those who had scattered throughout the country involved more research. Nearly all the Wessyngton slave descendants were eager to take the tests and were excited to learn about their African roots. Most of the people in Robertson County know about my ongoing research. My pastor, a Gardner descendant, was so thrilled about taking the test that he wanted me to explain how DNA testing works to the church congregation. Even a descendant of the white Washington family, Stanley Frazer Rose, appreciated the potential of my Wessyngton DNA project. He paid for a considerable number of tests.

The Wessyngton DNA project included descendants from several branches of Washingtons who came to Wessyngton from the late 1790s through the early 1800s, the Terry family who arrived in 1838, the Gardner family in 1839, the Lewis family in 1843, the Scott, Green, Cheatham, and several other families. Participants included eleven men and seven women. Many of the families have married through the generations, causing some individuals to have multiple lines originating at Wessyngton. Most of the participants live in Tennessee within a short radius of the Wessyngton Plantation; others live as far away as California. I have had several people take the test whom I have never met. One was a cousin who is a professor at UCLA.

The majority of the DNA tests were performed by African Ancestry Inc., DNAPrint Genomics, AncestryByDNA, Family Tree by DNA, and African DNA. I submitted so many tests that one of the companies cooperated by giving me substantial discounts.

The project involved three types of DNA tests: the MatriClan, which traces ancestry through the maternal lineage; the PatriClan, which traces the paternal line; and an admixture test, which is an estimate of a person's entire genetic composition such as: 90 percent African, 7 percent European and 3 percent Native American.

DNA test results were consistent with historical records regarding the slave trade. Most of the earliest Wessyngton families came from Virginia. During the peak of the slave trade, most Virginia slaves came from the present-day region of Nigeria, particularly the Ibo. Test results for many of the Wessyngton slave descendant families indicated descent from the Ibo and Yoruba of Nigeria. The DNA of a great-great-grandson of Emanuel Washington came back with a 100 percent statistical match with the Ga of Ghana and the Ewondo of present-day Cameroon. Testing between two

DNA Test Results of African American Wessyngton Descendants

DONOR 1ST GENERATION	AFRICAN NATION OR OTHER	PRESENT DAY COUNTRY	% MATCH	2ND GENERATION
Bob W. Washington	Ewondo/Ga	Cameroon/Ghana	100%	Bob Washington
Jabari Mahiri	Ewondo/Ga	Cameroon/Ghana	100%	Nathaniel Washington
Lamar Washington	Ibo	Nigeria	100%	Henry Lee Washington
Calvin Darden	Ibo	Nigeria	100%	William Darden
Thomas Washington	White	Germany, Poland, Norway	99.30%	Marcus Washington
Robert Jr. Terry	Ibo/Yoruba	Nigeria	99.40%	John Robert Terry
Silas P. Gardner	Mbundu	Angola	100%	Silas T. Gardner
Miles Scott	Balanta	Guinea-Bissau	100%	Lonzo Scott
Ken Lewis	Hezhan/Han	China	100%	John T. Lewis
Theodore Lewis	Hezhan/Han	China	100%	John T. Lewis
Charles Gardner	Fulbe/Berber	Niger/Morocco	99.20%	Catherine Pitt Gardner
Beverly Hill Shelley	Somali	Somalia	99.70%	Lillian Bowman Hill
Clara Wheeler Morton	Yoruba	Nigeria	99.70%	Mandy Washington Wheeler
Mary F. Washington Trotter	Temne	Sierra Leone	99.70%	Maggie Polk Washington
Joanne King	Mende/Kru	Sierra Leone/Liberia	99.70%	Mattie Barbee Burns
Beverly Northington Hughes	Mende/Kru	Sierra Leone/Liberia	99.70%	Charlesetta Ellis Northington

*100% match indicates donor is seven to eight generations removed from an African ancestor.

male descendants of Emanuel Washington came back with identical results.

Only one male lineage tested revealed unexpected European ancestry. According to geneticists approximately 30 percent of African American males have received results indicating European ancestry due to forced miscegenation during slavery. The results from a Washington descendant in San Antonio indicated that his male line ancestors were from Germany, Norway, and Poland. He was very disappointed. The same man had several lines that came from Wessyngton. He was delighted when I told him his distant cousin's test revealed descent from the Mende of Sierra Leone through their common maternal ancestry. There were other slaves from Wessyngton who had European ancestry, but this

	GENERATIONS BACK TO FIRST WESSYNGTON ANCESTOR			
3RD GENERATION	4TH GENERATION	5TH GENERATION	6TH GENERATION	7TH GENERATION
Amos Washington	Emanuel Washington	Godfrey Washington		
Richard Washington	General Washington	Emanuel Washington	Godfrey Washington	
Henry Washington	Gabriel Washington	Allen Washington		
Curtis Darden	Demps Darden	Hezekiah Washington	Allen Washington	
Jesse Thomas Washington	Thomas Washington	Irvin Washington		
John Terry	Wiley Terry	Dick Terry		
Sam Gardner	Will Gardner	Daniel Gardner	Aaron Gardner	
Daniel Scott	Dick Scott			
Will Lewis	John Lewis			
Will Lewis	John Lewis			
Mattie Washington Pitt	Ella Williams Washington	Fannie Ricks Williams		
Marion Otey Bowman	Mattie Green Otey	Marion Simms Green	Ary Washington	
Jenny Washington	Jenny Washington	Jenny Washington	Jenny Washington	
Mary Lewis Polk	Minerva Washington Lewis	Sally Washington	Esther Washington	
Bessie Darden Barbee	Mary Terry Darden	Margaret Lewis Terry	Melissa Washington Lewis	Sarah Washington Cheatham
Atlanta "Missie" Williams Ellis	Geneva Terry Williams	Rachel Washington Terry	Mary Washington	Sarah Washington Cheatham

could be proven through documentation and physical appearance of descendants. A test for some of the Lewis descendants revealed ancestral ties to the Hezhan and Han people of China, which was really surprising.

DNA can be used to prove or disprove family legends such as having Native American ancestry in the absence of supporting documentation. I took a DNA admixture test that indicated that I have some traces of East Asian ancestry. I contacted the company performing the test to inquire about the results. They asked if I had any Native American ancestry; they said it sometimes shows up as East Asian. This is consistent with family lore regarding my great-great-grandparents Henny Washington and Bob White having Native American ancestry.

DNA Lineages of Wessyngton Descendants

Morocco
(Berber)

Guinea-Bissau
(Balanta)

Niger
(Fulbe)

Ghana (Ga)

Nigeria

Cameroon
(Ewondo)

Somalia
(Somali)

Liberia
(Kru)

(Ibo)
(Yoruba)

Sierra Leone
(Mende)
(Temne)

Angola
(Mbundu)

When families have different surnames, DNA testing can be used to prove descent from a common ancestor. This occurred with the Washington and Darden families when one male descendant of Allen Washington (born 1825) used the Darden surname and the other did not. Their descendants were aware of the kinship although some of the present-day descendants did not know exactly how the relationship originated. Y-chromosome testing on the Dardens (descendants of Allen's son, Hezekiah Washington) and one of Gabriel Washington's (Allen's other son) descendants showed that both males had identical genetic markers and descended from the Ibo people of Nigeria.

While many situations were resolved by DNA testing, others were more challenging. The origins of Fannie Williams were one of the most mysterious of all the groups tested. According to some of Fannie's descendants, she was a full-blooded Indian. Other descendants said that she was only half Native American. It had been passed down that Fannie was part of the Cherokee removals during the Trail of Tears and she was separated from her family as a young child. Some said she was free; others said she was a slave. Conflicting documentation only complicated matters. The death certificates of three of her children (Ella Williams Washington, Robert Williams, and Wash Williams) all listed her with a different maiden name—Garrison, Keaton, and Ricks, respectively. Census records also had inconsistent information. Some census records listed Fannie's birthplace as either Tennessee, Virginia, or West Virginia. The 1910 U.S. Census listed Fannie as being born in Virginia, and both her parents as being born in Africa. Fannie's portrait gives credence to the theory that she was at least part Native American. Her distinct features were dominant among some of her descendants. The results of her great-granddaughter's DNA test to trace Native American ancestry through the maternal line came back with negative results. Another test indicated that Fannie's maternal lineage had connections to the Berber people of

Morocco and the Fulbe of Niger. An admixture test on another great-granddaughter indicated 18 percent East Asian/Native American ancestry. This test supported Fannie's Native American ancestry likely came through her father's line.

I used DNA testing for other research purposes. I always wondered how close the relationship was between President George Washington and Wessyngton's founder. The Washington family and the slave descendants had told me that they were close cousins. In the Washington Family Papers I found that in the 1930s and 1940s the family had spent considerable effort documenting that relationship. I had been in contact with a descendant of the president's uncle, and Stanley Frazer Rose was able to locate the last direct male-line descendant of Joseph. Once the results came back, it showed that the genetic connection could only be proven centuries earlier, from 800 to 1200 when both families descended from William de Hertburn, the owner of Wessyngton Manor in England.

Just as in the case of President Jefferson and Sally Hemings, I had hoped that DNA could have proved or disproved the paternal connection between George Augustine Washington, Wessyngton's owner, and Granville Washington, his valet. Unfortunately, I have not yet located a descendant of Granville who I can test.

DNA can help African Americans find our true heritage, which has been severed over the centuries. Most people feel that it is good to know who we were before slavery. Only time will tell what our DNA will reveal about our distant past, and how we will use that information in the future.

Epilogue:
To Honor Our Ancestors

———•◦•———

Well into the latter decades of the twentieth century, Wessyngton was a working tobacco farm with close connections to the African American community. George A. Washington 2d was the last Washington at Wessyngton to carry that surname. The family formed the Wessyngton Corporation, which controlled the plantation. The family gave Felix "Ditt" Terry, who had cared for George in his later years and had maintained the property, considerable acreage that is used for tobacco production. His son Jerry continues tobacco farming there more than two hundred years after the plantation was established.

The plantation was placed on the National Register of Historic Places in 1971. Wessyngton was sold out of the family in 1983 after 187 years of Washington ownership.

Glen and Donna Roberts, the new owners of Wessyngton Farms, have done extensive renovations to the mansion and grounds and operate the plantation as a cattle farm. They have been gracious in sharing Wessyngton with my family and me, the community, and family-reunion groups interested in their history. In addition to the mansion, Wessyngton has quite a few of its original buildings: a gazebo, the two-story brick smokehouse where the famous Washington Hams once hung, the brick kitchen and laundry room with servants quarters above (now a garage), the

Felix "Ditt" Terry, Dorothy Terry, Mary Terry Cole, Jimmy Cole, and Jerry Terry at Wessyngton Plantation.

Felix "Ditt" Terry (1924–2007).

ice house, the Washington family cemetery, the slave cemetery, a restored slave cabin, the stock barn, tobacco barns, and numerous outbuildings.

African American descendants from Wessyngton now live all over America. They became physicians, lawyers, poets, teachers, civil rights activists, ministers, painters, artists, authors, bankers, brokers, professional athletes, movie stars, airplane pilots, business owners, accountants, genealogists, writers, singers, entertainers, policemen, and government and public officials.

The Great Migration out of the South that occurred during the late 1800s, early 1900s, and up to the 1970s has ended, and the trend has reversed. Many African Americans are heading back south. Today the South offers opportunities unheard of by previous generations. New economic prospects as well as family ties have led African Americans to return and have attracted those born in the North as well.

Today in Robertson County, there are more actual Washington

descendants than any other family. Hundreds of direct descendants of Aaron and Betty Gardner still reside in the county with probably more African Americans carrying the Gardner name than any other surname. The Gardners have held an annual family reunion since 1935 and they visited Wessyngton in 2006. The Terry family is well represented in the area and is very large. When I drew a family tree spanning ten generations for their family reunion in 2003, it included 850 descendants of from Dick and Aggy Terry; the total has grown to more than a thousand. The Terry family has a biannual reunion that includes a tour of Wessyngton. The descendants of Dick and Anna Scott also hold a family reunion biannually in Springfield that is well attended.

The Antioch Baptist Church has a thriving membership after 140 years of service. Each year, on the fourth Sunday in May, the church celebrates its homecoming. People from all over the country attend, bringing their families back to the communities where they once lived. Each year, near Wessyngton Plantation, the Eighth of August Celebration takes place. This event commemorates locally

Washington family reunion at Wessyngton Plantation, 2000.

Washington family at Wessyngton Plantation slave cemetery, 2000.

the date when all slaves were emancipated in 1865, and hundreds of people from all over the country return for the celebration just as they have since the end of the Civil War.

----••••----

For all the solitary hours during long nights and weekends I have spent doing research and writing, it is the coming-together of people that has made it all worthwhile. Descendants of Bob and Maggie Washington have held an annual Washington family reunion for decades. Through my research efforts, in 2000 the reunion was expanded to include other descendants of Emanuel and Henny Washington and Allen and Jenny Washington. More than two hundred descendants gathered from places as far away as Illinois, Indiana, and Ohio. Participants covered six generations and ranged in age from one to ninety-six. This was the first time some family members had met since their families left the plantation in the early 1900s. They toured Wessyngton Plantation, and I gave a brief history of our family and other slave families on the plantation. Then we gathered at the Wessyngton slave cemetery, where a monument had been erected in 1995 to honor our ancestors and others buried there. After a dedication prayer, we closed with the spiritual "Walk with Me, Lord." It was a touching event that Nashville's CBS affiliate televised over five days.

One of the most positive results of my journey has been seeing the increased interest among African Americans in learning about our own histories. Over the years, many people have contacted me; the network is expanding and people are communicating. The ability to discover much more about our history and ourselves is growing. Young African Americans react very favorably to this new sense of positive identity; I am always especially pleased when this happens.

The story of Wessyngton Plantation is now part of America's history. I have tried to tell the story of African Americans with names. They were real people, not just an anonymous population often written about as "the slave," or "unknown slave," or "former slave." Had I not taken such a strong interest in the "unnamed former slaves" in the picture in my social studies book and gone beyond its initial presentation, I would never have learned about my deep and rich heritage. The history of Wessyngton Plantation has touched my life and the lives of many people. This book is a tribute to those African Americans who came before and a beacon of hope for those who will follow.

Acknowledgments

———•◦•———

My deepest appreciation and gratitude goes to so many people who have assisted me in my thirty-year journey. Special thanks go to all the elders from my childhood for sharing their memories with me and answering my never ending questions, to my family and extended family, other Wessyngton families and friends for their moral support, and the Washington family for sharing their stories, photographs, and support. These include:

Charlotte Fykes Anderson, Chantel Baker, Georgia M. Cobbs Baker, John F. Baker Sr. (1922–1987), Joe T. Baker Jr., Joe T. Baker Sr. (1947–2001), Steven Baker, Michael Black, Alice Lewis Buchanan (1911–2003), Cora Washington Burns (1899–1984), Peter Byrd, Joseph R. Cobbs Sr. (1905–1973), Ann Nixon Cooper, Calvin Darden, Janie Darden Couts, Allison Curd, Stacye Dowlen Sr., Jerry L. Durrett Jr., Mary Washington Edmondson, Clarence Scott Ellis (1923–2007), Marie Bell Ellis, Minnie Washington Ellis, Catherine Pitt Gardner, Charles Gardner, Reverend Sam Gardner (1901–1999), Reverend Silas P. Gardner, Cordell Howell, Beverly Northington Hughes, Harriet Bowling Jones, Betty J. Killings, Gertrude Terry Killings (1903–1996), Joann King, Julie Otey Lee, Ken Lewis, Theodore Lewis, A. E. Lockert, Jabari Mahiri, Mae June Williams McGlothen (1924–2005), Clara Wheeler Morton (1927–2007), Sallie Washington Cobbs Nicholson (1909–1995), Dianna Washington Northington, Ronald Otey, Henry Polk (1907–1990), Miles Scott, Beverly Hill Shelley, Mary Anne Terry

Sparkman, Nathaniel Stone (1931–2006), Pearl Crockett Stone, Annie Bell Terry (1914–2003), Felix "Ditt" Terry (1924–2007), Jerry Terry, Mattie Terry (1889–1982), Robert Jr. Terry, Frankie Townsend, Johnnie Baker Townsend, Kevin Townsend, Narcissus Terry Traughber, Mary Francis Washington Trotter, Ken Varner, Argene Washington, Bob Washington (1897–1977), Bob W. Washington, Baxter Washington (1903–1988), Caribel Washington, Carl Alex Washington, Carrie Williams Washington (1894–1993), Reverend Henry Washington, Joseph Washington (1895–2002), Lamar Washington, Maggie Polk Washington (1904–2003), Maxine Williams Washington, Oscar Washington Jr., Richard Washington, Thomas Washington, Willie D. Washington, Woodard Washington (1891–1985), Ola Baird Wells (1903–1995), Bessie Washington Cox (1927–2005), Lucy Washington Wilcox (1901–1980), Annie Mae Terry Williams (1904–1995), Celesta Williams, Christopher Williams, Herschel Williams (1898–1993), Robert B. Williams Sr. (1931–2001), Leland Wells Brown Woodard (1895–1984), Donald Wynn, and Goldena Lewis Yates (1905–1991).

I want to sincerely thank the many descendants of the Washington Family for answering my many questions, sharing their memories of Wessyngton, photographs, documents, and other Wessyngton memorabilia: C. Dewees Berry III, Douglas Berry, William Berry, Allen Blagden, Joseph W. Blagden Jr., Thomas Blagden Jr., Thomas Blagden Sr., George Preston Frazer (1908–2003), James Stokes Frazer III, Marshall Gaither Frazer, Eleanor Hardy, Mary Washington Holley, Jane T. Hotchkiss, Augustus Kinsolving, Richard Longstreth, Zelime Matthews, Mary "Robin" Robinson Pinckard, Stanley Frazer Rose, Anne Kinsolving Talbott (1942–2007), Williard Williams, and Sydney Williams.

So many other people helped me along the way with information about their ancestors, life in earlier times, and with editorial suggestions: John Blow, Sandi Craighead, Pam Drake, Bettye Glover, Nila Gober, Ted Ground, Katherine Harbury, Mary Sue Head, Tim

Henson, Gail Holman, Bill Jones, Mark Lowe, Betty Whitman McClaran, Emily C. Rose, Karen Beard Smith, Mai Southall, Mary Catherine Sprouse, John Talbott, and William H. Washington.

Special thanks go to Glen and Donna Roberts for graciously sharing Wessyngton with me and all those interested in its rich history.

Libraries, museums, archives, and research organizations held the history I delved into over so many years. The staffs of these organizations untiringly helped me in my research, and I thank them. Tennessee State Library and Archives (TSLA), Nashville, Tennessee: Ann Alley, Catherine E. Carmack, Ruth Jarvis Clements, Marilyn Hughes, Chaddra Moore, Wayne Moore, Lynn Sawyer, Jerri Steward, Harry Stokes, and John Thweat. Robertson County Archives, Springfield, Tennessee: Tonia Allen, Kay Dorris, Yolanda Gibb Reid. Gorham-McBane Public Library, Springfield, Tennessee, Robertson County Museum, Springfield, Tennessee: Linda Dean. Metro Historical Commission, Nashville, Tennessee: Ophelia Paine and Linda T. Wynn. Tennessee State University Afro-American Historical Conference, Nashville, Tennessee: Dr. Bobby L. Lovett, Gayle Brinkley-Johnson, Dr. Reavis Mitchell. Austin Peay State University, Clarksville, Tennessee: Dr. Yvonne Prather. Midwestern Archaeological Research Center (MARC), Normal, Illinois: David W. Babson, Kermit L. Baumgartner, Melanie A. Cabak, Mark D. Groover, Jerry Moore, and Dr. Mildred Pratt. Virginia State Library and Archives, Richmond, Virginia. Swem Library, Williamsburg, Virginia. Sussex County Clerk's Office, Courtland, Virginia: Gary Williams. African Ancestry, Inc., Washington, DC.: Dr. Rick Kittles and Gina Paige.

When it was time to let go of my thirty-year project, I was thrilled that my agent, Paul Bresnick, understood my passion and found a perfect home for me at Atria Books, a division of Simon & Schuster. My editor, Malaika Adero, guided my book with creativity and enthusiasm, and Isolde Sauer and the Simon & Schuster staff and freelancers—Deirdre Amthor, Annette Patricia Byrdsong, Yona

Deshommes, Paul Dippolito, Douglas Johnson, Navorn Johnson, Patricia Romanowski, and Jim Thiel—brought my book through the process with great attention to each detail.

As I thank each person for their assistance in the creation of my book, I take responsibility for any errors of fact or interpretation.

Notes

Abbreviations

TSLA: Tennessee State Library and Archives
WFP: Washington Family Papers

Chapter 3. We Walked Every Step of the Way from Virginia to Tennessee

1. Dr. Hanif Wahab, curator of the Harriet Tubman Museum and Cultural Association of Cleveland, Ohio, personal communications, 1991. Joseph Nwonkwo (Nigerian), personal communications, 1997. Dr. Uche Ogike (Nigerian), University of Nigeria, personal communications, 2004.
2. 1795–1860 Birth Register of Slaves. WFP, TSLA.
3. Maggie Polk Washington, interview by John Baker, 1995.
4. Blow Family History, compiled by Augusta B. Fothergill, 1927, Blow Family materials, Robert Bolling Batte Collection, Virginia State Library and Archives.
5. Mattie Terry, interview by John Baker, 1980.
6. Blow & Milhaddo to Hon. Thomas Jefferson, Richard Blow Papers, Swem Library, College of William and Mary.
7. Slave Bill of Sale, by Micajah Blow to Joseph Washington, 1802, WFP, TSLA.
8. Will, Joseph Washington Sr., 1803. WFP, TSLA.
9. Southampton County, Virginia tax records 1782.
10. Sussex County, Virginia tax records 1793.
11. Southampton County, Virginia tax records 1794–1798.
12. Walter Durham, *The Southwest Territory, 1790–1796* (Piney Flats, Tenn.: Rocky Mount Historical Association, 1990), 28.
13. Dr. B. L. Branch, interview by George A. Washington 2d, August 4, 1917. Joseph E. Washington, "Address of Hon. Joseph E. Washington, May 24th 1915 On the Occasion of the Reunion at Wessyngton of the One Hundredth Anniversary of the Birth of his father George Augustine Washington," WFP, TSLA. Adapted from speech with additional information included in brackets.

14. Ibid.

15. Ibid.

16. Ibid.

17. Land grant, 640 acres, to Moses Winters, North Carolina Land Grants 1784, Book G-7, 97–98.

18. Ralph Winters, *Hospitality Homes and Historic Sites in Western Robertson County, Tennessee* (Clarksville, Tenn.: self-published, 1971), 16, 127.

19. Weston Goodspeed, *History of Tennessee from the Earliest Time to the Present: Together with an Historical and a Biographical Sketch of Montgomery, Robertson, Humphreys, Stewart, Dickson, Cheatham and Houston Counties* (Nashville: Goodspeed Publishing, 1886; reprint, Columbia, Tenn.: Woodward & Stinson Print. Co., 1972), 830.

20. Joseph E. Washington, "Address of Hon. Joseph E. Washington, May 24th 1915 On the Occasion of the Reunion at Wessyngton of the One Hundredth Anniversary of the Birth of his father George Augustine Washington," WFP, TSLA. Adapted from speech with additional information included in brackets.

21. Joseph Washington, interview by John Baker, 1997.

22. Land sales contract, 60 acres, Hugh Lewis to Joseph Washington, 1798, Robertson County Tennessee Deed Book B, 193.

23. Deeds, WFP, TSLA.

24. Marcus Huish, *The American Pilgrim's Way in England* (London: Fine Art Society, 1907), 295–298.

25. Joseph E. Washington, "Address of Hon. Joseph E. Washington, May 24th 1915. Adapted from the speech with additional information included in brackets.

26. George A. Washington, 2d (b. 1879), Genealogy Notes, 1930s. WFP, TSLA.

27. Joseph E. Washington, "Address of Hon. Joseph E. Washington, May 24th 1915." Adapted from the speech with additional information included in brackets.

28. Reuben Thwaites, ed., *Travels West of the Alleganies: Made in 1793–96 by André Michaux: in 1802 by F. A. Michaux: and in 1803 by Thaddeus Mason Harris, M. A.* (Cleveland: Arthur Clark, 1904). Alfred Crabb, *Journey to Nashville: A Story of the Founding* (Indianapolis: Bobbs-Merrill, 1957), 82–96.

29. Andrew Washington to Joseph Washington, September 1804 (Southampton County, Virginia) WFP, TSLA.

30. Land sales contract, Moses Winters Jr. and Aaron Winters to Joseph Washington, February 9, 1802, Robertson County, Tennessee Deed Book, Book A, 115.

31. "Articles of Agreement," WFP, TSLA. "Indenture" [sales contract], Joseph Washington to Moses Winters Jr. and Aaron Winters, February 9, 1802, WFP, TSLA. Will, Moses Winters, signed July 9, 1798, and proved Octo-

ber 1798, Robertson County, Robertson County Wills—Abstracts from Book I, 1796–1811, TSLA microfilm, p. 30.

32. "Survey" and "Indenture" [sales contract], Moses Winters Jr. and Aaron Winters to Joseph Washington, February 9, 1802, WFP, TSLA. Will of Moses Winters, signed July 9, 1798 and proved October 1798, Robertson County, Robertson County Wills—Abstracts from Book I, 1796–1811, TSLA microfilm, p. 30. Land sales contract 204 acres, Moses Winters Jr. and Aaron Winters to Joseph Washington, 1802, Robertson County, Tennessee Deed Book, Book A, 115.

33. Joseph E. Washington, "Washington Genealogy Notes in Preparation for Publication" (1913–1915), 27. Joseph E. Washington, "Address of Hon. Joseph E. Washington, May 24th 1915," WFP, TSLA.

34. Weston Goodspeed, *The Goodspeed Histories of Montgomery, Robertson, Humphreys, Stewart, Dickson, Cheatham, Houston Counties of Tennessee* (Nashville: Goodspeed Publishing, 1886; reprint Columbia, Tenn.: Woodward & Stinson, 1972), 837.

35. Acts of Tennessee 1796–1830, W (Pt. 1), 38A.1.

36. H. Phillips Baco, "Nashville's Trade at the Beginning of the Nineteenth Century," *Tennessee Historical Quarterly*, 1956, 30–36.

Chapter 4. We Built That Big House Brick by Brick

1. Slave bills of sale and correspondence in WFP, TSLA.

2. Joseph E. Washington, "Address of Hon. Joseph E. Washington, May 24th 1915," WFP, TSLA.

3. Dunn vs. Washington, November 9, 1812, WFP, TSLA.

4. Will, Archer Cheatham Jr., February 10, 1823, WFP, TSLA.

5. Tax returns, Robertson County, Tennessee, 1813, WFP, TSLA.

6. Birth Register of Slaves, 1795–1860, and Slave bills of sale, WFP, TSLA.

7. N. Minor to Joseph Washington, May 10, 1814, WFP, TSLA.

8. James Clayton to Joseph Washington, June 23, 1819, WFP, TSLA.

9. Joseph E. Washington, "Address of Hon. Joseph E. Washington, May 24th 1915," WFP, TSLA, adapted from speech.

10. Ibid.

11. Gifford Cochran, *Grandeur in Tennessee: Classical Revival Architecture in a Pioneer State* (New York: J. J. Augustin, 1946), 11, photos 33.

12. Lucy Washington Helm, "The Story of Wessyngton Farms" (speech presented at the Query Club, Louisville, Ky., May 11, 1945), WFP, TSLA.

13. Mattie Terry, interview by John Baker, 1980.

14. Joseph E. Washington, "Address of Hon. Joseph E. Washington, May 24th 1915," WFP, TSLA, adapted from speech.

15. W. Clayton, *History of Davidson County, Tennessee* (1880, reprint, Nashville: Elder Bookseller, 1971), 266–269. John Wooldridge, ed., *History of Nashville* (Nashville: H. W. Crew, 1890), 399–405. I. Blandin, *History of*

Higher Education of Women in the South (New York: Neale Publishing, 1909), 273–281.

16. Martha Susan Washington to Mary C. Washington [1824], and November 4 [1824]. Receipts, Joseph Washington from Nashville Female Academy, 1820–1824, WFP, TSLA.
17. "Wessyngton Sees 150th Fall," *Nashville American,* October 15, 1969.
18. Joseph E. Washington, "Address of Hon. Joseph E. Washington, May 24th 1915," WFP, TSLA, adapted from speech.
19. Acts of Tennessee, 1796–1830, W–Part 1.
20. Joseph E. Washington, "Address of Hon. Joseph E. Washington, May 24th 1915," WFP, TSLA.
21. Ibid.
22. George A. Washington, visa for Cuba, January 14, 1836, WFP, TSLA.
23. George A. Washington to Mary C. Washington, May 8, 1836, and Mary C. Washington to George A. Washington, February 15, 1842, WFP, TSLA.
24. Bill of Sale from James Hicks to Joseph Washington for slave Godfrey, January 3, 1821, WFP, TSLA.
25. Will, Archer Cheatham Jr., February 10, 1823, WFP, TSLA.
26. George A. Washington to Joseph Washington, September 23, 1833, WFP, TSLA.
27. Richard Cheatham to George A. Washington from Washington, DC, February 4, 1838, WFP, TSLA.
28. George A. Washington to Mary C. Washington, March 22, 1839, WFP, TSLA.
29. George A. Washington to Mary C. Washington, April 12, 1839, WFP, TSLA.
30. Will, Jacob F. Young, Robertson County Will Book 17, p. 302, March 1858.
31. Reverend Sam Gardner, interview by John Baker, 1979.
32. Benjamin Simms to George A. Washington, May 6, 1839, WFP, TSLA.
33. Benjamin Simms to George A. Washington, May 7, 1839, WFP, TSLA.
34. Lucy Washington Helm, "The Story of Wessyngton Farms," 1945.
35. Ibid.
36. Account Book, Joseph Washington, 1834–1842, WFP, TSLA.
37. Ibid.
38. Ibid.
39. Yolanda Reid and Rick Gregory, *Robertson County, Tennessee: Home of the World's Finest, Celebrating 200 Years* (Paducah: Turner Publishing, 1996), 35.
40. Receipt, John C. Grimes to Joseph Washington, June 16, 1836, WFP, TSLA.
41. Cedar Hill Homecoming '86 Committee, *A Circle of Memories: Cedar Hill and Surrounding Area* (Cedar Hill, Tenn.: 1986), 4.
42. Reid and Gregory, *Robertson County Tennessee,* 35–36.
43. Ibid.

44. Slave bills of sale 1801–1843, WFP, TSLA.

45. Birth Register of Slaves, 1795–1860, WFP, TSLA.

Chapter 5. By the Sweat of Their Brows:
The Largest Tobacco Plantation in America

1. William B. Lewis to Adelaide L. Washington, December 6, 1842, WFP, TSLA.

2. William B. Lewis to George A. Washington, June 15, 1845, WFP, TSLA.

3. G. S. Moore & Son Real Estate Agents, "Wessyngton" (Springfield, s.p., 1983).

4. William B. Lewis to George A. Washington, December 6, 1845, WFP, TSLA.

5. William B. Lewis to George A. Washington, May 11, 1845, WFP, TSLA.

6. Marina B. Cheatham to George A. Washington, December 28, 1844, WFP, TSLA.

7. George A. Frazer to Stanley F. Rose, Stanley F. Rose, interview by John Baker, 2005.

8. I. Blandin, *History of Higher Education of Women in the South* (New York: Neale Publishing, 1909), 273–281. John Wooldridge, ed., *History of Nashville* (Nashville: H. W. Crew, 1890), 399–405.

9. George A. Washington to Jane Smith, May 28, 1849, WFP, TSLA.

10. Ibid.

11. Mary C. Washington to George A. Washington, June 3, 1849, WFP, TSLA.

12. Ibid.

13. Joseph E. Washington, "Washington Genealogy Notes in Preparation for Publication" (1913–1915), 38. WFP, TSLA.

14. Contract, George A. Washington and Anne Pope, July 18, 1849, Receipts, George A. Washington to Anne Pope, 1849–1871. WFP, TSLA.

15. Anne H. Pope to Jane (Jenny) S. Washington, July 27, 1849. George A. Washington to Jane S. Washington, November 7, 1849, WFP, TSLA.

16. Anne H. Pope to Jane S. Washington, August 18, 1849, WFP, TSLA.

17. Jane S. Washington to Anne H. Pope, September 11, 1849. Anne H.Pope to Jane S. Washington, July 27, 1849, August 7, 1849, August 18, 1849, WFP, TSLA.

18. Anne H. Pope to Jane S. Washington, August 7, 1849, WFP, TSLA.

19. Anne H. Pope to Jane S. Washington, August 9, 1849, WFP, TSLA.

20. George A. Washington to Jane S. Washington, November 7, 1849, WFP, TSLA.

21. George A. Washington to Jane S. Washington, January 24, 1852, WFP, TSLA.

22. Joseph E. Washington, "Washington Genealogy Notes in Preparation for Publication" (1913–1915), 37–38, WFP, TSLA. Smith Family Bible, private collection Sydney M. Williams. Anne K. Talbott to Stanley F. Rose, personal correspondence, 2006.

23. Jane S. Washington, "Lines on the Death of Little Mary," December 18, 1854, WFP, TSLA.
24. Family registers, Washington Family Bible, WFP, TSLA.
25. Wilbur Creighton Jr. and Leland R. Johnson, eds. *The First Presbyterian Church of Nashville: A Documentary History* (Nashville: First Presbyterian Church, 1986), 53–62. George A. Washington to Jane S. Washington, January 29, 1852, WFP, TSLA.
26. Lucy Washington Helm, "The Story of Wessyngton Farms," 1945.
27. Catherine E. Carmack, "A Tennessee Planter Family in Transition, 1849–1867" (MA thesis, Middle Tennessee State University), May 1995, pp. 13–14.
28. Jane S. Washington to George A. Washington, September 22, 1864, WFP, TSLA.
29. Lucy Washington Helm, "The Story of Wessyngton Farms," 1945.
30. George A. Washington to Joseph Washington, December 17, 1847, WFP, TSLA.
31. Yolanda Reid and Rick Gregory, *Robertson County Tennessee Home of the World's Finest Celebrating 200 Years* (Paducah: Turner Publishing, 1976), 53.
32. Kermit L. Baumgartner, "A Short History of Wessyngton Plantation," in David Babson, ed., *Families and Cabins, Archaeological and Historical Investigations at Wessyngton Plantation* (Normal, Ill.: Midwestern Archaeological Research Center Illinois State University, 1994), 18.
33. Compiled from Slave Schedules, 1850 and 1860 U.S. censuses.
34. Compiled from Slave Schedule, 1860 U.S. census.
35. Emily Burke, *Reminiscences of Georgia* (Oberlin: James Fitch, 1850), 233.
36. Bills for Runaways and Hired Negroes, WFP, TSLA.
37. Major William B. Lewis to Governor of Kentucky, January 5, 1843, WFP, TSLA.
38. R. M. Johnson to Major William B. Lewis, March 10, 1843, WFP, TSLA.
39. Slave bills of sale, WFP, TSLA.
40. George A. Washington to Robert D. Carr, January 24, 1842, WFP, TSLA.
41. Benjamin Simms to George A. Washington, March 18, 1847, WFP, TSLA.
42. Andrew Jackson Jr. to George A. Washington, May 24, 1855, WFP, TSLA.
43. William B. Lewis to George A. Washington, March 19, 1855, WFP, TSLA.
44. Diary, George A. Washington, March 12, 1859, WFP, TSLA.
45. George A. Washington, Unsent letter to *Union American*, ca. December 1860, WFP, TSLA.
46. U.S. Bureau of the Census. Robertson County, Tennessee, 1850, 1860.

Chapter 6. It Takes a Whole Village

1. Peter Kolchin, *American Slavery 1619–1877* (New York: Hill and Wang, 1993), 139–140.
2. Major William B. Lewis to George A. Washington, June 26, 1844, WFP, TSLA.

3. Major William B. Lewis to George A. Washington, December 25, 1846, WFP, TSLA.

4. Herbert G. Gutman, *The Black Family in Slavery and Freedom 1750–1925* (New York: Random House, 1976), 91.

5. Ibid., 89.

6. Brenda E. Stevenson, *Life in Black and White: Family and Community in the Slave South* (New York: Oxford University Press, 1996), 230.

7. Kenneth M. Stamp, *The Peculiar Institution: Slavery in the Ante-Bellum South* (New York: Vintage Books, 1989), 342.

8. U. S. Pension Application #897678, Reuben Cheatham Washington.

9. Diary, George A. Washington, 1851. WFP, TSLA.

10. J. W. Kendall to George A. Washington, August 28, 1854, WFP, TSLA.

11. Declaration for Pension, 1907, Otho Washington, Company B, 40th Regiment United States Colored Infantry Volunteer. National Archives Washington, DC, Pension #2520072.

12. Lerone Bennett Jr., *Before the Mayflower: A History of the Negro in America, 1619–1964* (Chicago: Johnson Publishing, 1978), 78.

13. List of men and boys on Wessyngton Plantation, 1838, WFP, TSLA.

14. List of men and boys on Wessyngton Plantation, 1856, WFP, TSLA.

15. Wilma King, *Stolen Childhood: Slave Youth in 19th Century America* (Bloomington: Indiana University Press, 1997), 7.

16. Medical bills, Wessyngton slaves and Washington family, 1841, WFP, TSLA.

17. Kathy Russell, Midge Wilson, and Ronald Hall, *The Color Complex: The Politics of Skin Color Among African Americans* (New York: Bantam Doubleday Dell, 1992), 12.

18. Bennett, *Before the Mayflower*, 259.

19. Mary Washington Holly, interview by John Baker, 2004. Stanley F. Rose, interview by John Baker, 2005.

20. George A. Washington 2d, Family Trees, WFP, TSLA. Sadie W. Frazer, Memoirs, Sadie Warner Frazer Papers, TSLA.

21. Mary Washington Holly discussions with Anne Kinsolving Talbott and her grandmother Anne Washington Blagden, 1993. As told to John Baker.

22. Bob Washington and Sallie Washington, interview by John Baker, 1976.

23. Harriet Bowling Jones White, interview by John Baker, 2005.

24. Maggie Polk Washington, interview by John Baker, 1980s.

25. Richard Carlton Fulcher, *Brentwood, Tennessee: The Civil War Years*, p. 25.

Chapter 7. Working from Can't to Can't

1. Negro Clothes Book, Jane S. Washington, 1858, WFP, TSLA.

2. Lucy Washington Helm, "The Story of Wessyngton Farms," 1945.

3. Bennett, *Before the Mayflower*, 78.

4. Estate Settlement, Edwin Washington 1804, WFP, TSLA.

5. Tobacco register, 1846–1864, WFP, TSLA.
6. James O. Nall, *The Tobacco Night Riders of Kentucky and Tennessee* (Kattawa: McClanahan Publishing House, 1992), 7.
7. Diary, George A. Washington, 1855, WFP, TSLA.
8. Ibid.
9. Lucy Washington Helm, "The Story of Wessyngton Farms," 1945.
10. Rev. Woodard Washington, Joseph Washington, and Lucy Washington Wilcox (sons and granddaughter of Gabriel Washington), interview by Caribel Washington, 1970s.
11. Joseph Washington, interview by John Baker, June 20, 1977.
12. Lucy Washington Helm, "The Story of Wessyngton Farms," 1945.
13. John McCline, *Slavery in the Clover Bottoms: John McCline's Narrative of His Life During Slavery and the Civil War* (Knoxville: University of Tennessee Press, 1998), 19–20.
14. Diary, George A. Washington, 1851, WFP, TSLA.
15. Slaves raising their own tobacco, 1850, WFP, TSLA.
16. Jane S. Washington to Mary Washington, March 14, 1865, from New York, New York, WFP, TSLA.
17. Will, David M. Wells, October 23, 1856, Robertson County Archives, Springfield, Tennessee.
18. Will, Mildred White, April 1864, Robertson County Loose Original Wills, Robertson County Archives, Springfield, Tennessee.
19. Lucy Washington Helm, "The Story of Wessyngton Farms," 1945.
20. George A. Washington to Mary C. Washington, April 12, 1839, WFP, TSLA.
21. Baxter Washington, interview by John Baker, 1980.
22. Diary, George A. Washington, January 4, 1851, WFP, TSLA.
23. Ibid.
24. Lucy Washington Helm, "The Story of Wessyngton Farms," 1945.
25. Negro Clothes Book, Jane S. Washington, 1858, WFP, TSLA.
26. Joseph Washington, interview by John Baker, 1997.
27. Account Book, Joseph Washington, 1838, WFP, TSLA.
28. Ann Nixon Cooper, interview by John Baker, 2006.

Chapter 8. I Couldn't Hear Nobody Pray

1. D. Ahern, S. Alvarez, L DeNunzio, and J. Orgaz, Antebellum Slavery: Plantation Slave Life Health/Mortality, http://cghs.dadeschools.net/slavery/.
2. Slave bill of sale Henry Gardner to George A. Washington, April 24, 1839, WFP, TSLA.
3. Lucy Washington Helm, "The Story of Wessyngton Farms," 1945.
4. R. W. January to George A. Washington, August 5, 1851, WFP, TSLA.
5. R. W. January to George A. Washington, December 22, 1851, WFP, TSLA.
6. Jane S. Washington to George A. Washington, January 14, 1854, WFP, TSLA.

7. Mary C. Washington to George A. Washington, June 8, 1840, WFP, TSLA.

8. Benjamin Simms to George A. Washington, January 16, 1842, WFP, TSLA.

9. Benjamin Simms to George A. Washington, April 15, 1846, WFP, TSLA.

10. Joseph E. Washington to Jane S. Washington, February 7, 1865, WFP, TSLA.

11. Slaves' medical bills 1815–1865, WFP, TSLA.

12. Charlotte Fykes Anderson, interview by John Baker, 2005.

13. Charles Joyner, *Down by the Riverside: A South Carolina Slave Community* (Chicago: University of Illinois, 1984), 148.

14. Drew Gilpin Faust, *Before Freedom Came: African-American Life in the Antebellum South* (Charlottesville: University Press of Virginia, 1991), 59.

15. John McCline, *Slavery in the Clover Bottoms: John McCline's Narrative of His Life During Slavery and the Civil War* (Knoxville: University of Tennessee Press, 1998), 22.

16. Joseph Washington, interview by John Baker, 1977.

17. Jane S. Washington to George A. Washington, January 24, 1851, WFP, TSLA.

18. Lucy Washington Helm, "The Story of Wessyngton Farms," 1945.

19. Ibid.

20. Preston Frazer, interview by John Baker, 1985. Information from his father, George Augustine Washington Frazer (1879–1962).

21. Preston Frazer, private memoir, 1997.

22. Mary Washington Holley, interview by John Baker, 2000.

23. Joseph Washington, interview by John Baker, 1997.

24. James O. Breeden, *Advice Among Masters the Ideal in Slave Management in the Old South* (Westport: Greenwood Press, 1980), 224.

25. Mary Holand Lancaster, transcriber, Minutes of Red River Baptist Church 1791–1826 Robertson County, Tennessee (Florence, Ala.: M. H. Lancaster, 1983), 146.

26. Ibid.

27. Ibid., 62.

28. Harriet Parks Miller, *Pioneer Colored Christians* (Clarksville, Tenn.: W. P. Titus, 1911, 1971), 19.

29. Sallie Washington Nicholson, interview by John Baker, 1979.

30. U.S. Pension Application #1255197, William H. Scott (aka Bill Washington), April 1930.

31. Frank W. Dunn Jr., interview by John Baker, 2002.

32. Obituary, Sam Washington, *Leaf Chronicle*, Clarksville, Tennessee, September 8, 1930.

33. Joseph Washington, interview by John Baker, 1977.

34. Joe M. Richardson, *A History of Fisk University 1865–1946* (University: University of Alabama Press, 1980), 29.

35. Yolanda G. Reid and Rick S. Gregory, *Robertson County, Tennessee: Home of the World's Finest, Celebrating 200 Years* (Paducah: Turner Publishing Company), 75.

36. Gregory G. Poole, *Robertson County, Tennessee Obituaries and Death Records 1802–1930,* (Nashville: Land Yatch Press, 1999), 91.

37. "Wessyngton Sees 150th Fall," *Nashville Banner,* October 25, 1969.

38. Mattie Terry, interview by John Baker, 1979.

39. Ibid.

40. Minnie Washington Ellis, interview by John Baker, 2006.

41. Michael A. Gomez, *Exchanging Our Country Marks: The Transformation of African Identities in the Colonial and Antebellum South* (Chapel Hill: University of North Carolina Press, 1998), 276.

42. Janet S. Hasson, *Widows, Weepers and Wakes: Mourning in Middle Tennessee* (Nashville: Belle Meade Plantation, 1995), 13.

43. Estate settlement of Catherine Black, February 5, 1855, Loose Papers, Robertson County Archives, Springfield, Tennessee.

44. "Death of Col. G. A. Washington," *Supplement of the Springfield Record Obituaries,* December 8, 1892, WFP, TSLA. Octavia Bond, "The Washington Family," *Nashville American,* October 10, 1909.

Chapter 9. Wessyngton Rebels

1. Rita A. Read, *Across the Plains: A History of Cross Plains, Tennessee 1778–1986* (Cross Plains: Cross Plains Heritage Commission, 1986), 22.

2. Petition, Mary Baird, 1856, Robertson County, Tennessee Loose Papers, Robertson County Archives.

3. John W. Blassingame, *The Slave Community: Plantation Life in the Antebellum South* (New York: Oxford University Press, 1972), 273.

4. Ibid.

5. Felix "Ditt" Terry, interview by John Baker, 2004.

6. Diary, George A. Washington, 1841–1863, WFP, TSLA.

7. Ibid.

8. Jane S. Washington to George A. Washington, January 4, 1852, WFP, TSLA.

9. Lady Terry Williams, "The Life of Lady Terry Williams," in *Reflections of the Past and Present,* August 1976; Annie Bell Terry, Idella Williams Ross, and Gertrude Terry Killings (granddaughters of Wiley Terry), interviews by John Baker, 1990s.

10. Exhibit State Museum, Nashville, Tennessee.

11. Mary C. Washington to George A. Washington, March 31, 1839, WFP, TSLA.

12. Benjamin Simms to George A. Washington, December 12, 1839, WFP, TSLA.

13. Bill of sale from Thomas Crutcher to William B. Lewis, March 30, 1816. Davidson County, Tennessee Deed Book, H 1809–1821.

14. Major William B. Lewis to George A. Washington, June 4, 1845, WFP, TSLA.
15. Diary, George A. Washington, 1841–1863, WFP, TSLA.
16. Ibid.
17. Diary, George A. Washington, April 25, 1851, WFP, TSLA.
18. Diary, George A. Washington, October 4, 1856, WFP, TSLA.
19. Slave bill of sale from Thomas Williamson to George A. Washington, January 6, 1838, WFP, TSLA.
20. Chris Booker, " 'I Will Be No Man's Slave' An Overview of African American Male History," *African American Male Research* (September/October 1997, vols. 1 and 2).
21. Ibid.
22. Maggie Polk Washington and Margaret Scott Couts, interviews by John Baker, 1996, 1997.
23. J. W. Kendall to George A. Washington, June 16, 1854, WFP, TSLA.
24. Diary, George A. Washington, April 22, 1854, WFP, TSLA.
25. Diary, George A. Washington, November 24, 1856, WFP, TSLA.
26. Jane S. Washington to George A. Washington, January 16, 1854, WFP, TSLA.
27. Mahala v. the State, 18 Tenn. 404–406 (1837), in Arthur Howlington, *What Sayeth the Law: The Treatment of Slaves and Free Blacks in the State and Local Courts of Tennessee* (New York: Garland Publishing, 1986), 170–171.
28. Reid and Gregory, *Robertson County Tennessee*, 47.
29. Howlington, *What Sayeth the Law*, 208–209.
30. Robertson County Circuit Court, Minutes, February 1853, 318–319, 335–336; October 1853, 392, 405; February 1854, 430, 441; June 1854, 464.
31. Reid and Gregory, *Robertson County Tennessee*, 47.

Chapter 10. Follow the North Star

1. John Hope Franklin and Loren Schweninger, *Runaway Slaves: Rebels on the Plantation* (New York: Oxford University Press, 1999), 16.
2. Runaway slave advertisement, *Nashville Whig*, June 1, 1814.
3. Runaway slave advertisement, *Nashville Whig*, November 3, 1819
4. Joseph H. Parks, *The Story of Tennessee* (Norman, Oklahoma: Harlow Publishing, 1973), 203.
5. George A. Washington to Robert D. Carr, January 24, 1842, WFP, TSLA.
6. Slave bill of sale for slave Jim belonging to Robert D. Carr to George A. Washington, March 25, 1842, WFP, TSLA.
7. Mary C. Washington to George A. Washington, June 3, 1849, WFP, TSLA.
8. Receipt Christian County, Kentucky, jail for slave Jack, September 24, 1838–October 3, 1838, WFP, TSLA.

9. George A. Washington to Mary C. Washington, April 12, 1839, WFP, TSLA.

10. Mary C. Washington to George A. Washington, June 8, 1840, WFP, TSLA.

11. Benjamin Simms to George A. Washington, June 22, 1840, WFP, TSLA.

12. Benjamin Simms to George A. Washington, January 16, 1842, WFP, TSLA.

13. Slaves' medical bills 1815–1865, WFP, TSLA.

14. Mary C. Washington to George A. Washington, September 4, 1853, WFP, TSLA.

15. Jane S. Washington to George A. Washington, January 14, 1854, WFP, TSLA.

16. Diary, George A. Washington, 1854, WFP, TSLA.

17. J. W. Kendall to George A. Washington, August 28, 1854, WFP, TSLA.

18. J. W. Kendall to George A. Washington, September 2, 1854, WFP, TSLA.

19. L. W. Brown to George A. Washington, September 25, 1854, WFP, TSLA.

20. Archer Cheatham to George A. Washington, November 10, 1854, WFP, TSLA.

21. Diary, George A. Washington, 1851, WFP, TSLA.

22. William F. Taylor to George A. Washington, March 28, 1861, WFP, TSLA.

23. Diary, George A. Washington, February 1, 1855, WFP, TSLA.

24. Robert E. Corlew, "Some Aspects of Slavery in Dickson County," *Tennessee Historical Quarterly* (December 1951), 344.

25. Diary, George A. Washington, 1856, WFP, TSLA.

Chapter 11. On the Road to Freedom:
Wessyngton Under Siege

1. Ed Cheatham to George A. Washington, April 20, 1840, WFP, TSLA.

2. George A. Washington to Editor, *Union and American* (Nashville), unsent letter, [November, 1860], WFP, TSLA.

3. Sara Norton to Jane S. Washington, [1860], WFP, TSLA.

4. Jane S. Washington to George A. Washington, April 17, 1861, WFP, TSLA.

5. Jane S. Washington, "Civil War in All Its Horrors" [after 1861], WFP, TSLA.

6. Joseph E. Washington, "Address of Hon. Joseph E. Washington, May 24th 1915, On the Occasion of the Reunion at Wessyngton of the One Hundredth Anniversary of the Birth of his father George Augustine Washington," WFP, TSLA. Adapted from speech with additional information included in brackets.

7. Stanley F. Rose, "Nashville and Its Leadership Elite, 1861–1869" (MA thesis, University of Virginia, 1965), 64.

8. Requisition receipt, September 1, 1862, WFP, TSLA.

9. Receipts, runaway slaves, 1862, WFP, TSLA.

10. Charlotte Fykes Anderson, interview by John Baker, 2006.

11. Bobby Lovett, *Blacks in the Union Army of Tennessee (1861–1866): Profiles of African Americans in Tennessee* (Nashville: Serviceberry Press, 1996), 10–11.

12. ———, *Profiles of African Americans in Tennessee* (Nashville: Tennessee State University, 1996).

13. Gen. James Buell, Military Records Order Regarding George A. Washington, March 11, 1862, WFP, TSLA.

14. Family registers, Washington Family Bible, WFP, TSLA.

15. Major William B. Lewis to George A. Washington, March 6, 1863, WFP, TSLA.

16. William L. Washington to Jane S. Washington, September 16, 1864, WFP, TSLA.

17. Jane S. Washington to William L. Washington, October 1, 1863, WFP, TSLA.

18. David C. Allen, *Winds of Change: Robertson County, Tennessee, in the Civil War* (Nashville: Land Yacht Press, 2000), 233.

19. List of slaves working for George A. Washington, 1863, WFP, TSLA.

20. Major William B. Lewis to George A. Washington, March 6, 1863, WFP, TSLA.

21. Major William B. Lewis to George A. Washington, February 24, 1863, WFP, TSLA.

22. Major William B. Lewis to George A. Washington, March 6, 1863, WFP, TSLA.

23. Jane S. Washington to William L. Washington, October 1, 1863, WFP, TSLA.

24. United States pension application, Miles Washington C768001.

25. United States pension application, Otho Washington C2520072.

26. United States pension application, Frank Washington C2478076

27. Ibid.

28. Affidavit, M. W. Winters, October 5, 1862, WFP, TSLA.

29. Major William B. Lewis to George A. Washington, May 1, 1863, WFP, TSLA.

30. Ibid.

31. Oath of allegiance, George A. Washington, May 6, 1863, WFP, TSLA.

32. George A. Washington, military passes, 1863–1865, WFP, TSLA.

33. R. B. Cheatham to Capt. Tom Berry, July 3, 1863, WFP, TSLA.

34. George A. Washington to Jane S. Washington, September 12, 1863, WFP, TSLA. George A. Washington to Jane S. Washington, September 14, 1863, WFP, TSLA.

35. Jane S. Washington to William L. Washington, October 1, 1863, WFP, TSLA.

36. Jane S. Washington to George A. Washington, September 19, 1863, WFP, TSLA.
37. Slave medical bills, 1815–1865, WFP, TSLA.
38. Doctor bills, 1863–1865, WFP, TSLA.
39. George A. Washington to Major William B. Lewis, December 14, 1863, WFP, TSLA.
40. Jane S. Washington to George A. Washington, February 29, 1864, and March 2, 1864, WFP, TSLA.
41. George A. Washington to Jane S. Washington, March 3, 1864, WFP, TSLA.
42. Jane S. Washington to George A. Washington, July 27, 1864, WFP, TSLA.
43. Mary C. Washington to Jane S. Washington, September 18, 1864, WFP, TSLA.
44. Jane S. Washington to George A. Washington, 1864, WFP, TSLA.
45. Family registers, Washington Family Bible, WFP, TSLA.
46. Lucy Washington Helm, "The Story of Wessyngton Farms," 1945.
47. Ibid.
48. Jane S. Washington to George A. Washington, July 27, 1864, WFP, TSLA.
49. Will, Drewry Bell, 1865, Robertson County Will Book, 644, Robertson County, Archives, Springfield, Tennessee.

Chapter 12. No Longer Under Washington Control

1. "An Unfortunate Shooting Affair," *Nashville Dispatch*, December 13, 1864, WFP, TSLA.
2. Stephen Ash, *Middle Tennessee Society Transformed, 1860–1870: War and Peace in the Upper South* (Baton Rouge: Louisiana State University Press, 1988), 164.
3. Jane S. Washington to William L. Washington, December 18, 1864, WFP, TSLA.
4. George A. Washington to Major William B. Lewis, January 13, 1863, WFP, TSLA.
5. William L. Washington to Jane S. Washington, January 1, 1864, WFP, TSLA.
6. George A. Washington to Jane S. Washington, March 3, 1864, March 8, 1864, WFP, TSLA.
7. George A. Washington to Jane S. Washington, July 24, 1864, WFP, TSLA.
8. George A. Washington to Jane S. Washington, July 25, 1864, WFP, TSLA.
9. Jane S. Washington to George A. Washington, July 27, 1864, WFP, TSLA.
10. Mary Washington to George A. Washington, July 1864, WFP, TSLA.
11. George A. Washington to Jane S. Washington, August 2, 1864, WFP, TSLA.
12. Jane S. Washington to George A. Washington, September 22, 1864, WFP, TSLA.

13. "An Unfortunate Shooting Affair," *Nashville Dispatch*, December 13, 1864, WFP, TSLA.
14. John Lawrence, "A Disgraceful Affair in Robertson County," *Religious Telescope* (Dayton, Ohio), December 28, 1864, WFP, TSLA.
15. Depositions, Granville Washington and Irene Washington, February 1, 1865, WFP, TSLA.
16. Deposition, Dr. John Dunn, February 1, 1865, WFP, TSLA.
17. Deposition, Irene Washington, February 1, 1865, WFP, TSLA.
18. Colonel Thomas J. Downey to Major B. H. Polk, December 9, 1864, WFP, TSLA.
19. Jane S. Washington to William L. Washington, December 18, 1864, WFP, TSLA.
20. Lucy Washington Helm, "The Story of Wessyngton Farms," 1945.
21. Lawrence, "A Disgraceful Affair in Robertson County."
22. Jane S. Washington to William L. Washington, December 18, 1864, WFP, TSLA.
23. Lawrence, "A Disgraceful Affair in Robertson County."
24. Colonel Thomas J. Downey to Major B. H. Polk, December 9, 1864, WFP, TSLA.
25. "An Unfortunate Shooting Affair," *Nashville Dispatch,* December 13, 1864, WFP, TSLA.
26. Lawrence, "A Disgraceful Affair in Robertson County."
27. Joseph E. Washington to Jane S. Washington, February 14, 1865, WFP, TSLA.
28. Lucy Washington Helm, "The Story of Wessyngton Farms," 1945.
29. Jane S. Washington to Mary C. Washington, March 16, 1865, WFP, TSLA.
30. Jane S. Washington to Mary C. Washington, March 14, 1865, WFP, TSLA.
31. Jane S. Washington to Mary C. Washington, March 16, 1865, WFP, TSLA.
32. Mary C. Washington to Jane S. Washington, December 1864, WFP, TSLA.
33. Jane S. Washington to Mary C. Washington, March 9, 1865, WFP, TSLA.
34. Lucy Washington Helm, "The Story of Wessyngton Farms," 1945.
35. Joseph E. Washington to Jane S. Washington, February 28, 1865, WFP, TSLA.
36. Joseph E. Washington to Jane S. Washington, March 10, 1865; March 27, 1865; WFP, TSLA.
37. Joseph E. Washington to Jane S. Washington, March 22, 1865, WFP, TSLA.
38. Mary C. Washington to Jane S. Washington, March 22, 1865, WFP, TSLA.
39. Receipts (2) for articles taken from Wessyngton Plantation by Union Army, April 14, 1865, WFP, TSLA.
40. Jane S. Washington to Mary C. Washington, February 26, 1865, WFP, TSLA.

41. Joseph E. Washington to Jane S. Washington, February 28, 1865, WFP, TSLA.
42. Jane S. Washington to George A. Washington, August 15, 1864, WFP, TSLA.
43. Jane S. Washington to George A. Washington, August 8, 1864, WFP, TSLA.
44. Jane S. Washington to Mary C. Washington, February 26, 1865, WFP, TSLA.
45. Jane S. Washington to Mary C. Washington, March 30, 1865, WFP, TSLA.
46. Joseph E. Washington to Jane S. Washington, February 28, 1865, WFP, TSLA.
47. Mary C. Washington to Jane S. Washington, March 1, 1865, WFP, TSLA.
48. R. F. Woods to George A. Washington, February 20, 1865, WFP, TSLA.
49. William L. Washington to Jane S. Washington, March 11, 1865, WFP, TSLA.
50. Joseph E. Washington to Jane S. Washington, February 9, 1865, WFP, TSLA.
51. Jane S. Washington to Mary C. Washington, March 9, 1865, WFP, TSLA.
52. Jane S. Washington to George A. Washington, August 8, 1864, WFP, TSLA.
53. Mary C. Washington to Jane S. Washington, April 3, 1865, WFP, TSLA.
54. Joseph E. Washington to Jane S. Washington, [spring] 1865, WFP, TSLA.
55. Joseph E. Washington to Jane S. Washington, March 27, 1865, WFP, TSLA.
56. Mary C. Washington to Jane S. Washington, March 29, 1865, WFP, TSLA.
57. Mary C. Washington to Jane S. Washington, December 1864, WFP, TSLA.
58. Joseph E. Washington to Jane S. Washington, February 28, 1865, WFP, TSLA.
59. Mary C. Washington to Jane S. Washington, March 5, 1865, WFP, TSLA.
60. Mary C. Washington to Jane S. Washington, March 3, 1865, WFP, TSLA.
61. Joseph E. Washington to Jane S. Washington, March 25, 1865, WFP, TSLA.
62. Joseph E. Washington to Jane S. Washington, March 27, 1865, WFP, TSLA.
63. Mary C. Washington to Jane S. Washington, March 31, 1865, WFP, TSLA.
64. Mary C. Washington to Jane S. Washington, December 1864, WFP, TSLA.
65. Jane S. Washington to Mary C. Washington, March 9, 1865, WFP, TSLA.
66. Lucy Washington Helm, "The Story of Wessyngton Farms," 1945.
67. Mary Washington Holley to Stanley F. Rose, private correspondence, July 2006.
68. Mary C. Washington to Jane S. Washington, March 3, 1865, WFP, TSLA.
69. Joseph E. Washington to Jane S. Washington, March 25, 1865, WFP, TSLA.

70. Jane S. Washington to Mary C. Washington, March 30, 1865, WFP, TSLA.
71. Joseph E. Washington to Jane S. Washington, February 23, 1865, WFP, TSLA.
72. Joseph E. Washington to Jane S. Washington, March 2, 1865, WFP, TSLA.
73. Bobby L. Lovett, *The African American History of Nashville, Tennessee 1780–1930* (Fayetteville: University of Arkansas Press, 1999), 68.
74. Union soldier's diary, March 20, 1865, in Stephen Ash, *When the Yankees Came: Conflict and Chaos in the Occupied South, 1861–1865* (Chapel Hill: University of North Carolina Press, 1995), 155–156.
75. George A. Washington to Jane S. Washington, July 18, 1865, WFP, TSLA.

Chapter 13. August the 8th

1. Account book, 1880, WFP, TSLA.
2. Jane S. Washington to George A. Washington, December 30, 1865, WFP, TSLA.
3. Joseph Washington, interview by John Baker, 1999.
4. Mattie Terry, interview by John Baker, 1977.
5. Lucy Washington Helm, "The Story of Wessyngton Farms," 1945.
6. Mattie Terry, interview by John Baker, 1979.
7. Joseph Washington, interview by John Baker, 1997.
8. Mary Washington to Joseph E. Washington, January 1, 1867, and January 24, 1867, WFP, TSLA.
9. Lucy Washington Helm, "The Story of Wessyngton Farms," 1945.
10. George A. Washington to Jane S. Washington, February 26, 1866, WFP, TSLA.
11. Jane S. Washington to George A. Washington, April 1865, WFP, TSLA.
12. George A. Washington to Jane S. Washington, July 25, 1865, WFP, TSLA.
13. George A. Washington to Jane S. Washington, July 18, 1865, WFP, TSLA.
14. George A. Washington to Jane S. Washington, June 10, 1866, WFP, TSLA.
15. Jane S. Washington to Joseph E. Washington, November 11, 1866, WFP, TSLA.
16. Mary C. Washington to Jane S. Washington, February 1865, WFP, TSLA.
17. Will, Mary C. Washington, November 16, 1860, WFP, TSLA.
18. Agreement, George A. Washington and William L. Washington, April 1866, WFP, TSLA.
19. George A. Washington to Jane S. Washington, June 10, 1866, WFP, TSLA.
20. Jane S. Washington to Joseph E. Washington, May 9, 1867, WFP, TSLA.
21. Jane S. Washington to Joseph E. Washington, December 2, 1866, WFP, TSLA.

22. Sharecropping agreement, John Lewis and George A. Washington, December 25, 1865, WFP, TSLA.

23. Jane S. Washington to George A. Washington, February 21, 1869, WFP, TSLA.

24. Ridley W. Wills II, *The History of Belle Meade: Mansion, Plantation & Stud* (Nashville: Vanderbilt University Press, 1991), 87.

25. Yolanda Reid and Rick Gregory, *Robertson County, Tennessee: Home of the World's Finest, Celebrating 200 Years* (Paducah: Turner Publishing, 1996), 69.

26. Jane S. Washington to Joseph E. Washington, January 20, 1869, WFP, TSLA.

27. George A. Washington to Joseph E. Washington, 1870, WFP, TSLA.

28. Jane S. Washington to Joseph E. Washington, November 8, 1868, WFP, TSLA.

29. Mary Washington to Joseph E. Washington, December 1, 1869, and April 29, 1871, WFP, TSLA.

30. Account books, WFP, TSLA.

31. Jane S. Washington to Joseph E. Washington, December 29, 1872, WFP, TSLA.

32. Jane S. Washington to Joseph E. Washington, December 30, 1866, WFP, TSLA.

33. Jane S. Washington to George A. Washington, January 4, 1866, WFP, TSLA.

34. Mary Washington to Joseph E. Washington, January 1, 1867, WFP, TSLA.

35. Jane S. Washington to Joseph E. Washington, February 1, 1869, WFP, TSLA.

36. Jane S. Washington to Joseph E. Washington, October 21, 1866, WFP, TSLA.

37. Jane S. Washington to Joseph E. Washington, January 12, 1873, WFP, TSLA.

38. Jane S. Washington to Joseph E. Washington, October 21, 1866, WFP, TSLA.

39. Jane S. Washington to Joseph E. Washington, September 9, 1869, WFP, TSLA.

40. Jane S. Washington to Joseph E. Washington, September 9, 1869, WFP, TSLA.

41. Mary Washington to Joseph E. Washington, May 5, 1869, WFP, TSLA.

42. Recipe book, Jane S. Washington, private collection, C. Dewees Berry III.

43. Jane S. Washington to Joseph E. Washington, November 1, 1866, WFP, TSLA.

44. Mary Washington to Joseph E. Washington, December 1, 1869, WFP, TSLA.

45. Jane S. Washington to Joseph E. Washington, October 6, 1872, WFP, TSLA.

46. United States Pension Application C2520072, Otho Washington.

47. United States Pension Application C2478076, Frank Washington.
48. Ibid.
49. Clinton and Ford Washington to Mr. D. D. Holman, January 2, 1866, Ref. No. A–6151, National Archives and Records Administration.
50. Bobby L. Lovett, *The African-American History of Nashville, Tennessee, 1780–1930* (Fayetteville: University of Arkansas Press, 1999), 79–80.

Chapter 15. The Church in the Hollow

1. Will, George A. Washington, September 8, 1888, George A. Washington, to Jane S. Washington, September 21, 1863, April 16, 1864, April 21, 1864, WFP, TSLA.
2. "Death Claims J. E. Washington, Notable Tennessean Succumbs to Typhoid at Home at Wessyngton," *Nashville Banner*, August 29, 1915.
3. Will, George Augustine Washington, September 8, 1888, WFP, TSLA. "G. A. Washington, Death of One of Tennessee's Most Prominent Citizens," *The Daily American* (Nashville), December 5, 1892.
4. "G. A. Washington," *The Daily American* [December, 1892].
5. Ralph L. Winters, *Hospitality Homes and Historic Sites* (Clarksville: self-published, 1971), 20.
6. J. B. Killebrew, *Life and Character of James Cartwright Warner: Memorial Volume* (Nashville: Publishing House of the Methodist Episcopal Church, 1897), 57–59.
7. Lucy Washington Helm, "The Story of Wessyngton Farms," 1945.
8. Ibid.
9. Preston Frazer, notations on article "Picture Pointed Youth Toward African Roots," *Nashville Tennessean*, June 3, 1979, Sadie Warner Frazer Papers, TSLA.
10. Major William B. Lewis to Seignora Peyton, October 21, 1842, WFP, TSLA.
11. Jane S. Washington to Joseph E. Washington, February 3, 1867, WFP, TSLA.
12. Bureau of Refugees, Freedmen and Abandoned Lands, 1865–1869, National Archives Microfilm Publication, M999, roll 34 "Reports of Outrages, Riots and Murders, January 15, 1865–August 12, 1868."
13. Ira Berlin and Leslie Rowland, *Families and Freedom: A Documentary History of African American Kinship in the Civil War Era* (New York: New Press, 1997), 189.
14. Lucy Washington Helm, "The Story of Wessyngton Farms," 1945.
15. Chapter XL Section 5 of the General Assembly of the State of Tennessee, Regarding the Rights of Persons of Color in the State of Tennessee.
16. Herbert Gutman, *The Black Family in Slavery and Freedom, 1750–1925* (New York: Random House, 1976), 419.
17. Jane S. Washington to Joseph E. Washington, November 8, 1868, WFP, TSLA.

18. Jane S. Washington to Joseph E. Washington, February 24, 1867, WFP, TSLA.
19. Records of the Assistant Commissioner for the State of Tennessee, Miscellaneous Records June 1865–1868.
20. Bobby L. Lovett, *A Profile of African Americans in Tennessee History* (Nashville: Tennessee State University, 1996), 5.
21. Yolanda Reid and Rick Gregory, *Robertson County, Tennessee: Home of the World's Finest, Celebrating 200 Years* (Paducah: Turner Publishing, 1996), 130.
22. Mary Washington to Joseph E. Washington, April 25, 1870, WFP, TSLA.
23. Joe M. Richardson, *A History of Fisk University, 1865–1946* (Tuscaloosa: University of Alabama Press, 1980), 6.
24. D. D. Holman to J. R. Lewis, June 23, 1866, Freedmen's Bureau Report for Robertson County, Tennessee.
25. Jane S. Washington to Joseph E. Washington, February 21, 1869, WFP, TSLA.
26. Ibid.
27. Jane S. Washington to Joseph E. Washington, December 29, 1872, WFP, TSLA.
28. Jane S. Washington to Joseph E. Washington, October 25, 1868, WFP, TSLA.
29. Jane S. Washington to Joseph E. Washington, November 16, 1868, WFP, TSLA.
30. Antioch Baptist Church Program Commemorating Its 115th Anniversary, 1984.
31. Mary Washington to Joseph E. Washington, October 6, 1869, WFP, TSLA.
32. Mary Washington to Joseph E. Washington, April 13, 1869, WFP, TSLA.
33. Woodard Washington, interview by Caribel Washington, 1970s.
34. Joseph Washington, interview by John Baker, 2002.

Chapter 17. Generations in Transition

1. Judge Henry B. Tompkins to Jane S. Washington, May 1, 1887, WFP, TSLA.
2. "G. A. Washington, Death of One of Tennessee's Most Prominent Citizens," *The Daily American* (Nashville), December 5, 1892.
3. "Death of Col. G. A. Washington," Supplement of the Springfield Record Obituaries. December 8, 1892, WFP, TSLA. Octavia Bond, "The Washington Family," *Nashville American,* October 10, 1909.
4. Will of George Augustine Washington, October 20, 1888, WFP, TSLA.
5. Ibid.
6. "The Late Mrs. Washington. Large Attendance at the Funeral Yesterday at Wessyngton," *The Daily American* (Nashville), February 14, 1894.

7. Obituary, Jane S. Washington, *Nashville Banner*, February 13, 1894.

8. Obituary, "Mrs. G. A. Washington Dead," *Nashville American* February 13, 1894, WFP, TSLA.

9. Ibid.

10. Memorandum on the St. Nicholas, Islip, Northamptonshire, the Washington Memorial, WFP, TSLA.

11. Ann Nixon Cooper, interview by John Baker, 1997.

12. Obituary, Granville Washington [August 1898], located in family Bible of Foster Washington.

13. "Colored Man's Suicide: Granville Washington Sends a Bullet Through His Head," *Nashville Banner,* August 22, 1898.

14. Will, Granville Washington, October 16, 1897, WFP, TSLA.

15. Ann Nixon Cooper, interview by John Baker, 1997.

16. Ibid.

17. "Hortense, Tennessee," *Nashville Banner,* April 25, 1913.

18. Ann Nixon Cooper, interview by John Baker, 1997.

19. Ibid.

20. Ann Nixon Cooper, interview by John Baker, 2000.

21. George A. Washington to Mary Washington, June 1907, WFP, TSLA.

22. Mattie Terry, interview by John Baker, 1979.

23. Obituary, "William Lewis Washington," *The Record* (Nashville), January 16, 1902, WFP, TSLA.

24. Notes, Sadie W. Frazer, Sadie Warner Frazer Papers, TSLA.

25. "Washington Hall," The Jean Durrett Collection, Gorham-MacBane Public Library.

26. Reverend Woodard Washington, interview by Caribel Washington, 1976.

27. Herschel Williams, interview by John Baker, 1997.

28. Winters, *Hospitality Homes and Historic Sites*, 23, and obituary, "Joseph E. Washington," *The Springfield Herald,* September 2, 1915.

29. Obituary, "Joseph E. Washington," August 29, 1915, WFP, TSLA. Obituary, "Joseph E. Washington," *Springfield Herald,* September 2, 1915. Obituary, "Joseph E. Washington," *Nashville Banner,* September 1, 1915.

30. "The Burial of a Washington," *The Nashville Woman's Magazine,* October 1915.

31. Obituary, "Joseph E. Washington," *Springfield Herald,* September 2, 1915.

32. "Death Claims J. E. Washington," *Nashville Banner,* August 28, 1915. "J. E. Washington Succumbs After Brave Battle," *Nashville Tennessean,* August 29, 1915. "Joseph E. Washington," *Nashville Tennessean,* August 29, 1915. "Hon. Joseph E. Washington," *Nashville Banner,* August 30, 1915. "Mr. Washington Laid to Rest," *Nashville Banner,* August 31, 1915. "Sleep with His Fathers: General Sorrow Attends Laying Away of Kindly Master of Wessyngton," *Nashville Banner,* September 1, 1915. "Joseph E. Washington," *Springfield Herald,* September 2, 1915. "Hon. Joseph E. Washington County's Leading Citizen Passes to Great Beyond," *Spring-*

field Herald, September 2, 1915. "The Burial of a Washington," *The Nashville Woman's Magazine,* October 1915.

33. "Farm Management Corporation Report on Wessyngton, Inc.," May 4, 1932, WFP, TSLA.
34. "Mary Bolling Kemp Washington, In Memoriam," *Nashville Tennessean,* March 26, 1946.
35. Jane S. Washington to George A. Washington 2d, September 2, 1893, WFP, TSLA.
36. Joseph Washington [son of Gabriel Washington] interview, 1970s, private collection, John Baker.
37. Diary, Washington family member, December 25, 1935, WFP, TSLA.
38. Account book, December 1935, WFP, TSLA.
39. Robert B. Williams Sr., interview by John Baker, 1997.
40. Maggie Polk Washington, interview by John Baker, 1998.
41. Deed, Robertson County, Tennessee Deed Book 57, page 204, 1906.
42. Goldena Lewis Yates, interview by John Baker, 1994.
43. Lester C. Lamon, *Black Tennesseans, 1900–1930* (Knoxville: University of Tennessee Press, 1977), 170.
44. "He Knows About Slavery First Hand: Woodard Washington," *The Messenger* (Madisonville, Kentucky), May 3, 1980.
45. Reverend Woodard Washington, interview by Caribel Washington, 1970s.
46. Ibid.
47. Maxine Williams Washington, interview by John Baker, 2000.
48. Mattie Terry, interview by John Baker, 1979.
49. Joseph Washington, interview by John Baker, 1997.
50. Mary Washington Holley, interview by John Baker, 1994.

Selected Bibliography
of Primary Sources

Tennessee State Library and Archives (TSLA), Washington Family Papers (WFP)

Account Books, 1813 to 1860

Civil War Records, 1863 to 1865
Slaves Enlisted in the Union Army, 1863 (USCT)
Testimony in Trial Depositions of Granville and Irene Washington, 1865

Correspondence
Joseph Washington and Andrew Washington, 1800 to 1810
Joseph Washington and William Washington, 1800 to 1810
George A. Washington and Joseph Washington, 1833 to 1848
George A. Washington and Mary Cheatham Washington, 1833 to 1865
George A. Washington and Major William B. Lewis, 1843 to 1865
George A. Washington and Jane Smith Washington, 1849 to 1880
Jane Smith Washington and Mary Cheatham Washington, 1861 to 1865
Jane Smith Washington and son Joseph E. Washington, 1861 to 1894
Joseph E. Washington and William L. Washington, 1865 to 1890

Diaries
George A. Washington, 1850 to 1860

Deeds
Land Purchases, 1798 to 1860

Genealogical Records
Genealogical notes of George A. Washington 2d, 1910s to 1940s
Wills, 1700 to 1964

Obituaries
George A. Washington, 1892
Jane Smith Washington, 1894

William L. Washington, 1902
Joseph E. Washington, 1915
Mary Bolling Wyndham Kemp Washington, 1946

Photographs
Slaves, Freedmen, Sharecroppers
Wessyngton Plantation and Homes
Washington Family

Speeches and Articles
Joseph E. Washington, "100th Anniversary Commemoration of George A. Washington's Birth," May 24, 1915.
Lucy Washington Helm, "The Story of Wessyngton Farms." Speech presented at the Query Club, Louisville, Ky., May 11, 1945.

Slave Records
Birth Register of Slaves, 1795 to 1860
Correspondence, 1804 to 1865
List of Men and Boys at Wessyngton, 1838
List of Men and Boys at Wessyngton, 1856
List of Runaway Slaves, 1838 to 1863
List of Slaves on Washington Home Place, 1860
List of Slaves Raising Their Own Tobacco, 1838 to 1863
Slave Bills of Sale, 1801 to 1843
Slaves' Medical Bills, 1815 to 1865
Tax Records on Slaves, 1813 to 1863

Newspapers, Tennessee State Library and Archives (TSLA)
The Nashville Whig
Nashville Banner
The Republican

Robertson County Archives, Springfield, Tennessee

Birth Records
Census Records
Church Records
County Minutes Books
Court Records
Death Records
Deeds
Genealogical Records
Land Plats
Loose Papers

Maps
Newspapers
Obituaries
School Records
Slave Records

Gorham-McBane Public Library, Springfield, Tennessee

Census Records
Deeds
Genealogical Records
Maps
Tax Records 1813 to 1900

Swem Library, College of William and Mary, Williamsburg, Virginia

Accounts Books
Blow Family Papers
Deeds
Slave Lists
Speeches and Articles
William Nivison Blow, "Tower Hill Before the Rebellion: A History of the Small
    Virginia Plantation Before the Civil War" [1893]

Wills

Southampton County Court Clerk's Office, Courtland, Virginia

Court Orders
Deeds
Minute Books
Slave Bills of Sale
Tax Records

Sussex County Court Clerk's Office, Sussex, Virginia

Court Orders
Deeds
Minute Books
Slave Bills of Sale
Tax Records
Wills

National Archives, Washington, DC

1850 U.S. Slave Schedule, Robertson County, Tennessee
1850 U.S. Slave Schedule, Todd County, Kentucky
1860 U.S. Slave Schedule, Robertson County, Tennessee
Freedmen's Register for Springfield, Tennessee, 1865
Freedmen's Labor Contracts for Robertson County, Tennessee, 1865

Interviews of African American Wessyngton Descendants by John Baker

Anderson, Charlotte Fykes
Buchanan, Alice Lewis (1911–2003)
Burns, Cora Washington (1899–1984)
Cooper, Ann Nixon (b. 1902)
Cox, Bessie Washington (1927–2006)
Edmondson, Mary Ann Washington
Ellis, Minnie Washington (b. 1923)
Gardner, Reverend Sam (1901–1999)
Howell, Cordell
Killings, Gertrude Terry (1903–1996)
Lee, Julia Otey
Lockert Jr., A. E.
McGlothen, Mae June Williams (1924–2005)
Morton, Clara Wheeler (1927–2007)
Nicholson, Sallie Washington (1909–1995)
Northington, Phyllis Washington
Otey, Ron
Polk, Henry (1907–1990)
Ross, Idella Williams (1907–1999)
Shelley, Beverly Hill
Sparkman, Mary Ann Terry
Stone, Nathaniel (1931–2006)
Stone, Pearl Crockett
Terry, Annie Bell (1914–2003)
Terry, Felix "Ditt" (1924–2007)
Terry, Jerry
Terry, Mattie (1889–1982)
Traughber, Narcissus Terry
Washington, Baxter (1903–1988)
Washington, Bob (1897–1977)
Washington, Caribel
Washington Sr., Reverend Henry
Washington, Joseph (1895–2002)

Washington Jr., Oscar
Washington, Maggie Polk (1904–2003)
Washington, Carrie Williams (1894–1993)
Washington, Helen Maxine Williams
Washington, Willie D.
Washington, Woodard (1891–1985)
Wilcox, Lucy Washington (1901–1981)
Williams, Herschel (1898–1993)
Williams Sr., Robert B. (1931–2001)
Williams, Annie Mai Terry (1904–1995)
Williams, Lady Terry (1878–1981)
Yates, Goldena Lewis (1905–1991)

Interviews and Correspondence with Washington Family Descendants

Berry, William
Blagden, Thomas
Frazer, George Preston (1908–2003)
Holley, Mary Washington
Hotchkiss, Jane
Pinckard, Mary Robinson
Rose, Stanley Frazer
Talbott, Anne Kinsolving (1942–2007)
Washington, William H.

Interviews and Correspondence with Descendants of White Tenant Farmers

McClaran, Betty Whitman

DNA Test Donors, African American Wessyngton Descendants

Curd, Allison
Darden, Calvin
Gardner, Charles
Gardner, Catherine Pitt
Gardner, Reverend Silas P.
Killings, Betty Jean
King, Joann
Lewis, Ken
Lewis, Theodore
Mahiri, Jabari

Morton, Clara Wheeler
Northington, Beverly
Scott, Miles
Shelley, Beverly Hill
Terry, Robert Jr.
Trotter, Mary Francis Washington
Washington, Bob W.
Washington, Lamar
Washington, Thomas
Washington, Willie D.

Selected Bibliography

Allen, David C. *Winds of Change: Robertson County, Tennessee in the Civil War*. Nashville: Land Yacht Press, 2000.

Ash, Stephen V. *Middle Tennessee Society Transformed, 1860–1870: War and Peace in the Upper South*. Knoxville: University of Tennessee Press, 2006.

Babson, David, ed. *Families and Cabins, Archaeological and Historical Investigations at Wessyngton Plantation*. Normal: Midwestern Archaeological Research Center, Illinois State University, 1994.

Bennett Jr., Lerone. *Before the Mayflower: A History of the Negro in America 1619–1964*. Chicago: Johnson Publishing Company, 1978.

Berlin, Ira, and Philip D. Morgan. *Cultivation and Culture: Labor and the Shaping of Slave Life in the Americas*. Charlottesville: University Press of Virginia, 1993.

Blassingame, John W. *The Slave Community: Plantation Life in the Antebellum South*. New York: Oxford University Press, 1972.

Burt, Jesse. *Your Tennessee*. Austin: Steck-Vaughn Company, 1974.

Faust, Drew Gilpin. *Before Freedom Came: African-American Life in the Antebellum South* Charlottesville: University Press of Virginia, 1991.

Franklin, John Hope, and Loren Schweninger. *Runaway Slaves: Rebels on the Plantation*. New York: Oxford University Press, 1999.

Goodspeed, Weston. *The Goodspeed Histories of Montgomery, Robertson, Humphreys, Stewart, Dickson, Cheatham, Houston Counties of Tennessee*. Nashville: Goodspeed Publishing, 1886; reprint Columbia, Tenn.: Woodward & Stinson, 1972.

Gutman, Herbert G. *The Black Family in Slavery and Freedom, 1750–1925*. New York: Random House, 1976.

King, Wilma. *Stolen Childhood: Slave Youth in 19th Century America*. Bloomington: Indiana University Press, 1997.

Kolchin, Peter. *American Slavery: 1619–1877*. New York: Hill and Wang, 1993.

Lovett, Bobby L. *The African American History of Nashville, Tennessee, 1780–1930: Elites and Dilemmas*. Fayetteville: University of Arkansas Press, 1999.

McCline, John. *Slavery in the Clover Bottoms: John McCline's Narrative of His*

Life During Slavery and the Civil War. Knoxville: University of Tennessee Press, 1998.

Mooney, Chase C. *Slavery in Tennessee.* Bloomington: Indiana University Press, 1957.

Reid, Yolanda, and Rick Gregory. *Robertson County, Tennessee: Home of the World's Finest, Celebrating 200 Years.* Paducah: Turner Publishing Company, 1976.

Russell, Kathy, Midge Wilson, and Ronald Hall. *The Color Complex: The Politics of Skin Color Among African Americans.* New York: Bantam Doubleday Dell, 1992.

Stampp, Kenneth M. *The Peculiar Institution: Slavery in the Ante-Bellum South.* New York: Vintage Books, 1989.

Vlach, John Michael. *Back of the Big House: The Architecture of Plantation Slavery.* Chapel Hill: University of North Carolina Press, 1993.

Walsh, Lorena S. *From Calabar to Carter's Grove: The History of a Virginia Slave Community.* Charlottesville: University Press of Virginia, 1997.

Williams, Derita Coleman, and Nathan Harsh. *The Art and Mystery of Tennessee Furniture and Its Makers Through 1850.* Nashville: Tennessee Historical Society, 1988.

Winters, Donald L. *Tennessee Farming, Tennessee Farmers: Antebellum Agriculture in the Upper South.* Knoxville: University of Tennessee Press, 1994.

Winters, Ralph L. *Hospitality Homes and Historic Sites in Western Robertson County, Tennessee.* Clarksville, Tenn.: self-published, 1971.

Illustration Credits

Many people graciously allowed me to include photographs from their personal collections. "Courtesy of Wessyngton descendant" indicates a photograph owned by African American descendants of Wessyngton Plantation. "Courtesy of Washington descendant" indicates a photograph in the possession of a descendant of the Washington family, founders of Wessyngton Plantation.

Page xii: Emanuel, Henny, Allen and Granville Washington. Courtesy of Washington family descendants.

Page 3: Sallie Washington. John F. Baker Jr. collection.

Page 7: Bob and Maggie Washington. John F. Baker Jr. collection.

Page 10: Birth register. Washington Family Papers, Tennessee State Library and Archives.

Page 11: Emanuel Washington. Courtesy of Jane T. Hotchkiss, Washington descendant.

Page 12: Talbott family. Courtesy of John Talbott.

Page 13: Wessyngton mansion. Courtesy of Jane T. Hotchkiss, Washington descendant.

Page 16: Mattie Terry. John F. Baker Jr. collection.

Page 24: Carrie and Guss Washington Jr. John F. Baker Jr. collection.

Page 25: Fannie and Wesley Williams. John F. Baker Jr. collection.

Page 27: Rachel and Wiley Terry. John F. Baker Jr. collection.

Page 29: Terry family. John F. Baker Jr. collection.

Page 36: Slave bill of sale. Washington Family Papers, Tennessee State Library and Archives.

Page 39: Joseph Washington. Courtesy of Joseph W. Blagden Jr., Washington descendant.

Page 42: Washington crest. Courtesy of C. Dewees Berry III, Washington descendant.

Page 44: Map to Wessyngton Plantation. Drawn by John F. Baker Jr.

Page 46: Andrew Washington. Courtesy of Stanley Frazer Rose, Washington descendant.

Page 50: Mary Cheatham Washington. Courtesy of Joseph W. Blagden Jr. Washington descendant.

Page 53: Slave cabins. Washington Family Papers, Tennessee State Library and Archives.

Page 55: George A. Washington. Courtesy of Stanley Frazer Rose, Washington descendant.

Page 57: Granville Washington. Washington Family Papers, Tennessee State Library and Archives.

Page 57: George A. Washington. Courtesy of Jane T. Hotchkiss, Washington descendant.

Page 62: Tobacco fields. Washington Family Papers, Tennessee State Library and Archives.

Page 64: Joseph G. Washington. Courtesy of Mary Washington Holley, Washington descendant.

Page 68: Fairfield mansion. Washington Family Papers, Tennessee State Library and Archives.

Page 71: Jane Smith Washington. Courtesy of Stanley Frazer Rose, Washington descendant.

Page 72: Forks of Cypress. Washington Family Papers, Tennessee State Library and Archives.

Page 77: Henny Jackson Smith. Courtesy of Robertson County Museum.

Page 80: Covered bridge. Courtesy of C. Dewees Berry III, Washington descendant.

Page 103: Richard Cheatham. Washington Family Papers, Tennessee State Library and Archives.

Page 103: Susan Cheatham. Washington Family Papers, Tennessee State Library and Archives.

Page 104: Fanny Saunders Cheatham. Courtesy of Peter Byrd.

Page 104: Harriet Cheatham Bransford. John F. Baker Jr. collection.

Page 105: Joseph and Marion Green. Courtesy of Beverly Hill Shelley, Wessyngton descendant.

Page 115: Slave cabins on hillside. John F. Baker Jr. collection.

Page 116: Slave cabin. Courtesy of Jane T. Hotchkiss, Washington descendant.

Page 117: Emanuel and Henny Washington family. John F. Baker Jr. collection.

Page 120: House servant. Courtesy of C. Dewees Berry III, Washington descendant.

Page 121: Servant stringing peppers. Courtesy of C. Dewees Berry III, Washington descendant.

Page 122: Wessyngton plots. Washington Family Papers, Tennessee State Library and Archives.

Page 131: Jane Washington. Courtesy of Charlotte Fykes Anderson, Wessyngton descendant.

Page 140: Olive Cheatham Bell. John F. Baker Jr. collection.

Page 170: Receipt for Davy. Washington Family Papers, Tennessee State Library and Archives.

Page 172: Rebellious Slaves on Wessyngton. Compiled by John F. Baker Jr.

Page 203: Granville Washington. Washington Family Papers, Tennessee State Library and Archives.

Page 204: Irene Lewis Washington. Courtesy of C. Dewees Berry III, Washington descendant.

Page 226: Thomas and Minerva Cobbs. John F. Baker Jr. collection.

Page 227: Cobbs family reunion. John F. Baker Jr. collection.

Page 232: Wessyngton servant in laundry. Courtesy of C. Dewees Berry III, Washington descendant.

Page 239: White sharecroppers. Courtesy of Jane T. Hotchkiss, Washington descendant.

Page 240: Black and white sharecroppers. Courtesy of Jane T. Hotchkiss, Washington descendant.

Page 242: Hog killing. Courtesy of C. Dewees Berry III, Washington descendant.

Page 242: Women processing pork. Courtesy of C. Dewees Berry III, Washington descendant.

Page 254: Polk family. John F. Baker Jr. collection.

Page 260: Daniel Gardner. Courtesy of Ken Varner.

Page 261: Gardner family. Courtesy of Ken Varner.

Page 262: Lewis family. Courtesy of Cordell Howell, Wessyngton descendant.

Page 263: Joseph and Fannie Scott. Courtesy of Cordell Howell, Wessyngton descendant.

Page 280: Baptism ceremony. Courtesy of C. Dewees Berry III, Washington descendant.

Page 287: Sarah Scott Harris, Emanuel and Henny Washington. John F. Baker Jr. collection.

Page 289: Memorial monument. John F. Baker Jr. collection.

Page 291: Joseph Washington. John F. Baker Jr. collection.

Page 297: George A. Washington. Washington Family Papers, Tennessee State Library and Archives.

Page 297: Jane Washington. Washington Family Papers, Tennessee State Library and Archives.

Page 298: Washington family. Washington Family Papers, Tennessee State Library and Archives.

Page 299: Joseph Washington family. Courtesy of Jane T. Hotchkiss, Washington descendant.

Page 300: Hostler. Courtesy of Jane T. Hotchkiss, Washington descendant.

Page 301: Wessyngton Division. Washington Family Papers, Tennessee State Library and Archives.

Page 303: Centennial Parade. Washington Family Papers, Tennessee State Library and Archives.

Page 308: Joyce Washington Nixon. Courtesy of Ann Nixon Cooper.

Page 308: Joyce Washington Nixon. Courtesy of Ann Nixon Cooper.

Page 309: Foster Washington. Washington Family Papers, Tennessee State Library and Archives.

Page 310: Grantz Washington. Courtesy of Ann Nixon Cooper.

Page 311: Ann Nixon Cooper. Courtesy of Ann Nixon Cooper.

Page 312: Emanuel, Henny and Winnie Washington. John F. Baker Jr. collection.

Page 313: William L. Washington. Washington Family Papers, Tennessee State Library and Archives.

Page 314: Washington Hall. Washington Family Papers, Tennessee State Library and Archives.

Page 315: Washington Hall. Washington Family Papers, Tennessee State Library and Archives.

Page 316: Glenraven. Washington Family Papers, Tennessee State Library and Archives.

Page 317: Washingtons at Glenraven. Washington Family Papers, Tennessee State Library and Archives.

Page 318: Wessyngton. John F. Baker Jr. collection.

Page 319: Five generations. John F. Baker Jr. collection.

Page 321: Jenny Washington and Geneva Gleason. John F. Baker Jr. collection.

Page 324: Austin and Anne Terry. Courtesy of Jane T. Hotchkiss, Washington descendant.

Page 327: Henny Jackson Smith. Courtesy of Jane T. Hotchkiss, Washington descendant.

Page 328: Wessyngton servant. Courtesy of Jane T. Hotchkiss, Washington descendant.

Page 329: Terry family. John F. Baker Jr. collection.

Page 330: Sellie and Callie Terry. John F. Baker Jr. collection.

Page 331: Nelson Washington. Courtesy of Charlotte Fykes Anderson.

Page 331: Irvin Washington. Courtesy of Charlotte Fykes Anderson.

Page 332: Arry Fort Pitt. Courtesy of Carl Alex Washington, Wessyngton descendant.

Page 332: Nicie Pitt Ross. Courtesy of Carl Alex Washington, Wessyngton descendant.

Page 334: Green family. Courtesy of Cordell Howell, Wessyngton descendant.

Page 335: Bowling-Bransford reunion. John F. Baker Jr. collection.

Page 336: Amos Washington. John F. Baker Jr. collection.

Page 337: Cora Washington. John F. Baker Jr. collection.

Page 337: Bob Washington. John F. Baker Jr. collection

Page 338: Servant with Pauline Washington. Courtesy of Jane T. Hotchkiss, Washington descendant.

Page 339: Guss Washington Sr. John F. Baker Jr. collection.

Page 341: Baxter Washington. John F. Baker Jr. collection.

Page 341: Sallie Washington. John F. Baker Jr. collection.

Page 343: George A. Washington 2nd. Courtesy of Jane T. Hotchkiss, Washington descendant.

Page 344: Gabriel Washington. John F. Baker Jr. collection.

Page 348: DNA Chart. Compiled by John F. Baker Jr.

Page 350: African Map of DNA lineages. Drawn by John F. Baker Jr.

Page 354: Terry family. Courtesy of Jane T. Hotchkiss, Washington descendant.

Page 354: Felix Terry Jr. John F. Baker Jr. collection.

Page 355: Washington family reunion. Courtesy of Richard Washington, Wessyngton descendant.

Page 356: Washingtons at slave cemetery. Courtesy of Richard Washington, Wessyngton descendant.

Index

Page numbers in *italics* refer to illustrations.

399